How To B[arcode] Quick Turn Real Estate Millionaire

Make Fast Cash With No Money, Credit, Or Previous Experience

Ron LeGrand

Dearborn™
Trade Publishing
A **Kaplan Professional** Company

Vice President and Publisher: Cynthia A. Zigmund
Acquisitions Editor: Mary B. Good
Senior Managing Editor: Jack Kiburz
Interior Design: Lucy Jenkins
Typesetting: the dotted i

Published by Dearborn Trade Publishing
A Kaplan Professional Company

Printed in the United States of America
04   05   06   10 9 8 7 6 5 4 3

Library of Congress Cataloging-in-Publication Data

LeGrand, Ron.
    How to be a quick turn real estate millionaire : make fast cash with no money, credit, or previous experience / Ron LeGrand.
        p.   cm.
    Includes index.
    ISBN 0-7931-8886-5 (pbk.)
    1. Real estate investment.   2. Real estate investment—Finance.
3. House buying.   4. House selling.   I. Title.
HD1382.5.L44 2004
332.63'24—dc22

                                                                    2004009127

C *o n t e n t s*

PART FOUR
SUCCESS

f you are ready to have cash, cash, and more cash, you have the right book in your hands, right now. It is going to change your life. It is written by the money insider's insider—the man who has studied everyone else in the profession and then originated brilliant new ways to earn, learn, and return massive amounts of cash in a flash.

Now, thanks to this book anyone can start with nothing and end up with a whole lot of something. That something you are going to end up with is several things, including a lot of great, profitable, cash-generating real estate. Plus, your self-esteem is going to go up. You will experience and express your new levels of self-confidence and feel good about yourself. You'll have a net worth that works and keeps on working, because the best income is residual income. Ron LeGrand is the King of Residual Income. He is a guy who has worked this program 24/7 for the past 20+ years and bought and sold over 1,500 homes in his own personal investment portfolio. He has written about it in a way that lets anyone duplicate his success.

Ron and I are great, grand, and terrific friends. I respect, admire, and appreciate him. I have met his students from around the country and have talked at his seminars. He is the real deal. If you want to make yourself eminently and immediately wealthy, this is the guy to follow.

If you ever get a chance, travel across cracked glass if you have to, so you can attend his live seminars. For sure, read and reread this book and listen to his tapes.

As a writer, Ron LeGrand writes commandingly good and motivational copy. It will get you from where you are to where you want to be—with inspiration—so you will have aspiration, to do the perspiration, with a little bit of dedication, to get to the destination that is worthy of you.

Enjoy reading my friend Ron's great, inspiring, and helpful book.

Mark Victor Hansen
Coauthor, *The One Minute Millionaire,* and
Cocreator, #1 *New York Times* bestselling series *Chicken Soup for the Soul*

In the early 1990s, our training business was growing so fast I knew we'd better get help from someone qualified to lead our students to success. The load on me was becoming more than I could handle.

I found such a man by accident one day while speaking at an event that he was attending. His name is Ray Rach, and I have to tell you, there would be a lot fewer millionaires in North America if I hadn't met Ray. His dedication to our student's success over the years has made a huge difference in the lives of many who needed that helping hand in low times or someone to brag to in high times. I've been with him on many tiring trips to my speaking locations in airports and hotels across the continent, and I've watched him put in numerous 16-hour days on the phone working with our students. His energy is contagious, and his attitude has been a model for many to follow.

We've been through a lot of good times together, and our share of bad times, and we always emerge on top. He's been there with quality advice the whole time. I'm proud to call him friend, and fortunate I taught that seminar way back then where Ray just happened to be attending.

When I first got involved with real estate, I was a dead broke auto mechanic trying to make enough money to make ends meet. There was no such thing as disposable income around my house. It was all disposed of before I got it. Thirty-five-years-old and bankrupt, I didn't have a clue what I wanted to be when I grew up; but I knew it wasn't fixing cars in the hot Florida sun.

The year was 1982. I saw an ad that said something like "Come learn how to buy real estate with no money or credit and get rich by next Thursday." That appealed to me because I had no money or credit and I kinda liked the rich idea. So I attended the free seminar.

The instructor got us all excited about real estate and showed us how people were buying real estate with no money down. Then he said that if you pay $450 and attend our two-day training this weekend, we'll show you all the secrets. I wanted in but I had a big problem—actually 450 big problems.

But something compelled me to find a way to get the money, and that's what I did. I borrowed it from two friends and showed up for the seminar. That decision changed my life forever, my family's life, and their family's lives for generations to come, not to mention hundreds of thousands of my students and their descendants into the millions. That one small split-second decision that could have gone either way made me millions of dollars and spawned countless numbers of millionaires all over North America and in countries I can't even pronounce.

In fact, most of the stuff taught in that seminar was over my head. I was clueless and could barely spell real estate. But I picked up one idea I felt I could use, and within three weeks I made my first $3,000 from real estate using no money or credit, as I had none of either. I immediately called my boss and said, "I'm upping my income . . . see you around!"

The biggest thing that seminar did was get me involved in real estate and committed to changing my lifestyle. For years I'd been looking for something but didn't know what it was. When I got my hands on that three grand, it became crystal clear that real estate was my future.

Fast-forward two years: I had amassed 276 units—some single-family, some apartments—not including some I sold along the way to live. I was a millionaire . . . on paper. I had over $1 million in equity two years after starting with no money or credit.

REALITY ARRIVES!

I sat down one Friday evening to pay my bills and realized my outgo was bigger than my income and my upkeep was becoming my downfall. All I had accomplished was creating a big, ugly mess. I'd spent two years buying the wrong properties the wrong way in the wrong areas for the wrong reasons. I built my empire on a house of cards, not on a solid foundation.

You see, I really didn't understand the real estate business. I just bought properties because I could without money or credit. I bought all the crap savvy investors wouldn't touch. They'd already been to the school I was about to graduate from—"The School of Hard Knocks." All my low-income properties in war zone areas with brainless tenants were sucking me dry, financially and mentally. My days were spent solving these tenants' petty problems and listening to all the worthless reasons why they couldn't pay rent.

I spent the next five years selling off my junk for dimes on the dollar. It took me seven years in the business to really understand it and get my life back. Oh, I made a good living during that time—several times my previous income—but I sure wish I'd have known myself back then and had the system that my students have now. On second thought, it wouldn't have mattered anyway. I wouldn't have listened. I'm a man, and men don't follow instructions. It's the way we're wired.

After about seven years in the business and over 400 houses later, I built an easy system to turn real estate into cash immediately, cash monthly, and cash later. I made it a real business anyone could operate from home to make obscene amounts of money. That's about the time I started teaching what I had learned. Somewhere along the line someone called me "The World's Leading Expert at Quick Turning Houses" and the name stuck.

In the late 1990s the information company I built went public with revenues exceeding $20 million annually from my books, tapes, and seminars.

Now fast-forward a few more years of teaching what I know while simultaneously doing what I teach, and I will admit I'm a weird dude. I've bought and sold over 1,500 houses and still do 2 or 3 a month with an average profit over $40,000 with the help of my ex-secretary, who spends 10 to 15 hours a week at real estate.

Over the years I've created a mountain of home study products; written millions of words in print; and shared the platform with past presidents, movie stars, actors, politicians, sports heroes, business leaders, superwealthy individuals from all professions, and some of the best speakers in the world. I've spoken to audiences as small as 20 and as large as 20,000 in hotel meeting rooms and coliseums all across North America.

I've gazed in amazement and sheer joy as so many thousands of my clients and new friends have pulled themselves out of financial mediocrity, or downright poverty, and made themselves financially independent millionaires and some even multimillionaires from the words that left my lips and the time we spent together.

So many of these new millionaires have now become leaders reaching out a hand to those in need to help them climb the ladder to success. My legacy has spread like a swarm of locusts, and millions will be affected or already have been by the positive impact I made with a few carefully chosen words that left my lips or got put in print at a time when students were ready to receive them and convert them to action. New generations will profit directly or indirectly from the words in this book because they attended one of my seminars, then used the information and passed it on. *When the student is ready, the teacher will appear.*

Much of my time now is spent in front of good people who are serious about getting rich and will do what it takes to become one of the 3 percent who can not only say but prove they have achieved true wealth.

People constantly ask me why I continue to teach. It's hard for them to understand why a multimillionaire would take the time to work with those who aren't.

My answer is simple, really. First, make no mistake about it; I get paid well for teaching. It's not a mercy mission, and we're not a non-profit organization. Second, I have to do something with my time; golf, fishing, and diving get old quickly. Making millionaires never gets old, and I can't think of anything I'd rather do in my life. It's fun to be me and I love doing it.

Besides, I've been married about 40 years to one woman. Her name is Beverly and between the "Honey, do's" (her requests) and the nine grandchildren (three live on our estate), it's nice to get away once in a while. Beverly says that even though we've been married 40 years, its closer to 3 if you take out my travel time.

Truthfully, I'm just a simple auto mechanic with a redneck background who barely got out of high school. I'd rather have a good hamburger than a steak. I hate wine and all other alcoholic beverages. I smoke cigars, listen to county music and jazz, and go to the movies a lot. We have horses, cats, a dog, and chickens; we grow stuff in our own garden and, yes, I even have my very own tractor I use to plow that garden.

So there you have it—the real me. Now let's spend the rest of this book on you and how I can add your name to our millionaire's club . . . quickly.

They both lost their jobs but gained financial freedom.

Stephanie and Jon Iannotti, *Lyndora, Pennsylvania*

Dear Ron,

3 years ago we started dabbling in Real Estate the Carlton Sheets way, which by the way, almost made us not want to do Real Estate at all. Then in November, we met YOU at the OREIA Convention in Columbus, Ohio. 1-1/2 hours with you changed our lives!!!

In June, I was able to go from a full time $50,000/yr. Administrative Asst. job to 2 days a week. Then in February, Jon left his job of 24 years in the steel mill, where he was making $80,000/yr. I was able to completely quit my job of 21 years. Without you and your teachings, Ron, this would not have been possible!

In a little over a year and a half we were able to replace our incomes and purchase our dream home, a new Avalanche, a Stingray speedboat, paid off our credit card debt, set up a great financial plan and achieved many of our personal and financial goals. All of the people that said we were CRAZY and that Real Estate stuff doesn't work, are really starting to see that they were very wrong. We have decided that trading hours for $$$$$ is certainly not the way to financial freedom. A JOB keeps you <u>Just Over Broke</u>!!! We now are Transaction Engineers, doing Lease Options, Options, Subject To's, Wholesale deals, Retail deals, Rehabs, Short Sales, Pre-Foreclosures, all using other people's money. We are getting ready to do our first Auction, thanks to what we learned at M.I.S.

Since attending M.I.S. earlier in December, we came home and 2 days later were able to get 4 deeds. We have another property that appraised for $630,000. They owe $500,000 and are willing to let us take an option. We are going to auction it off too.

None of this would have been possible without having met you Ron. Jon is really excited, he purchased your Platform Speaking Home Study Course and has been studying in between getting these deals done. This will be another stream of income for us, as well as a way to give back to others who want to learn how to become "<u>Unemployed</u>" and "<u>Financially Free</u>." What a great feeling to be in control of your own destiny and to not have someone tell you when, where and how to do something. Our lives are like a never-ending vacation now. We are in debt to you Ron. You convinced us that we needed to get our ROTH IRA set up A.S.A.P., good thing you did, because we just barely were able to qualify this year and I can guarantee that we will be over the income limit next year, hopefully after our first auction.

We have included copies of just some of our checks, as well as some pictures so that you can see, we are just ordinary people following the system that you teach, and we are on our way to MILLIONAIRE STATUS. See you at the top SOON!!!!!!

Fondly and Respectfully,

Stephanie + Jon Iannotti

Stephanie & Jon Iannotti
Iannotti Realty Solutions, Inc.
Lyndora, PA

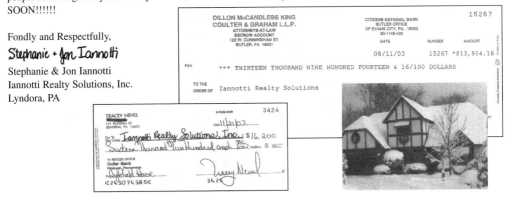

HOW TO GET STARTED AS A REAL ESTATE ENTREPRENEUR

During my travels, one question comes up repeatedly in my conversations with students: "How do I get started?" In our relentless pursuit of the dollar, we sometimes get sidetracked and forget the basics. Each time I've personally lost track of the fundamentals, it has resulted in another expensive seminar at "idiot school." I don't care how smart you are—or think you are—this business has rules like any other. If you forget the rules, or fail to learn them in the first place, it'll cost you, believe me.

During my career of buying and selling over 1,500 houses, I've made a lot of mistakes. Some were very costly, not only in money but also in needless anxiety. When I look back, I see that most of those screwups could have been avoided if I had stuck to my own advice.

Yes, I realize this is only a book. You'll read it, toss it aside, and go on about your business. That's OK, but at least read it two or three times before you drop it in the circular file. It just might save you a lot of grief.

Let's talk about getting started. I'll lay down the basic principles for those who are new to the business, and along the way you old pros may pick up some pearls of wisdom from "the guru," too. This book is loaded with pearls.

There are three reasons to be in any business:
1. Cash now, in a lump sum
2. Cash flow daily, weekly, and monthly
3. Cash in the future

Some people get into business under the mistaken impression that cash in the future is more important than cash flow now. How many times have you heard of people going one, two, or even three years in a start-up business before they show a profit?

This kind of foggy thinking keeps the bankruptcy courts full. Only idiots would start a business knowing they'd have to endure a negative cash flow for such an extended period of time. I know, there are rare exceptions when it may work, but for the sake of this book I'll assume if you're in the real estate business, your situation is *not* one of the exceptions. Therefore, if you're operating with a negative cash flow, you've qualified for a seminar in The School of Hard Knocks. If there is one thing I know for certain, it's this: *Negative cash flow has no place in the life of an intelligent real estate entrepreneur!*

So if you're just beginning, concentrate on creating income streams that put money in your pocket, not on businesses that suck it out. Take care of today's cash needs before worrying about building an empire. Focus on cash flow now, growth later. You see, you can't get to the future without first going through the present.

HOW DO YOU KNOW WHERE TO START?

Now it's time to get to the heart of this question. And by the way, don't feel that you're the only person who's ever asked it. Unfortunately, the answer isn't the same for everyone, even though I'm sure you'd like a clear-cut solution that would make it easy—some magical technique that would apply to everyone, would never fail, would be easy to do, and would require no education or money. It's not impossible to create such a system, but it wouldn't be the same for everyone. I could only provide such a plan after spending a lot of time with you to find out what makes you tick, what your likes and dislikes are, your strong and weak points, your skills and abilities. No two people are alike. Many have similar wants and desires, but few are alike in ability or drive.

Because we don't have the option of this kind of one-on-one right now, I'll do the next best thing and in these pages show you how you can find your own best system. Unfortunately, it's hard to pick the right approach when you know very little about any of them. So how can you get this kind of information? You have it in your hands.

The material laid out for you comes from over 22 years of trial and error and millions of dollars in real estate transactions. It's the beginning of a whole new lifestyle if you use it. The next best thing I would suggest is to make sure, when I or my staff gets anywhere near your area to conduct a seminar, that you attend. My seminars have changed thousands of lives.

Ultimately, the answer of where to start must come from within you. But because there *is* a way to explore your options with no pain and little cost, I think that way is the wisest course of action. That way is to take a little time to get some basic information on which ideas float your boat. It sure saves a lot of time saddling the wrong horses!

The second step in the plan is to *learn the basics*. Don't confuse this with learning everything there is to know before doing anything. That's the worst success killer in the business. It's called "paralysis of analysis." If you try to get all the answers before you saddle up for the ride, you'll never experience the thrill of the chase. Not only that, but the longer you wait, the harder it gets.

Don't expect to be an expert before you begin. Perfection leads to paralysis!

There are two ways to get an education. The first is at The School of Hard Knocks. The tuition in this school is very expensive and time consuming. In today's environment of readily available information, only a fool would choose this route. It's hard, it's long, it's expensive, and it's laded with death traps that kill dreams and eliminate fortunes. Most people never graduate from this school because the price and the sacrifices are just too high.

Those few who have graduated have a lot of stories to tell, but I've never met one of them who didn't wish he or she could've taken an easier route. Yes, there is another route! It's less painful, a lot quicker, and costs only a fraction of Hard Knocks University.

Anyone can enroll, regardless of race, creed, sex, or financial condition. Graduation comes with fewer scars, and the success rate is many times greater than it is when you take the hard, expensive route. What school am I referring to?

THE UNIVERSITY OF PRIOR LEARNING

The only people qualified to teach at this school are those who have gone before you and paved the way in whatever endeavor you choose. Learning from the right teachers is always cheaper, without exception, regardless of what it costs.

The number of people who think it's cheaper to get answers on their own never ceases to amaze me! My friend, if there's one important message you get from this book, please let it be this: *The cost of education is always cheaper than is the price of ignorance!*

Regardless of the business you're in, there are always those who have gone before you, willing to teach you what they know. However, it's a big mistake to believe that information of this quality is free. There's an investment to be paid. Just remember this:

Free advice is almost always worth what it cost, but good advice is almost never free!

I don't say that because I'm in the information business and get paid to give good advice. I practice what I preach and will pay handsomely to learn what I don't know, especially if it will help me make money.

Before I continue, I have to clarify one thing. There's a big difference between those who are *willing* to teach and those who are *qualified* to teach. It's your responsibility to distinguish between the two; but don't get upset if you choose incorrectly sometimes. There are lots of phonies who bill themselves as experts. If you mistakenly pay to see one, it's just another part of your education.

At the same time you're learning the business, you'll also learn who's qualified to teach it and who isn't. I'm just suggesting that before you hire a consultant, attend a seminar, or act on financial advice, ask yourself:

To whom are you listening?

Listening to the wrong people will put you exactly where they want you to be—broke. Learn to separate the wheat from the chaff as you seek out your sources. And . . .

Never take financial advice from someone who isn't making several times your income!

Your accountant or your lawyers are probably not competent to teach you how to make money. The average accountant makes $38,000 per year. The average lawyer makes $58,000. Can they teach you to be rich? Obviously, the same question applies to your friends, associates, and your brother-in-law. If they ain't rich, they ain't qualified!

Step three in the plan is to proceed immediately to your first deal. Don't pass Go. Don't wait for all the answers. It's far better to do it right away than to do it right.

In fact, you should learn to operate in the real estate business without taking any financial risk at all. That way, any mistake you make won't be devastating. If you haven't learned a risk-free plan yet, start small until you do.

The key is movement, not perfection. Even if your first deal isn't as good as those that made it into my book, it will still be a very important deal in your career. So get on with it. Get all the answers as you go, not before you start.

Reading books and listening to tapes are great ways to gain an understanding of something, and that's important. But they cannot teach you how to do it. It takes practice, practice, practice. Which brings me to one of the most adhered to of all business myths: *Practice makes perfect.* This is nothing but caca!

Only perfect practice makes perfect!

Doing the same old stupid things every day only makes you older and more frustrated, not richer or wiser. You should be constantly trying to improve your craft. Don't fall into a trap of complacency and get so full of yourself that you quit learning. There's always someone who knows more about your business than you do.

How many times have you heard people say, "You can't teach me anything; I've been doing this for 20 years!"? Yet when you take a close, hard look, these people don't know much more now than they did 20 years ago! They haven't grown or expanded their knowledge, and the world is passing them by. Anyone who has been doing anything in the

He made $252,125 his first year.

Clyde R. Goulet, *Lake Mary, Florida*

Lake Mary Realty, Inc.

Dear Ron,

Well, this letter has been a long time coming, and when I saw you in Phoenix I was reminded once again that I owed you this letter of appreciation. I have just wrapped up my first full year using your system and I knew I had a fairly decent year, but after going through the files and putting it all on paper, I simply can't believe it. In one year, basically as a one-man show, I netted in cash and equity a respectable $252,125.63. That does not include the deal I am working on now that will net a very conservative $35K in equity when all is said and done once it closes in January.

I did this with a combination of wholesaling, rehabbing, retailing, and lease-optioning. The largest deal grossed $43,126.11 and the smallest deal netted $2,798.50. One of the astounding things was that this was accomplished by just doing 14 deals, just a little over one a month. It's a little scary to think sometimes what will be produced in 2004 when I really get serious about this business.

The large deal was a property I picked up that was going into foreclosure and needed about $10K in work. I got it under contract, obtained a hard money loan for both the purchase and some of the rehab and sold it a few months later for over a $30,000 net profit. The small deal was a wholesale deal where I never owned the property but just got it under contract and assigned the contract to a rehabber. By just what I like to call "getting in the way" of a transaction, I earned myself a payday.

Before meeting you and learning your system I had bought properties in ways I thought were creative only to find out I was buying other people's headaches. I can't tell you how much your easy to follow system has helped me focus on the aspects of the business that will get you wealthy and keep you out of trouble. Thanks to you we are about three or four months away from being totally debt free, including paying off our home mortgage.

Thanks again Ron, I am hoping to get to another live training event as I really want to keep on top of any new and cutting edge techniques that may have been developed. I have enclosed the closing statements from the rehab deal I mentioned as well as a copy of the check. I also sent along a copy of the spreadsheet, my old accountant's habits die hard. Take care and God bless.

Sincerely,

Clyde R. Goulet
Lake Mary Realty, Inc.
Lake Mary, FL

business world for 20 years should be filthy rich, or that person is definitely not qualified to be your mentor.

The real trick to getting started fast is learning how to avoid some of the deep potholes you may find in the early part of your journey. Let's examine a few common causes of failure so you'll be able to see them coming and steer clear before they stop you dead in your tracks.

Lack of Money or Credit

Actually, this is not an obstacle. The good thing about the real estate business is that it doesn't take money or credit to get rich. If you don't believe that, I'll introduce you to dozens of students who'll prove it to you in this book. When you begin, concentrate on methods that don't require any cash, at least none of your own. These nothing-down methods require less than a few hundred dollars. Just remember one thing though: When you start making money, don't forget the methods you used to get it and begin doing stupid things that involve foolish risks! Just keep building your empire, conserving capital, and avoiding risks.

Lack of Time

The question to keep asking is not whether you have time. Instead, ask whether it's worth your time. Every human being alive has the same number of hours in a day as you. Donald Trump, Ted Turner, Bill Gates, and you and I all have the same 24 hours to use in each day. The only thing that separates superachievers from the masses is what we choose to do with our time. That's it! Like it or not, that is the big difference.

This is a fact you can accept, deny, or ignore. Whichever you do, you'll still have to deal with allocating your time to become a superachiever. You have no choice. Ninety-five percent of what we do every day doesn't mean spit. You owe it to yourself and your family to . . .

*Find out what will produce the most income
for you and give it your laser beam focus!*

The only way to never fail is to never try. However, true failure and stress come from staying at a job you hate. Unfortunately, the one pothole that stops more success vehicles than any other is . . .

Fear of Failure

It's not a matter of taking a chance. It's a matter of giving yourself a chance. There's nothing wrong with occasional failures as long as you're failing forward. Then you're actually succeeding. No individual success or failure is final. My advice: Concentrate on your future success and forget your past failures.

> *There comes a time when you must turn*
> *and face the tiger.*

Ask yourself, "What have I got to lose?" As Willie Mays used to say, "It's not my life and it's not my wife, so why worry?!" Think about the things you can change and forget those you can't.

There's no way you'll ever get rich without failing. You just ain't that good. Neither am I, nor is any human being ever born. Life and business are a never-ending series of mistakes. Any problem solved will be immediately replaced with another, more complicated one. So quit crying over spilled milk and go milk another cow.

Wealth Comes from Chaos

So go make a big mess! The whole world expects you to fail anyway; why let them down? The difference between you and them is you're failing forward. If you're gonna hang around me, that's the only acceptable kind of failure. Just keep floundering and failing until you're so rich it just doesn't matter anymore. It sure beats the alternative!

> *The best way to predict your future*
> *is to create it.*

ABOUT THIS BOOK

I've laid out each chapter in this book as a step-by-step guide that takes you through the process of quick turning a house and the benefits of doing so.

Throughout the book, you'll find testimonials from students to demonstrate the change that has taken place in their lives. Although this may be an unusual way to create a book, I can't think of anything more important for you to read than the success of those who started with nothing but commitment and overcame adversity, some becoming multimillionaires very quickly.

Obviously, we have removed the phone numbers, dates, and account numbers from checks, but everything else is just as we received it except the layout in order to accommodate this book.

Many thanks to these contributors and may *your* contribution be in the next edition.

"Deals are my art form. Other people paint beautifully on canvas or write wonderful poetry. I like making deals, preferably big deals. That's how I get my kicks."

Donald Trump

Ty and Margarita Leon-Guerrero, *Fairfield, California*

Team Realty.Com

Ron LeGrand-Global Publishing, Inc.

Dear Ron,

My family & I can't thank you enough. We were introduced to you and your "real estate courses" in 2001 by a friend. At the time, my wife, Margarita & I were already considered to be "Young & Successful Real Estate Professionals" by most people's standards. We both began as real estate agents in 1994, working "half days" (from 8am-8pm -12hrs a day, and sometimes more). We both worked "hard" and achieved a high level of success together, selling and closing 100+ transactions per year...then we met you Ron.

Your systems, and more importantly "your MINDSET" and "approach" to Buying, rehabbing, and selling real estate was an amazing "AWAKINING of my personal FINANCIAL GENIUS"!

In the last 24 months since we met you Ron, **We've personally purchased over 40+ houses, sold 25 houses with over $1,000,000 in income!!!** (this is in addition to our regular real estate sales business) We also grew our net worth to over $2,000,000! (See the attached copies of a few checks)

"The LESS I do, the MORE I Make $"

"The less I do, the more I make" is the new theme of our business today. Today I approach my business as a "Transaction Engineer", NOT an "on-call, cold calling realtor". We've hired & trained a "team" of people to support us. Today I buy "ugly houses", "foreclosures" and "pretty houses", in addition to selling 100+ transactions as a real estate broker (simply because I still enjoy it). We also leverage our position as a real estate company by offering our "traditional listing-for-sale" clients 2-3 options such as:

a) All Cash "fast close" offer (wholesale pricing without commissions & hassles)
b) Guaranteed sale within 30 days or I'll buy it! (Wholesale pricing)
c) Retail / traditional listing (a normal agency listing with commissions)

Today we're living OUR Dreams! Margarita, my wife, enjoys being a full-time mom (by choice) to our newborn daughter, Mya, 12 yr. old son Miguel, & 13 yr. Daughter Corina and I rarely work more than 35 hrs. a week, 38 weeks a year (BY CHOICE: besides, you can only enjoy "so many" rounds of golf before golf gets boring too).

We look forward to continued success working with your tools and ideas.
THANKS RON & THE ENTIRE STAFF AT GLOBAL PUBLISHING!
Sincerely,

Ty & Margarita

$167,576.52
$40,089.41
$119,901.82

Part One

WINNERS
ALL AROUND

1

YOU CAN GET A BIG CHECK IN DAYS, NOT YEARS

started in the real estate investment business after attending a two-day seminar back in 1982. Luckily, one or two things I learned there worked. I quickly discovered a whole new world of opportunity was out there that I'd never been exposed to—a world built around using my brain, not my back, with huge paydays and freedom from swapping hours for dollars.

Not long after that seminar, I had 276 rental units. That may sound wonderful, but I sat down to pay the family utility bills one day and discovered there wasn't enough money to cover them, which led me to take a hard look at how I had been operating. I had become a paper millionaire quickly. It had been easy to accumulate equity, but I had no cash. And I couldn't eat equity or pay bills with it. That's when I started to look for cash flow. It was this chain of events that led me to develop the quick turn method to generate fast cash.

You can make $10,000 to $100,000 or more in this business with just one deal, even in a low-priced market. It doesn't take many deals like that each year to make a good living. This book is full of real-life examples of people who have reclaimed their lives after I showed them the magical world of quick turn real estate.

Most people work all their lives to get pensions equal to half the wages they were earning—wages that didn't even cover their bills. You have the opportunity to take the future in your own hands and build cash flow that will continue whether you have a job or not.

The first step is to take care of today's cash flow needs before you start building your empire. Once those needs are met and you possess the ability to generate cash, there are countless ways to turn the cash into a consistent flow and provide for a secure retirement.

YOU DON'T HAVE TO WAIT

Some people think the only way to make money in real estate is to buy a rental property; sit on it for 20 or 30 years; contend with bad tenants, plugged toilets, and negative cash flow; and then sell for a profit. But that assumes there is something left of the house and that inflation hasn't decreased the property's value. It also assumes that during the holding period the owners don't get so frustrated with the property management they just quit, which is what happens to many people.

My intention is not to discourage the use of real estate as a retirement tool or to indicate that people shouldn't hold property for the long term. In fact, I honestly believe the greatest profits take time to develop. Huge fortunes have been amassed (some accidentally, it must be admitted) by the people who sat on a property for a long time, then awakened one day to find the value increased by 10 or 20 times the purchase price.

But most people don't have the luxury of time or the blind luck to make money while they sleep. And most are not properly equipped with knowledge and a clear-cut action plan before they start to buy properties. I've seen many people who think owning a few houses will make them rich enough in five years to retire and go fishing all day. More often, the opposite happens. The houses drag down the owners, who weren't properly trained to deal with the realities of real estate ownership. Those owners didn't have the knowledge you'll get from this book— knowledge that will keep you in control.

THE GOOD NEWS

If your intentions are to buy real estate to generate more cash, and if you want to have the cash now rather than years from now, listen up. There is a way to do just that. It involves flipping houses fast, or what I call "quick turning."

I have bought and sold more than 1,500 houses for fast cash profit. Along the way, I developed a system that anyone who has the desire and willingness to learn can duplicate and make work for them, regardless of their financial condition. We're going to study all the aspects of this system, step-by-step, in the following chapters.

If you think you need a lot of money and good credit or you have to be a genius to make money in real estate—it just isn't so! In this book, you'll learn how to convert houses to fast cash, no matter where in North America you live and regardless of whether you're wealthy or flat broke. In fact, if you're broke, you may actually have an advantage, because you have no choice but to *learn* before you leap. Those who have money tend to leap before they learn, then blame their failure on the system, the economy, their spouses, their mothers-in-law—everyone, except themselves. In this or any other business you have to learn the fundamentals before leaping.

These are the three basic reasons to buy non-owner-occupied real estate:

1. Quick cash profits
2. Monthly cash flow
3. Long-term growth

"But wait," you say, "what about tax shelters?" Forget tax shelters! Those days are gone. Many properties bought for tax shelters before the 1986 tax change were soon owned by the Resolution Trust Corporation (RTC) or the lending institution. This is especially true for such large properties as apartment and commercial buildings that were sold for a fraction of their former value. Today, tax benefits are a bonus, not a reason to buy.

Once you're sure your family's needs are being met, you can afford to invest in some "keepers" for long-term growth. You'll learn more about that strategy in the following chapters. For now, I'll assume you want to know how to make fast cash without using your money or credit.

WHY REAL ESTATE?

One thing is sure: People always need a place to live! Why not be in a business that will never lack customers? Why not work at something that produces paychecks in the thousands, whether you are involved part-time or full-time? How would you like to go where you want, when you want, stay as long as you want, and never worry about what's happening while you're away? And then there's the recognition you'll get for being a person who can find houses for people who never thought they could be homeowners.

Best of all, why not be in a business that's recession proof? You'll learn how to make money with real estate in spite of the economy, interest rates, or the market situation. The only real difference between the "haves" and the "have-nots" is knowledge converted to action.

When I started in 1982, the prime rate was 18 percent. Times were tough. Money was tight and chaos rampant in the real estate industry. Realtors were dropping like flies, and Wall Street had no kind words for real estate.

Yet somehow I managed to buy 23 properties my first six months in business without using a dime of my own money and made an average profit on each deal of $17,000 per house. Me . . . a dead broke auto mechanic with no previous real estate experience and a bankruptcy on my record. Even though I was new and clueless, I managed to make more money in my *first* six months than I had made the previous year swapping hours for dollars 60 hours a week.

Today my experience is quite normal for thousands of my students who exceed their job income quickly with real estate. You'll read about a few in the following chapters. It didn't take me long to learn that *wealth comes from chaos,* and when everyone else is complaining how tough times are, smart people smell opportunity and find a way to capitalize.

LITTLE OR NO MONEY OR CREDIT NEEDED

There are two ways to lose in my world. One, write a big check to buy a house. Don't write a big check and you can't lose a big check. It ain't rocket science. You can buy all the houses you need, including your own

From 15-hour workdays to a $163,000 first year.

Roger Ketchum, *Gladewater, Texas*

"There's Security In The ARK

Housing Authority, Inc.
Gladewater, TX • 75647

Dear Ron,

For some time now I have been intending on writing you to share my story with you and your staff. Your offer to be famous for just doing a little bragging is just the boost I needed to take the time to write. The bragging you will read below is not so much a testimony to what I've done, but more to what your system has done for me.

A little over a year ago I was working two jobs; I had a paper route from 3am to 6am and then my regular job from 7am to 5pm. I would leave my house at 2:30am and return home around 5:30pm. I was taking prescription medication to help me rest and to help me cope with those long 15 hour days. In October, I ordered your systems (Red, Blue, & Green). For the next 30 days, for 3 hours a day during my paper route, I did nothing but listen and study your systems. By the end of October I gave up my paper route and in November, I resigned from my full time job and pursued real estate full time.

A year later, I have structured 12 deals on single family houses totaling $1,111,000. My income from those deals totals over $163,000 and that was only working part-time. To date, I have optioned 5 houses, am currently working on UGLY house #4 & #5, which I am rehabbing and retailing, and have had 2 houses deeded to me. In addition, I currently have 2 short sales in the works.

From the first CD I listened to, I had no doubt that if I followed your step by step instructions and did what you said to do I could not help but be successful. There were those around me who were skeptical, but not anymore. They won't admit it but I believe they are a little envious of what has happened in my life as a result of your incredible, easy to follow system.

A year ago I had no life; I worked long difficult hours and saw no way out of the trap that I was in. I had succumbed to the realization that this was my life and there was nothing I could do about it. Then along comes Ron LeGrand; you and your system literally sprung me free from that trap. I now not only have a life, but a wonderful life. I now work only when I choose to and my income has tripled. I received much more than financial independence from your systems, I received my life back. I can't begin to express my thanks. **Thank you Ron LeGrand... you're the man!!**

Sincerely,

Roger Ketchum

Roger Ketchum
Housing Authority, Inc.
Gladewater, TX

My 1st UGLY House Deal
(Shreveport, LA)

Purchased for $55K cash — (Used $80K in private funds from local businessman whom I found using the "Do you have an IRA or any other investment capitol that is safely and consistently paying you at least 12% return?" strategy.)

Spent $35K on repairs & updates
Sold 88 days later on May 5th for $127K.
Net on my 1st UGLY House deal $36,827.38!! Did not take the time to make a copy the check but have sent you a portion of the HUD-1 and copy of the deposit slip!

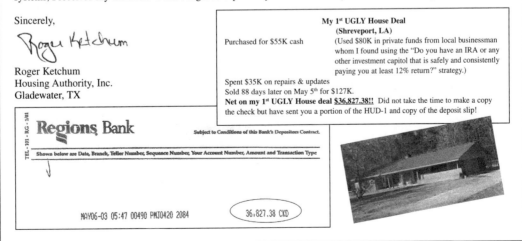

TEL - 101 - KG - 1/01

Regions Bank

Subject to Conditions of this Bank's Depositors Contract.

Shown below are Date, Branch, Teller Number, Sequence Number, Your Account Number, Amount and Transaction Type

MAY06-03 05:47 00490 PMJ0420 2084

36,827.38 CKD

primary residence without spending a dime of your own money. You'll see a preponderance of evidence of that in this book.

Second, you lose in my world by guaranteeing debt. We don't apply for loans, fill out an application, and suck up to bankers in my world. Your credit won't be needed; if you use it, you're doing business incorrectly and setting yourself up for a fall. Stay out of banks—I'll show you how my students and I are buying millions of dollars in real estate with no personal liability. If you insist on breaking this rule, I can promise you your empire will be built on a house of cards, not on a solid foundation.

There's actually a third way you can add to this list of ways to lose in real estate—one of equal importance to the first two. That way can be avoided, however, by following a rule that will make the difference between whether you love this business or hate it:

Don't make promises you can't keep.

If you don't lie to the people you deal with and simply tell it like it is . . . you won't have to remember who you lied to last. What an amazing idea. We simply deal with those who want to deal with us and forget the rest. More on that later.

IT WORKS EVERYWHERE

Where there are people who live in houses, there are people who want to sell houses and others who want to buy, regardless of the economic climate or geographic location. It was that way before you were born and it'll be that way after you're gone.

I tell my students if it doesn't work where you live, you can always move. But as soon as you're out of town, it'll start working for everyone else. If *you* say it won't work, it never will. I believe the best place to do a deal is in your own backyard. If you can't do deals where you live, moving won't help. Only training can fix the problem—not a U-Haul truck.

EVERY DAY'S A PLEASURE TO GO TO WORK

When I was a mechanic, I hated to go to work. I went because I thought I had to. Groceries were a requirement around my house. I'd work 12-hour days and come home with burnt hands, greasy fingernails, and a lousy attitude.

Then I got into real estate. I couldn't wait to go to work. Every day was exciting. I was in charge—on fire with passion for my work.

As a mechanic, weekends and vacations were what I lived for. As my own boss, I didn't want to quit on weekends; I wanted to work. To this day I take vacations because my wife says we should. Personally, I'd prefer a postcard, but when you've been married as long as I have, you learn to do what you're told. We've been married for nearly 40 years, and she's still putting up with me. Four children and nine grandchildren later, here's the secret to marriage that's worked for me!

You can be happy, or you can be right.

If I were you, gentlemen, I'd commit this to memory. It'll save you a lot of arguments.

As I write this, over 20 years after I got into real estate and over 1,500 houses later, and after training more than 300,000 students, doing hundreds of seminars, and creating a mountain of products . . . I still can't wait to get out of bed and go to work.

Some folks think that's the definition of a workaholic. I can assure you those folks are broke. You see, when you can't wait to get at what you love, even if it appears to be work to others, there's no such thing as stress in your life. Stress is for job slaves who hate what they do.

People without a mission
don't understand missionaries.

Here's a pilot who does it all.

Paul and Denise Andrews, *Port Charlotte, Florida*

Dear Ron,

    Just wanted to touch base with you and share a little of what we are up to. I know there are skeptics in your seminars and wonder if the techniques you teach actually work. Well I'm here to say absolutely **YES!** Attached are copies of a stub and some checks. Each check was earned using a different technique I learned from you.

    The first is a copy of a check stub for $5518.00 from a house I got the deed to (yes people will give you houses) and my tenant/buyer cashed me out. What this doesn't include is the up front $4000.00 option fee, the escrow refund (yep, your letter worked great concerning escrow refunds), insurance refunds, and monthly cash flow. I held the house less than a year and made $10,000.00.

    The next one is a check for $4000.00 which was basically a wholesale flip. People take "anywhere" in my newspaper ad literally. I got a call from a guy who said he had a house in Louisiana and wanted to know if I was interested. I said yes, went to my computer and logged on, found an interested investor in the area where the house was located, cut a deal and when the house was purchased, collected $4000.00 for putting the deal together.

    The next check is for $8600.00. This one was earned with an option. Denise **was** a Physical Therapist doing home health care at the time. While she was treating a patient a lawn care guy noticed the "We Buy Houses" signs on her car and waited for her to come out from her patient's house. He gave her the name and number of a guy who was dealing with an estate property. The guy lived out of state and wanted it "handled". I optioned it and then within a week sold my option for a total of $9000.00 ($400 up front, the balance at closing).

    The last check for $49,056.17 was earned on a cash deal. Using Kathy Kennebrook's Marketing Magic. We got a response to one of our mailings, the owners were interested in selling and asking $70,000.00. The first words out of my mouth when I called them was "What is the least you'll take if I pay you cash and close quickly", their reply $60,000.00. I made an appointment to go see it and found it in very poor condition. I called them back and told them it was in worse shape than I anticipated and asked "is that the best you can do?" their reply "$55,000.00", My reply — **"SOLD!"** we put close to $54000.00 into it and sold it for $170,000.00. I do want to add one thing; I sold this one using a Realtor. We had some family issues to deal with and I didn't have time to sell it myself as I normally do, so I listed it. Had I sold it myself I would have made almost $58,000.00.

    Yes I'm still flying at this time, I was supposed to be downsized out this year but things were temporarily postponed so Denise quit her job first.

    Sincerely,

    Paul & Denise Andrews

PROFIT $49,056.51

WORKING FROM HOME: NO LARGE INVESTMENT OR FRANCHISE FEE

I worked from home for two years until Beverly, my wife, told me to get an office. Until recently I worked from an office outside my home, where I did real estate and built other businesses. Today I'm back in my home with an outside office I visit occasionally to pester my daughter Vicki, who runs our publishing business called Global Publishing Inc.

Most of my students start working from home and just stay there. Many are making in excess of a million dollars a year from their home. Your biggest investment will be in your education. There you don't have a choice. There are only two ways to get a business education: the easy way and the hard way. As most of us do, I chose the hard way.

Obviously, the best way to learn any business is to follow a proven system and do no pioneering. I've made millionaires all over North America and other countries—people who chose to follow my system. Some did so immediately, whereas others tried it their way for a while and then came back to my way. Some tried it their way and were never seen again.

You get to decide whether you choose the easy way or the hard way. And remember this . . .

If you think education is expensive,
try ignorance.

Fortunately, for you there's plenty of training available beyond this book. We have courses, live trainings on all aspects of quick turn real estate, and mentoring on the phone as well as seminars near where you live. The options are all on my Web site at **http://www.ronlegrand.com.**

A PART-TIME BUSINESS THAT PRODUCES A FULL-TIME INCOME

Anyone spending more than 10 or 15 hours a week buying houses is wasting most of his or her time. I'll be the first to tell you that's exactly what most people do.

It's easy to be busy. It's more difficult to be productive. The real art is to be productive without being busy. Do the right things and that's exactly what will happen to you. Do the wrong things and you'll feel like real estate is just another job sucking up all of your time.

People forget, or never learn, what business is supposed to be about. It should free up your time so you can enjoy life and do the things you can't do as a job slave. Business is supposed to provide for you and your family and make life easier, not drag you into an endless vacuum of always being busy but never getting rich.

The most important lesson I ever learned in business is one of the toughest for most people to incorporate into their business and life, but doing it can make you filthy rich. By not doing it, your life will pass by in an endless parade of minutia. Here's the big lesson, my credo, and what has contributed to the success of so many of my millionaires:

The less I do, the more I make.

This is not about being busy. It's about making money—a lot of it. I'll suggest to you that the busier you become, the less you'll make.

Here's another wake-up call for you: If you can't do real estate part-time, you won't do any better at it full-time. More on this later.

"All people are self made. Only the successful people admit it."

Unknown

He went from a job to 100 houses and multimillionaire status in five years.

Winston Barlow, *Kingsland, Georgia*

RON TO THE RESCUE.....

In 1997 I was employed as a mechanical supervisor at a paper mill making $74,000.00 a year. Upper supervision asked me to do something which was unethical, immoral and actually illegal. It's a long story so I'll spare you the details. I refused to follow their orders and they said that if I didn't, they would fire me. I told them that my integrity was more important than my job and they fired me. I ended up getting my job back, but things were never the same. I had decided that somehow I wanted to put myself in a position where a man would not have control over my destiny. That someone could not pull the rug out from under me even if I did what was right. I prayed about direction and it was constantly on my mind. I now believe that God implements a universal law of attraction that when you pray or have something constantly in your thoughts, the solution will be attracted to you as what happened to me.

I received a postcard about this thing called, The Cash Flow System, by Ron LeGrand that taught you how to generate income with Creative Real Estate Investment. I decided to check it out. I remember when it arrived, I could not believe how simple and risk free the information was. I said, "I can do this" and actually had over 30 units by the time I attended my first conference with Ron. All with no money down. Since then, I've attended many conferences (at least 2 to 3 per year). I started doing the business with no computer, filling in the blanks on offers by hand and doing everything myself including repairs. As my business grew I hired a secretary and set up an office in my home. Eventually, I had to hire out my repairs and grew out of my home office to a little small office down town. One year later we had to move into a larger office, hired another girl in the office, brought on a full time maintenance man and brought my brother on board when he lost his job at the same paper mill where I had quit my J-0-B. After being in business over fifty years, they went out of business 1 year after I left (Guess they needed me more than I needed them.) I had set a goal to own 100 houses in a life time. That goal was accomplished in less than 5 years, and our deals continue to get bigger and better. Life is good.

Ron, I thank you for coming to my rescue. My life has totally changed because of you. In the last two years I've been to Mexico, Africa, Aruba and several areas of our beautiful USA. In a few months, I'll be hunting Red Stag in New Zealand and my wife is going to the Holy Land. We now live in a beautiful 3200 sq ft. brick home in the country with screened in heated swimming pool surrounded with the privacy of acres of Georgia pines. Last Thursday night, my wife and I were having dinner out by the pool and I was discussing my goals. As I told her my goals of doing high dollar house deals, commercial properties and platform speaking, she says, "I hope you're not getting too wrapped up in the money." I laughed and said, "you don't understand: It's no longer about the money. I'm happier than I ever have been in all my life". I don't need more money. It's now the chase. Inside every man is the desire to conquer. That's why we hunt and fish, and the bigger the game the more exciting the conquer. Real Estate has become not only a passion but a way of life for me. I Love It. Ron, true success is impacting the lives of others and if I can impact just one person as you have my life. I feel that my life will be a success.

Thanks Ron,

Winston Barlow
President, Residential Property Solution Inc.
Kingsland, GA

2

EIGHT MYTHS ABOUT MAKING MONEY

There are those who always seem to have all the money they could ever need. Then there are those who work and toil all their life and yet never seem to get ahead financially. Which of these two categories do you fall in?

Have you been brainwashed into thinking the only way people get really rich is to inherit a lot of money or just get lucky? The reason most of us think this way is because we haven't been taught by self-made millionaires. Instead, we've learned from those who really don't know a thing about accumulating wealth. The advice you're about to read has been culled from those who have amassed fortunes.

One of the most important points you'll learn is that a surplus of money starts first in the mind. As soon as you understand and can implement this, you will have made a giant step toward true financial prosperity. Here are some myths about money that need to be put to rest now so you can get on with your financial life.

MYTH NUMBER ONE: "FINANCIAL SECURITY LIES WITH HAVING A GOOD-PAYING JOB WITH A GOOD COMPANY."

This may not have been a myth 40 years ago, but times have changed. Today, relying on an employer to give you lifelong financial security can be downright dangerous! Unless, of course, you're getting stock options and riding the coattails of a public offering.

What gives you the right to expect your employer will never lay you off someday if the economy takes a downturn? Or what if you're just let go one day because your department has been "reorganized"? Then there's the possibility of your company's being bought out by another company, and this new company may decide your position is no longer needed.

True security comes from within, not from someone or something else. We all need to accept personal responsibility for our financial future by building up our own income and cash reserves. Real financial security lies within our own business and not with someone else's business. As long as you're exchanging dollars for hours, your chances of creating true wealth are very slim.

If you ever expect to make real money, you must first put yourself in a position to do so.

MYTH NUMBER TWO: "A PENNY SAVED IS A PENNY EARNED."

This myth doesn't really sound like a myth, does it? In reality, a penny saved is really a penny earned. Saving your spare change will actually add up to a nice little savings after a few years—maybe even enough to buy you a gold watch when you retire. If you want to retire rich, I'd suggest you take control of your own future and make sure when you check into the nursing home, you own it free and clear.

Do some number crunching and you'll find after you take into account taxes and inflation, any investment that doesn't produce a true annual return of at least 10 percent is actually losing money! It pains me to say this, but you can even use your cash to buy real estate and get a much higher return than 10 percent. Of course, if I've trained you, you

"While my coworkers went out the door worried about their futures, I went out with a smile on my face."

John Walton, *Tampa, Florida*

Real Opportunities

Dear Ron:

Just wanted to let you know about a junker that I just rehabbed and sold, and to thank you for all of the training that made this deal possible. I am an Environmental Chemist in an industry that was thriving until the government changed the rules. The company I was with went out of business along with most of its competitors. While my coworkers went out of the door worried about their future, I went out with a smile on my face and excited about putting together deals such as this one.

This house was the most extensive rehab yet. It needed a new roof, electrical, plumbing, windows, stucco, and had a severe settling problem. Most investors were scared off by the amount of work. But I had listened to you and knew that the extra work was simply just me signing a check.

We purchased the house for $37,000, did $57,750 in repairs, and sold it for $150,000. Enclosed is a copy of the check from closing, which included our profit of $55,250. Wow, that sure is better than working as a chemist.

Oh, also thanks for getting us set up with an internet site, because we sold it to a couple from Connecticut that was moving to Tampa. They saw the house on the internet, signed a contract and sent in a deposit, and got approved for the mortgage. All this before they came down to see the house.

Thanks again for all your support and training. We are looking forward to many more deals like this.

Sincerely,

John Walton

John Walton

| COASTAL SECURITY TITLE OF FLORIDA, INC. | COLONIAL BANK | 4983 |
| ESCROW ACCOUNT
3750 GUNN HIGHWAY, SUITE 2C
TAMPA, FL 33624-4005
(813) 908-3848 | 63-8978/2631 | |

PAY

$144,858.42

**One Hundred Forty Four Thousand Eight Hundred Fifty Eight dollars & Forty Two cents **
**$144,858.42

TO THE ORDER OF **REAL OPPORTUNITIES, LP**

File No. 2A3864 801 E. River Drive

AUTHORIZED SIGNATURE

Tampa Bay's Leader in Creative Real Estate

should know you can get all the real estate you want without using your cash. Then you can put that cash into passive investments to grow at a high rate of return while you actively create cash by buying and selling real estate. Then when you don't want to be active anymore, your passive pot will provide for you the rest of your life.

Money you leave buried in real estate can grow only at the rate that real estate grows, which will be the same whether your cash is buried or freed up to grow passively.

MYTH NUMBER THREE: "ALL DEBT IS BAD."

Some believe all kinds of debt are bad. However, there are two kinds of debt: good debt and bad debt. Consider bad debt as the type that puts you in debt for long periods of time (and in some cases for a lifetime). Run-of-the-mill consumer debt such as charge card debt for jewelry, material trappings, and impulse purchases are examples of bad debt that should be avoided like the plague. For compulsive credit card purchasers whose cards are always at their maximum, the best financial strategy is getting and staying out of bad debt.

So what type of debt is good? Any type of debt for creating wealth is obviously a wise debt. Fortunately, in the real estate business we can buy all the property we want without borrowing money. We simply take over the debt that comes with the property.

There's a big difference between personally guaranteed debt and nonrecourse debt. As you know, I vigorously object to guaranteeing any long-term debt to buy a single-family house. But I've got folks everywhere making a lot of money by taking over existing debt without recourse ("subject to"). It's become the mainstream or foundation of their business.

This kind of debt produces income. Bad debt produces only outgo. That kind of debt is why we have a country full of job slaves trying to keep up with their bad debt. Let's start thinking like a bank and do more collecting than paying because your debt is producing more revenue than it costs.

A late night call changed her life.

Ronda Marcum, *Liberty, Indiana*

Dear Ron,

I can not find the right words to say thank you for the way you have changed my life. I was one of those people waking up at 3:00 am watching late night TV and wondering how are we going to pay these bills. After watching your program night after night I finally made the call, attended the seminar and purchased every course offered that day. Now, the only question I ask myself is why didn't I do this sooner. I am a new student of one year and having the time of my life with my new career.

I have been wholesaling the junkers this past year. I have had 15 closings and earned approximately $75,000.00. I could not have done this without you. There is no doubt in my mind you are definitely the man with a plan and I will be following in your footsteps. You have shown me how to enjoy financial freedom again.

This is going to be a good year for me thanks to you. I have a 2.5 million dollar deal that will generate a nice monthly cash flow, equity, employment for my kids, and it has opened the door for many new opportunities for me. Enclosed you will find a few copies of some of my closings. Thanks again for everything,

Sincerely,

Ronda Marcum
Liberty, IN

ABSTRACTS OF RICHMOND, INC.
CUSTODIAL ESCROW ACCOUNT
25 N. 8TH ST.
RICHMOND, IN 47374
(765) 935-7020

945

FIRST BANK RICHMOND NA
RICHMOND SHELBYVILLE CENTERVILLE CAMBRIDGE CITY
71-7079-2749
9450

	DATE	AMOUNT
Four Thousand Two Hundred Sixty Six and 26/100*********************************	3/4/03	$4,266.26

PAY TO THE ORDER OF RHONDA MARCUM

MYTH NUMBER FOUR: *"THE GOVERNMENT WILL TAKE CARE OF ME."*

Much of our society has been lulled into a false sense of security provided by others. Social Security, unemployment insurance, welfare, food stamps, and other governmental meddling into our lives have created a dependent, "can't-save-myself" class of Americans. This type of pseudo-security has caused great harm to those who have subscribed to it. True security can come only from knowledge, education, confidence, initiative, invention, self-reliance, ability, and innovation. That it comes from others is only an illusion.

Putting too much emphasis on security can be paralyzing. It can cause a person to live in fear, avoid any and all risks, be indecisive, and ultimately live a dull ho-hum life. All things worthwhile in life involve some risk taking: marriage, love, starting your own business, moving to a new city, and so on. Those who don't venture out of their security bubble will never know the true potential of what life can bring.

Some people spend their life playing not
to lose instead of playing to win.

MYTH NUMBER FIVE: *"FAILURE IS BAD."*

Failure is bad only if you perceive it as such. For those who look at failure as an opportunity to learn and a temporary setback, it can be a building block to bigger and better things. But many are conditioned to be ashamed of failures and mistakes. This leads to a fear of failure, which becomes a great hindrance to any success that may be looming on the horizon. Those who develop a positive attitude toward failure can conquer the destructive emotions of fear, shame, and guilt. You must be able to put into perspective what others may think about you and continue on your quest for success.

In my experience, the biggest fear is not about failure but the fear of rejection. Most people are worried sick about what others say or think of them. Who cares? It doesn't matter what the morons say. Let them talk, criticize, and complain. The truth is if you knew what was really going on in their life, you wouldn't care what they think. You will fail; I guarantee it. In fact, failure is a prerequisite for success. You see . . .

It's impossible to succeed without failing first.

Life is one failure after another. Those who create wealth simply manage to succeed a few more times than they fail.

MYTH NUMBER SIX: "BEING WEALTHY IS ALL ABOUT MATERIAL POSSESSIONS."

There is more to being wealthy than "he who dies with the most toys wins." There's a huge difference between accumulating money and being wealthy. It's not uncommon for real estate entrepreneurs to become so engulfed with a love for what they're doing they may not realize for months they've become millionaires.

Above all, never pursue money at the expense of your health, peace of mind, loving relationships, and just enjoying personal activities. Money is a means of creating wealth; wealth is a means of creating a great life.

I know this is hard to believe if money's a problem in your life, but real wealth is in the thrill of the chase. Wealth creates power. Power creates more opportunities to be in control. Control creates more chases and therefore more thrills.

You don't need a million bucks in the bank to feel wealthy—you need freedom. Cash flow creates freedom. If you have enough cash coming in, you'll begin to feel wealthy, regardless of your bank balance. Now use that cash to generate more, and pretty soon your money's working for you instead of the other way around.

Incidentally, if you've got a million bucks sitting around in a bank account, you've got mush for brains. That's for old ladies and the uneducated who don't understand that banks are paying you less than inflation is costing.

He lost his job and found his future.

Joe Hession, *Carmel, Indiana*

Dear Ron:

Five years ago this week my executive job of 25 years evaporated in one day. Three years ago this month I met you—thankfully!

As you know, I invest in both residential and commercial real estate—a total transaction engineer.

Here's a sampling of last year's deals. I had purchased this home (Coil) at the local property tax lien sale for about $5,000. We completed a $7,000 rehab after securing the deed and title, then sold it on contract with my buyer getting a mortgage earlier this year. We received $76,832 at closing.

I purchased this house (Riverside) for $13,000. It was vacant, ugly and had termites. I wholesaled it to a realtor rehabber for $34,000 and received a check for $32,700 at closing. No property taxes, no utilities, and no holding costs!!!

We acquired this home (36th St.) for approx. $10,000 and then completed a $14,000 rehab. Then, I executed a lease/option agreement receiving $5,000 non-refundable option consideration, $750 per month and a sales price of $91,500.

This 4 bed/2 bath two story (Ft. Wayne St.) was purchased for $15,500. After completing a quiet title action, I secured a work for equity buyer at $76,900.

Finally, I sold an office/warehouse complex and completed a 1031 exchange into this strip center (Thompson). The 1031 exchange allowed me to defer approximately $400,000 in taxes and leverage up to a newer property with far better cash flow. I also had $113,000+ of tax free borrowed funds wired into our account at closing. My anchor tenant's monthly rent more than services the seven figure, non-recourse debt on this property.

More importantly, it would be impossible for me to put a value on the wonderful friendships I have made with other students while attending your events during the last three years. Many of them will last a lifetime.

Ron, I cannot begin to thank you enough for the knowledge, inspiration and friendship you have imparted to me over the last three years. You've made a huge difference in yet another life. God bless and best wishes.

Joe Hession
Carmel, IN

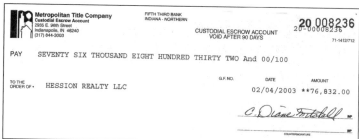

MYTH NUMBER SEVEN: "THE ACQUISITION OF WEALTH IS A WIN/LOSE GAME."

If the rich keep getting richer, do the poor keep getting poorer? Thanks to inaccuracies in the media and omissions at our nation's universities, the truth regarding this matter is seldom heard. Here's a bit of reality for you on the situation: Your *not* becoming rich will benefit no one; but your becoming rich benefits others in an abundance of ways.

Wealthy individuals build factories, which create jobs that help the economy. They invest in real estate, which provides housing to renters who cannot afford to buy their own home. They also make tax contributions to the community and support churches, charities, scholarships, and the like. It's a fact the more wealth you create for yourself, the more wealth and opportunities you create for others.

How would you like to live in a country of mostly poor folks? Well, here's some bad news—you do. Folks maybe not at poverty level but barely getting by. Are you one of these folks? If the answer is yes, why? You have no one to blame but yourself. Don't get mad at me; I'm not your boss. I didn't make the conscious decision to be broke; you did. Spend more time creating assets that pay instead of liabilities that suck you dry and your situation will change quickly.

MYTH NUMBER EIGHT: "YOU MUST HAVE MONEY TO MAKE MONEY."

That's the biggest lie since "the IRS is here to help." People who think this way will die broke. The truth is . . .

If you can't make money without money, you can't make money with money.

Now, I didn't say *no* money was needed. I just said it doesn't have to be your money. You should be using OPM (other people's money), and I wrote this book to show you how to do just that.

The greatest fortunes are made through leverage, and, fortunately, real estate is the highest leveraged vehicle on the planet. Hey, if you

$216,426 on 8 deals in 4½ months.

Sean Queen, *White House, Tennessee*

Ron,

I've needed to send you a thank you letter long before now but I know as it is often said, "It's better late than never." **THANKS A MILLION!!** I can't thank you enough for what you've taught me and how your training has helped me net **$216,426.97** on 8 deals in only 3 months, since the end of May this year!

After a successful 7 years in the car business, I can now see the daylight at the end of the real estate tunnel and I know I made the right choice to switch careers. I won't miss those long hours at night, weekends, or holidays that I used to work while I missed out on my kids' ball games and birthday parties. You'll never know what this switch in careers has done for me and my family. Without your help I could never have done it!

I know this testimonial is not like some of your other students who have made more on one deal than my 8.

I am still excited anyway. Instead of a big deal coming around once in a while, I am very happy to see the results of a system that I have learned from you which has proven to me that this business will supply a very comfortable income month in and month out, not just once in a while.

Here is the information on the 8 deals to show the profit on each. I have enclosed copies of checks and the Hud-1 settlement statements for each deal.

1. 268 Sunset Blvd.: I purchased this home for **$36,000.00**. I then got a loan for **$56,000.00** giving me **$20,000.00** for rehab and holding costs. I spent a little more than **$20,000.00** which ended up being a total of **$22,236.93**. I raised the price to cover my buyers closing costs and sold it for **$94,100.00**. **My net profit on this deal is $28,479.34.**

Net check $30,716.27
Rehab cost overage -$2,236.93
Net profit $28,479.34

2. 1538 Straightway Ave.: I purchased this home for **$34,500.00**. I then got a loan for **$62,000.00** giving me **$27,500** for rehab and holding costs. I only spent **$16,842.07**. I raised the price to cover my buyers closing costs and sold it for **$77,000.00**. **My net profit on this deal is $20,705.99.**

Net check= $10,048.06
Loan funds not used = $10,657.93
Net profit = $20,705.99

3. 284 35th Ave. N.: I purchased this home for **$46,500.00**. I made a split funded offer for half up front and the other half in 6 months which she accepted. Not knowing whether or not I wanted to keep it for a rehab or flip it, I decided to run an ad worded like you taught me to test the market for a flip. The day after the ad ran I put it under contract with my new buyer for **$62,000.00** with a **$5,000.00** earnest money check. Before I contracted with my new buyer I could tell he was teetering on the phone, so to push him over the edge I told him he could, pay me **$42,000.00** up front and the rest in 5 3/4 months. It worked great. I owe her **$23,240.00** and he owes me **$20,000.00**. **My net profit on this deal is $14,401.57.**

Net check = $12,641.57
Earnest money = $5,000.00
$17,641.57
- $2,340.00
Net profit = $15,301.57

4. 1609 Baptist World Ctr. Dr.: I purchased this home for **$63,000.00** "subject to" the mortgage. I had to pay **$8,954.60** to bring the mortgage current. I spent **$3,892.33** to rehab it. I raised the price to cover my buyers closing costs and sold it for **$112,243.00**. **My net profit on this deal is $37,168.18.**

Net check $50,015.11
Reinstate -$8,954.60
$41,060.51
-$3,892.33
Net profit = $37,168.18

5. 808 Jones Ave.: I purchased this home for **$52,640.20**. I then got a loan for **$68,000.00** giving me **$15,359.80** for rehab and holding costs. I only spent **$8,376.28**. I raised the price to cover my buyers closing costs and sold it for **$96,717.00**. **My net profit on this deal is $31,289.27.**

Net check = $17,305.75
Earnest money = $7,000.00
Loan funds not used = $6,983.52
Net profit $31,289.27

6. 1504 Heritage View Blvd.: I purchased this home for **$56,699.23**. I then got a loan for **$70,000.00** giving me **$13,300.77** for rehab and holding costs. I only spent **$8,149.64**. I raised the price to cover my buyers closing costs and sold it for **$98,500.00**. **My net profit on this deal is $25,097.57.**

Net check = $19,946.44
Loan funds not used = $5,151.13
Net profit = $25,097.57

7. 2521 Slaydon Dr.: I purchased this home for **$62,900.00** subject to the mortgage. I had to pay **$2,906.34** to bring the loan current. I didn't get a loan and I never touched it. I sold it for **$94,203.00**. **My net profit on this deal is $25,500.88.**

Net check = $28,407.22
$2,906.34
Net profit $25,500.88

8. 2018 Skyline Dr: I purchased this home for $89,900.00. I put **$13,000.00** down and financed the rest. Periodically I paid principal payments to reduce the balance and interest—while it was lease optioned. I got a **$5,000.00** non refundable option deposit and just recently, got cashed out with a net check at closing for **$52,003.63**. **My net profit on this deal is $32,384.17.**

Net check = $52,003.63
Earnest money = $5,000.00
$57,003.63
Down pmnt., principal pmnts. + closing costs - $24,119.46
Net profit $32,884.17

That's a total of **$216,426.97** on 8 deals in 4 1/2 months! It used to take me 12 to 14 months to make that and I know it is only going to get better.

Thanks again!!
See you in Vegas.

Sincerely,

Sean Queen

don't write a check to buy a house and make money on the deal, your return is infinite. It doesn't get any better than that. That's OPM.

Do you want to be a millionaire? Simply acquire $10 million worth of houses with $9 million of nonrecourse (subject to) debt and bingo! you're there. Relax, that's only 66 houses worth $150,000 each. What's the big deal? I've got students buying that many houses in one year. What if it took you three or four? Of course, that probably means you're still exchanging hours for dollars. This plan requires you to keep the houses, but what's wrong with that? Buy some, sell some, and keep some. Now you have the best of both worlds.

Wealth is like a house—it needs a good, solid foundation or it will fall apart. People who have taken the time and effort to build solid foundations of successful characteristics can proceed with the business of creating their houses of wealth—doing the framing, laying the bricks, and so forth—with the security that comes from knowing that what they're building is very likely going to last for a long, long time and no one can lay them off or fire them.

Once you know how to buy real estate correctly and understand clearly what to do with it, then you truly have created security. No one can take the knowledge away once you have it.

"You should always buy houses as if you're broke."

Ron LeGrand

He bought his home with no money down while attending my seminar.

E. Bowden, *San Jose, California*

Dear Ron,

Thank you for the valuable information, insight and motivational inspiration that you provided me in the recent Ron LeGrand seminar. If the individuals sitting in your seminar realized the value and power of the information that was at their fingers tips, they would realize that this is truly bigger than any pre-IPO stock tip that they could have gotten in the dot.com boom times.

Prior to taking a 3-day seminar such as this, I had purchased 2 homes. Each time it was the very traditional method and painful process that everyone is all too familiar with in dealing with lending institutions, and the construction of new home developments. However, after taking your class, those days are a thing of the past for me!! As we all know education not utilized is wasted, and actions speak louder than words. Allow me to share my story as an inspiration to those in your seminar today.

On the third day of my initial seminar in real estate, I happened to meet a couple, who like me was interested in learning more creative ways to buy and sell real estate properties. They had just purchased another home in Saratoga, Calif, which they were about to close on, and currently owned a 2 1/2 year old home in San Jose, and a condo in Saratoga.

They were interested in finding someone who wanted to purchase the home in San Jose, and eventually even sell their condo in Saratoga before the end of the year. All of this certainly caught my attention – especially any property that was for sale by owner. At the end of the seminar we met in the bar and had a drink, got to know one another and discussed the seminar, as well as their problem.

Within an hour, I offered up a solution. I'd buy the home at their purchase price if they'd give me my terms! Needless to say, we adjourned to their home and after a walk through, we sat down at the kitchen table and worked out the terms of the deal. I was back the following day with a contract and we finalized the paperwork within 4 days.

I purchased my first home for nearly no money down, simply a DOLLAR, and therefore NO BIG CHECKS, no personal signature for the debt. The title wasn't in my name and I moved into it within 45 days. All this due to the fact that I diminished my risk with an advanced education in real estate, the things I never was taught in school.

Thanks to the Ron LeGrand organization for your inspiration and support. I've been living in my pretty home deal for the past 7 months, and I'm working my next deal, an UGLY home – with 4.6 acres of undeveloped land attached. Can't wait to share that story with you!! This is a reality, all anyone has to do is overcome their FUD Factor (Fear, Uncertainty and Doubt), and anything is possible!!

Sincerely,

E. Bowden
San Jose, California

3

EVERYONE WINS OR
I WON'T PLAY

Some outsiders are under the impression the only way to make money in quick turn real estate is to take advantage of people. They picture all of us investors literally stealing houses and putting old ladies out on the street. Or they perceive us as tyrannical landlords wearing big black hats operating slum properties unfit for human habitation. Such perceptions are not just erroneous—they demonstrate total ignorance.

In all the years I've been an investor buying more than 1,500 houses, not once have I ever put a gun to a seller's head and said, "Sign or die." In fact, many times I've found myself hoping the seller wouldn't work with me because I didn't like the looks of a deal. But I went ahead and bought anyway to get the seller out of a jam. That's not what I'd suggest you do. It's better to walk.

Many people don't understand the valuable services real estate entrepreneurs perform for the public. Of course, I wouldn't buy a house if I couldn't make a profit from it, but in many cases I could have walked away and been happier than if I had bought. However, the seller's needs pushed me to take on some project or other that may not have been the best use of my time.

In looking at the real estate business, several elements must be considered: First, the business is more than money. Money is only the by-product of a specialized activity that provides one of life's necessities—shelter. Think about the last sad story you heard about a family home lost to foreclosure. Maybe you, yourself, have been through hard times and lost your house to a bank. How would you have felt about an investor's providing you with a solution when no one else could or would? I can tell you from experience few things in life are more humiliating and stressful than having lenders hounding you almost daily, demanding payments you can't cough up.

Going through that process destroys self-esteem, breaks up marriages, and can even cause health problems—or worse. I once bought a house whose owner—the father of three children—had committed suicide under the stress of pending foreclosure. That experience gave me a new outlook on life. At the same time I was buying the widow's house at eight o'clock one Saturday night, trying to help her stop crying, I decided my measly little problems didn't amount to a hill of beans compared with hers.

She had three kids, but she had no income, no job, no food, and now no husband. All of a sudden I switched from the mind-set of "How cheaply can I get this house?" to "How much can I afford to give this lady?" She owed about $26,000 on a $50,000 house (remember this was in the early 1980s), and the monthly payment was $280. She was four months behind on her payments, and the house needed about $2,000 in repairs. She told me if I would give her $1,000 and make up her payments, she would deed the house to me.

Now, I'm no angel, and I'm usually pretty reluctant to give up a buck unless it's absolutely necessary, but that night was an exception. I reached into my wallet and handed her $500 cash. Then I told her once I had checked her title and she was out of the house, I would give her an additional $3,500. That's $3,000 more than she was asking. Needless to say, she was elated, and I had won a friend for life.

But who really got the best bargain? Yes, I made money on the house and could have made $3,000 more. But the most important result of the deal: I was on a high for weeks afterward, and I had learned a lesson that will stick with me for life: *You can't help someone up a hill without getting closer to the top yourself!*

Remembering that experience still gives me goose bumps. And I'm sure, as your career progresses, you'll have the opportunity to help a similar family solve its problems.

SAVING HOUSES FROM THE WRECKING BALL

In addition to the human element, of course, there's also the matter of the houses themselves. Think of all the houses that are rehabbed by investors every week. If investors don't buy them, who will? What happens to them?

The answer is they get bulldozed, or they just sit there until they are boarded up and condemned, then fall down on their own. True, every once in a while an owner/occupant buys a property to fix up and occupy. But for every one of those, 100 get rehabbed for profit by people like us. We're providing a service to our community by improving the looks of the neighborhood, as well as by increasing the stock of the houses and the community's tax base. That, in turn, generates more revenue for the city.

In addition, rehabbing requires contractors and laborers who benefit from the work. All rehabs require more materials, which are supplied by vendors who buy from manufacturers—all businesses that create jobs and employ people. And the process generates fees for professionals such as surveyors, Realtors, appraisers, termite inspectors, closing agents, title clerks, attorneys, and so on. Stop the rehabbing of houses, and all those people would suffer directly or indirectly; many couldn't exist. So, yes, people who buy and fix houses are certainly performing a public service.

SHARING THE WEALTH

Let's look at aspects of real estate investing that have nothing to do with the rehabbing process itself. Have you ever known people who have had to make two house payments simultaneously because they purchased a new home before the old one was sold?

Who besides an investor is going to offer debt relief when the house doesn't sell? Real estate brokers? Hardly. Realtors attempt to sell houses at little or no risk to themselves. Making a seller's payments while tying up a house for six months is not part of their service.

Could a seller rent the house to a tenant? Possibly. More often than not, all the seller would wind up with is an expensive lesson in landlording and a bigger problem. Renting the house could also make it extremely difficult to sell. It would rarely be clean, and getting access to it would be complicated. Of course, the tenant would not be cooperating with the seller if it meant that when the house was sold, the tenant would have to move.

So we investors step in and take over payments and repairs, and we usually get the house sold in time. The seller's problem is solved, and we have provided a valuable service.

Believe it or not, while we're working to help sellers by saving them from the foreclosure machinery of the big bad banks, we're also performing a service for those banks. And that service, too, trickles down to a wider public. If investors didn't buy houses out of foreclosure or afterward, who would? If the only market were owner/occupants, you would see a drastic decline in housing prices. Moreover, the conditions for getting a loan would become terribly stringent. These factors would slow demand drastically, and all related industries would suffer, many of them evaporating.

Yet another very important group of people benefit from investors' work in real estate. What about all those owner/occupants who wouldn't have a home of their own without us? I have sold hundreds of houses to first- and last-time homebuyers. Many of them needed help solving minor problems and overcoming hurdles. I can honestly say some would never have been able to buy had I not made it possible.

Sometimes I helped them get financing. Sometimes I was the bank and owner financed for them. Without my being the bank and allowing them to bypass rigorous qualifying procedures, most of these people would still be renters today. Usually, investors are the only owner-financing game in town.

Without us, owner financing would be almost nonexistent.

So are we providing a public service by understanding creative financing? You bet. We are providing a service that is extremely important to those families who couldn't own a home any other way. Incidentally, if it weren't for investors, who would own rental property, and where would all the tenants live?

True, as you become more and more involved with real estate investing, you may get the feeling you're not always appreciated. Sometimes we get a lot of flack from government employees, real estate professionals, and other people who don't understand the business. But rest assured investors will be around as long as people need places to live. There is plenty of business to go around, and investors can make money without making anyone suffer. If any deal is not win-win, just don't do it. Move on.

> *"You can't help someone up a hill without getting closer to the top yourself."*
>
> Unknown

"I have recently surpassed $1,000,000 in this business."
Richard Roop, *Woodland Parks, Colorado*

Bottom Line Results, Inc.

Entrepreneurial Marketing. Real Estate Investments. Equity Loans

Dear Ron,

This letter is long overdue. I have made over $1,000,000 in my real estate business since taking your courses. Although I have shared some of my successes with you and your students at several of your events, I've never taken the time to thank you in writing and share the actual results I have achieved in my Real Estate business. Even though I am always looking and learning, you deserve the most credit since I have yet to find a better source for practical instruction on how to make money as a Real Estate Entrepreneur. After buying and studying your 3 course modules, I purchased my first property (with none of my own money).

To date, I have been involved in 70 properties. Because I have been able to make multiple profits on a few of these houses, I have done a total of 89 real estate transactions. Since getting started, I've collected $479,000 in cash plus $464,000 equity in contracts, notes and properties I have acquired. I still own 16 of these homes and control another 9, which means I am managing 25 properties today. Five of these properties I got just in the last month.

The bottom line is that I have made an average profit of $13,471 on each of these properties, without losing a dime on any of them for a total of $930,000 in cash and equity. I also have other income from notes, flipping paper, positive cash flows, and brokering private loans. Taking into account this additional income, I have recently surpassed $1,000,000 in this business. What is my net? My overhead has grown over the years to about $9,000 a month but now I have 2 employees helping me do 3 or 4 deals each month. This year my company will net over $300,000 in cash and equity.

QUICK TURN TOOLS

4

FIVE WAYS TO PROFIT

Quick turn transactions fall into five main categories: (1) rehabbing and retailing; (2) wholesaling; (3) getting the deed; (4) lease options; and (5) options. Almost everything you do in the real estate investing business will follow one of these methods.

REHABBING AND RETAILING

Buying houses low and selling them high is called *retailing*. This is the most easily understood method of investing in real estate because of the countless books and tapes on the subject. It's the art of buying at a low price, often doing some repairs, and then selling at retail price and usually cashing out. A lot of money is made through this method. Some people do it part-time, turning 2 or 3 houses a year, and make more money at it than they make on their regular jobs. Others do it full-time and turn 40 to 80 houses a year with an average profit from $20,000 to $35,000 per deal.

In the following chapters you'll find a plan for locating these basically ugly houses, making offers, estimating repairs, and selling quickly.

If you attempt to do this type of deal from a book, I have to caution you a lot can go wrong, but obviously I can't cover every detail here.

Rehabbing and retailing houses is very profitable, but it's also the hardest way to make money in real estate and is layered with costly entanglements. Frankly, it's not where I'd suggest you start your career unless you simply can't control that internal burning desire to make something ugly into something pretty.

A lot of satisfaction comes from rehabbing, and there's a lot to learn. However, if you have a choice to make money an easy way or a hard way, my guess is you'd take the easy way. I know I would; in fact, the older I get, the easier I want it.

But if you can't resist the urge to buy and renovate, here are some tips not covered in later chapters:

Tip 1. Buy in areas where qualified buyers want to live, not in war zones where bullets fly and little white bags change hands on street corners.

Tip 2. Pay close attention to my MAO (maximum allowable offer) formula in Chapter 7 and buy well below the MAO. If you pay too much for the house, you'll be working for nothing—or worse.

Tip 3. Never close your purchase without confirming your assumptions, that is, after repaired value and repair estimates. Do your due diligence and get the purchase appraised as completed; buy title insurance; have a termite inspection; get repair estimate(s) from qualified contractors; and get estimates to fix any other traps you can avoid.

Tip 4. Always borrow more than you need to buy and repair. The job will always cost more, take longer, and yield less profit than you expect. You better have a cash reserve. Chapter 11 covers where to get the money to buy "junkers," even if you're dead broke, bankrupt, and have bad breath, BO, and no friends or family and just got released from the federal penitentiary.

Tip 5. Keep a tight leash on contractors. They'll play you like a yo-yo, which can—and probably will—be one of your biggest learning experiences in The School of Hard Knocks. But, hey, don't worry; I graduated from that same school top of my class, and I survived.

Former school teacher netted $37,438 on one deal!

Stephanie Bombei, *Tampa, Florida*

Dear Ron,

We wanted to show you our check for our latest deal in Tampa, Florida. My father, husband, and I began our real estate investing career a little over a year ago and with every deal we have made numerous mistakes, but each time have learned and made a little more. I am a former middle school teacher and run our business full time while my husband and father still hold full time jobs. We have attended your MMBC two times and are excited to be going to MIS in Las Vegas in March.

This was a retail deal we purchased for $50,000. We renovated the house (primarily ourselves – don't scream) for $ 7,000 which included a new A/C unit, carpet, paint, new kitchen and bathroom, and termite treatment. When completed, it appraised for $119,000, and while we were trying to sell it, we found because of the area it was in the people who loved it couldn't qualify for a mortgage. Using the creative financing methods we learned from you we were able to help a couple qualify for a 90% first mortgage and take back a small second. We raised the sales price from $95,000 to $119,000 since we made it easier for them to purchase the home and in turn got cashed out. Now the second mortgage is only icing on the deal! With this one deal only we netted **$37,438.64!!** I look at this check and I can't believe we really did it!! Thank you so much for showing us the path to financial freedom.

Best Regards,

Stephanie Bombei, Brian Bombei, and Ed Skorupa
Sunchoice Properties, LLC

10581

SUPERIOR SERVICE TITLE INC.
TRUST ACCOUNT
6570 30TH AVENUE N.
SAINT PETERSBURG, FL 33710
(727) 344-3880

AMSOUTH BANK
SAINT PETERSBURG, FL 33710
63-466/631

PAY TO THE ORDER OF: Sunchoice Properties LLC $***94,438.64

Ninety-Four Thousand Four Hundred Thirty-Eight and 64/100*** DOLLARS

MEMO 2208/Sunchoice to Rice/Seller's Proceeds

AUTHORIZED SIGNATURE

Tip 6. Don't tie up your cash. Tying it up is a good way to become a motivated seller. The greater your need to sell, the longer it will take. Ron's law!

Tip 7. Do a nice renovation job. It'll pay handsome dividends in saved holding costs and in satisfied customers who'll send you more buyers.

Tip 8. Find a good loan processor or mortgage broker to get your buyers financed. It's the difference between success and failure. This person has your paycheck in his or her control, so make sure the person you find knows his or her business and follows up.

Tip 9. Master the art of selling houses as fast as humanly possible. Slow selling is the biggest weakness for most yet one of the easiest to fix. If you sell houses the way most untrained investors do, it'll be a while before you get paid.

Tip 10. Never do your own repairs. If you do, you're working as a laborer, not an investor. You make money by locating and buying good deals, not swinging a paint brush. If you adhere to Tip 4, it won't be a problem; you'll have the money. Some people tell me fixing houses is their therapy. I say if you lay hands on a house, you need therapy.

Tip 11. Get trained at this craft of quick turning real estate before you have to pay an ugly price for your education. Education is a lot cheaper than ignorance.

Go to **http://www.ronlegrand.com** and check out our five-day training taught by student turned teacher Robyn Thompson. When I met her, she worked for IBM and was a part-time waitress. Now she rehabs about 50 houses each year, netting about $23,000 each. Put that in your calculator and see if it's better than your job pays.

Robyn has become one of the best in the country at this, and I'm proud to say "I knew her way back when." Now she's a nationwide trainer, author, lecturer, guru, and sweetheart of a lady. I affectionately call her "the hatchet lady." Others call her "the Queen of Rehab." Her contractors call her "Mama."

Their first deal taught them some valuable lessons while they were making $60,000!!

Gene and Laura Bauerle, *Huntingdon, Pennsylvania*

E.R.B & SONS, Inc.

Ron LeGrand

This is a letter of thanks for caring to teach others what you know about real estate and finances. Also to tell you about a deal I did and what I learned from it. This home was in the foreclosure process but the bank was giving the owner a chance to list it. The house was an ugly 2 bed 1 bath.

He was asking $60,000 but he owed the bank $80,000. I offered $50,000. They accepted it but it took 3 months for them to sign the agreement.

The ARV was $130,000, needing $40,000 in repairs, which made my MAO $51,000. After we settled I decided to change the house to a 3 bedroom 2 bath for a better market. It took 9 months to complete. I sold it for $179,900 and put over $60,000 in repairs and carrying costs. The house took 45 days to sell and another 3 months to settle. I owned it over 13 months. The buyer's home inspection picked up mold in the basement so the house needed to be tested and then remediated, which at the last minute was another unexpected $2,000.

What I learned from this is to keep mold in consideration when doing repairs and clean it up yourself and save the last minute problems, which also come with a big last minute bill.

Also, like Ron says, hire contractors and get it done faster and spend your time making more offers and don't use your own money because it's not worth the stress. This lead was from a call I placed to a Realtor listing a house on my street. I asked him about the listing, then gave him some info on what I do with ugly homes and he called me 2 days later with a pocket listing. Somebody in his office asked him if he knew of anybody that would want a handyman special. This happened to also be the first offer I ever made on a junker.

Again Ron I would like to thank you for giving us the tools to become everybody's dream to be worth MILLIONS.

Sincerely,   Gene & Laura Bauerle

WHOLESALING

The second method of investing in real estate is *wholesaling*. This is an entire business in itself and generates super-fast profits, usually without ever acquiring the title on the property. It's not uncommon to pick up a check at closing, with the seller and buyer present at the same time. Many times I have earned thousands of dollars within two or three days of finding a deal. Successful people in the wholesale business are accomplished at locating good deals and marketing them—primarily to people who are in the rehabbing and retailing business. The first purchaser is willing to take a smaller, fast profit and leave the larger profit to an investor with the time and money to buy, repair, and sit on the house until it's sold.

Some of my students are making a good income by buying and then reselling immediately only once or twice a month. These deals require no money, no credit, and no bosses. Believe me, if you locate a deal, someone is waiting to buy it from you. Finding bargains for bargain hunters is the easiest and quickest way I know to pick up a check for at least $5,000. The whole process shouldn't take more than 15 to 20 days from the beginning to the end.

In Chapter 6 I discuss ways to find these junkers, and Chapter 10 covers selling them quickly. The only difference between wholesaling and retailing is in the exit strategy you use. It's the same house—ugly!

Here are some wholesaling tips not discussed in detail in later chapters:

Tip 1. Don't pay too much. Remember, you're selling to bargain hunters. Leave them plenty of room to make a profit or you won't find a buyer. That means they should net at least 20 percent of the sales price after all expenses.

Tip 2. If the house is in a war zone, you better be paying war zone prices. "Buy 'em so cheap you can sell 'em so cheap your buyers can't refuse 'em." The biggest market is landlords looking for low-income rentals. Buy well below the MAO discussed in Chapter 7.

Tip 3. Your only exit is to sell for all cash quickly. Make sure your buyers can get the cash and aren't relying on bank financing. Don't allow buyers to learn banks won't finance junkers at your expense. If a buyer can't close in 15 days or less, find another buyer.

Tip 4. Use an assignment of contract and let your closing agent collect your fee. See Chapter 10 for details and Appendix A for the assignment.

There's really not that much to learn about wholesaling. It's an easy business. I have students all over North America doing one to ten deals a month and netting a low of $3,000. Some make more on one wholesale deal than most people make in a year on their job.

GETTING THE DEED

The third method of real estate investing involves acquiring ownership of houses by taking over the existing debt. The common term used is a *"subject to clause"*—you take title subject to the underlying financing. This method doesn't involve credit because you are not assuming the loan. Title stays in the seller's name but transfers to you. This is the most common technique used by real estate investors today and is literally making millionaires all over the free world.

The normal exit strategy is to sell for cash to a qualified buyer immediately or to install a lease purchase tenant until that tenant gets financed at a later date, a topic I cover in Chapter 10.

To use the "subject to" clause requires you to go beyond what you may consider normal or reasonable. There are three issues some people have a hard time coping with here, and they keep a lot of folks from reaching the big profits. Get past them and it's worth a fortune to you. These are the three issues:

1. *People deed their house to you and the loan stays in their name.* You'll get the house but will not assume the debt or accept personal liability. Instead, you'll *take over the debt,* which is called taking title "subject to." The loan shows on the seller's credit report until it's paid off and, yes, the seller's credit is in your hands. The only kind of seller who will do this is one that *needs* to sell, *not wants* to sell (more on this in Chapter 6). The need to sell must outweigh the concern about credit or you won't get the deed.

High school drop-out makes $20,000 on a quick wholesale deal!!

Victor R. Favela, *Los Angeles, California*

Dear Ron,

Yet another Wholesale Flip! Who would have thought that a .37 cent investment (stamp) would put $20,000 in my pocket, solve a seller's personal challenge, increase property values, and end blight in the inner-city?

I found a distressed property, tracked down the owner and sent a letter. The seller called and was delighted someone was crazy enough to take this "problem" off her hands. After coming to an agreement on price I Wholesale Flipped the property to another investor who specializes in rehabs for $20,000.

The property sat vacant for approximately 10 years before I got involved. After repairs, the property was sold for $27,000 and a deserving family moved into it. This was my second Wholesale Flip and I have continued to do more. My mission is to end blight in the inner-city and thanks to your training it is becoming a reality one property at a time. The best part is I don't put up any money, other than modest advertising costs and my credit is a non-issue.

It's difficult for many to believe that an unemployed, former U.S. Navy Squid (sailor) and high school drop-out from East L.A. can do as well as I've done. I've included pictures of the property I've discussed in this letter as well as a picture of me and of course my company car...yup, that's a 5 series BMW. Thanks again Ron for giving me my life back and helping erase all those supposed boundaries.

Sincerely,

Victor R. Favela
Los Angeles, CA

Life sure does change after Ron...

Yup, that's a 5 series BMW.

Some sellers couldn't care less about their credit—it's already shot before they call you. Other sellers have good credit but want debt relief now and simply believe you'll do what you say. There is no written personal guarantee on your part, and you are only morally obligated to do what you promise you'll do.

2. *People give you thousands of dollars in free equity if you let them.* Equity is "pie-in-the-sky" money that doesn't exist until the property is cashed out at retail price. Debt relief and a long list of other motivating factors compel many people to give away equity in exchange for peace of mind. If you understand this and stop trying to psychoanalyze other people's motives, you can quickly amass millions in free equity that you can turn into cash with a little training.

3. *The lender can call the loan due because the title transferred without the loan's being paid off.* There's a due-on-sale clause in all loans now that gives lenders this right. That's the bad news. The good news is that lenders hate real estate—it's a plague to them. They're in the money business. Rarely will lenders call a loan due when someone is willing to make the payments, and that's assuming they even learn it transferred before they get paid off.

But let's play worst-case scenario. If the lender did call it due, that won't affect your credit. You didn't guarantee the note. No one will be knocking on your door collecting your assets, except for this house. Your name wouldn't be mentioned in a lawsuit unless you are foolish enough to take title in your own name. (More on this in Chapter 13 on land trusts.)

Will the lender's calling the loan due affect the seller's credit? Yes, it will. That's why I or my students never get a deed "subject to" without also getting what I call a CYA letter signed by the seller. It's a simple disclosure whereby the seller acknowledges having been made aware the loan will stay in the seller's name and that the bank could call the loan due. Any sellers who'll deed you their house will sign a CYA letter; if not, don't take the house.

We'll cover how to buy and sell these extremely profitable and easy-to-do deals in later chapters. Try to overcome your objections and apprehensions here and keep an open mind. I have over 300,000 students to date, and I'd bet over 60 percent of them have bought free houses on a

Elementary school principal specializes in "subject to" deals!!

Hannah J. Liddiard, *Lexington, Michigan*

We Buy Houses
Sunrise Home Buyers LLC

Hey, Ron!

Just writing to let you know what a great time I'm having buying houses "subject to" the existing mortgages. When I first heard of this concept, I had what is probably a very typical reaction: "Why would <u>anyone</u> in their right mind deed their house over to me, while leaving the mortgage in their own name?" Hmmm...could only be someone way behind in their payments whose credit is already trashed, right?? WRONG!!

In my first seven months of buying houses "Ron's way," I have had four owners deed their houses over to me, subject to their mortgages — and three out of the four were current on their payments!! Only one was in pre-foreclosure. The details are summarized below. Needless to say, "getting the deed subject to" has now become one of the favorites in my toolbox of strategies. I am averaging just under $26,000 per house of instant equity the day I buy (with more long-term profit if I lease-option them for a while).

I'M A BELIEVER NOW!!! This is a very powerful tool, AND it provides lots of juicy tax breaks that I can claim as the <u>owner</u> of the house. Here are the four "subject to" deals so far:

<u>State Road</u> Taken for $99,000 current 1st mortgage (sellers are continuing to pay their 2nd mortgage payment of $195 because the payments would have been too high for me to lease-option it to the future buyer). L/O for $120,000. Instant equity: $21,000. Seller Motivation: Retired folks who had moved to Florida for health reasons and couldn't get this house in Michigan sold through realtor. Their out-of-pocket of about $1,000 per month here was eating up their retirement pension, since they'd already bought something in Florida.

<u>Lakeshore Road</u> Taken for $115,000 1st mortgage (had to put in about $7,000 of private lender money to bring this one current on top of the $108,000 owed on the principal). L/O for $152,000. Instant equity: $37,000. Seller Motivation: Major medical problem had put them into pre-foreclosure — they sold to me and moved nearer to family in another state to start over with new jobs (and a salvaged credit record).

<u>Metcalf Road</u> Taken subject to $120,000 current 1st plus $5,000 moving money (owners paid next two payments). L/O for $149,000 with $500 "off" to install own new carpet and paint walls. Instant equity: $24,000. Seller Motivation: To move in with his ailing, elderly mother a.s.a.p.

<u>Myrtle Street</u> Going to sign the "subject to" papers this afternoon on this one! Taking over current 1st of $107,000, they will pay next two payments after moving out. Bread-and-butter houses should easily sell for $120,000 or L/O for $125,000+. Instant equity: $15,000-20,000. Seller Motivation: Tried to sell for 8 months with realtor, and are about to lose their chance to buy their "dream house" in same neighborhood.

This SURE beats the heck out of working as an elementary principal or curriculum coordinator for the public schools!! Attached is a photo from my "school administrator" days—you won't catch me in a suit very often now. I also don't set an alarm clock unless I'm at a Boot Camp!! Thank you SO MUCH for making this new life possible. I wake up every day excited to jump into my deals.

2004 will be MY YEAR!!   Yours, Hannah

"subject to" basis. Who knows, it might even work for you. I've bought over 400 houses "subject to" and not once has a lender called the loan due.

LEASE OPTIONS

The fourth method of investing in real estate is to *lease option* properties from sellers to control the properties without taking title. This method works on houses in any price range and with any underlying financing. You can reap big profits without ever owning the house while at the same time paying no closing costs to buy or sell, doing no repairs, and using very little or no money.

The objective is to either sell for cash or install a tenant/buyer to lease purchase from you until he or she cashes out or until you can cash out immediately by getting enough free equity. This technique is sometimes referred to as a "sandwich lease." You're the meat in the sandwich.

Buying with a lease option overcomes all the objections I just discussed, because the title doesn't go from the seller to you until your buyer gets new financing in the future. Therefore, a bank can't call the loan due and the seller's credit is not in your hands. However, you must still get free equity, or there's no reason to get involved.

You'll find and sell these deals the same way you do all the others. The only difference is you're leasing instead of buying. Your agreement must give you the right to buy at a fixed price—usually the loan balance—and the right to sublet to a tenant. You totally control the property during this term you agree to, and the seller can't reverse the agreement unless you default. It's truly control without ownership.

You should only lease option attractive houses ready to be occupied, and the maximum deposit to the seller is $100. If the seller wants more money, get the deed or get the door.

Honestly, in today's market I won't do a lease option. It's too easy to get the deed, and I'd rather have ownership than control for two main reasons:

1. When I get a deed, I never have to contact the seller again for any permission or signature. I own the house just as legally, morally, and ethically as if I had paid cash but not true for lease options.

The seller in a lease option transact can always be a problem later after you've solved the problem and are about ready to cash out.

2. I can depreciate a house I own, but I can't depreciate one I lease. On a house I bought for $150,000 (the loan amount I took over), that came to about $5,000 a year I get for free through a tax write-off.

When people call you to buy their house, they usually want to sell, not rent it. Buying is a conclusion, even if the loan is in their name. Of course, there are times when lease optioning makes sense—perhaps it's the only way you'll get the deal—so you should be prepared. All it takes is a little training and a couple of agreements to be in business—a multi-million-dollar business I might add.

OPTIONS

Using the *options* method of investing, you simply agree to option a property at price A with the intent to sell at Price B. You hope that price B is higher than price A; the difference is your profit. This is a risk-free technique that's producing huge paychecks for some of my students. The biggest as of this writing is from an Orlando, Florida, student who made *$2,450,000 on one deal in 43 days with a $100 investment.*

His name is Marco Kozlowski, a 30-something guy I stole from the job market and turned into an assassin. In his first year in business, Marco acquired 119 deeds on "pretty" houses in the Orlando area. Then he started raising his sights and working with ultraexpensive houses. Once he learned it doesn't cost a nickel more or take any more time or resources or risk to deal with multi-million-dollar houses as it does to deal with hundred-thousand-dollar houses, there was no stopping Marco.

He found a wealthy guy who had an $8,600,000 house on the market for four years with a Realtor. It was vacant and one of five the guy owned; at that price it was obviously a pretty cool pad with all the bells and whistles, including a dock and waterfront. After three months of going back and forth, the seller agreed to option the house to Marco for $4,000,000. So much for our previous discussion about getting free equity! This house was a pain to the seller; he didn't want or need it, and the money meant nothing to him. In addition, he had a $5,000,000 yacht parked at the dock. Marco optioned the house for $4,000,000 and got a bunch of free "stuff" in the house with the deal. His total deposit was $100 to the seller. He later admitted he forgot to even give him that.

Marco then called an auctioneer and scheduled an auction for 43 days later. He persuaded the auctioneer to call some end consignment houses in order to load the place up with art, furniture, and other stuff to sell at the auction with the house and the yacht.

Over 300 people attended the two-day auction. The house sold for $5,600,000, the yacht for $4,300,000, and the stuff for almost $1,000,000. Marco netted $2,440,000 altogether on this one deal, with no money, no credit, no risk, and no promises he couldn't keep. I was with him the day he got the wire transfer from the closing. He was a mental wreck all day until it came.

Now Marco has turned teacher and trains others to do what he does in a three-day event, where he actually auctions off a house he optioned or took "subject to" during the training. You can learn about it by calling **800-567-6128** or at **http://www.ronlegrand.com.** Marco's my hero and, as of this writing, holds the record for the largest check so far, but a few others are on his tail.

Actually, options are nothing more than retailing a house for cash. You simply bypass the repair process and remove all risks. When you think about retailing houses to an owner-occupant, you usually conjure up all the negative things that come with that part of our business: Where do I get the money to buy and fix the house? What if I underestimate the repair costs? Where do I find a good contractor who'll work cheap? What if my contractor stiffs me? What if I can't sell the house? How do I make payment on a vacant house if I'm barely surviving now?

I bet you could throw a few more fears in the pot. In fact, within the next few pages you'll learn what could be a full-time (or part-time) business that could easily—and I really mean *easily*—net you more money than your job does.

Not only will you make more money, but we'll eliminate the following negatives while we're at it:

- I need money. *(You won't need much.)*
- I need credit. *(You won't borrow a cent.)*
- Repairs scare me. *(You won't be doing any.)*
- I'm afraid the house won't sell. *(If it doesn't, you won't lose a nickel.)*

He made $2,450,000 on one house in 43 days with a $100 investment!!!!!!
Marco Kozlowski, *Orlando, Florida*

Dear Ron,

Thanks a million…well actually 2,500,000 to be exact. I just closed on that south Florida deal and I should gross around 2.5 million in that ONE deal!!!

I owe it all to you. You gave me the foundation I needed to help me put the pieces together to make it happen. Am I glad I kept coming to ALL your events. It was only after repeating MIS the third time that I realized what I should be doing to make my fortune…and I did!

(slow learner I know)

Thanks so much! and I hope you enjoy the cigars!

Marco

THE FOLLOWING WIRE WAS CREDITED TO YOUR ACCOUNT:

USD AMOUNT   1,878,986.72

TRANSACTION REF:

IMAD:
ID:

ORIGINATOR: SURITEC IND.
SENDING BANK: LLOYDS BANK INT.
BENEFICIARY: KEMBO INVESTMENT TRUST

ID:
ID:

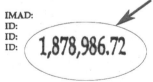

PAYMENT DETAIL: REF: SEC/536245

- I don't want anyone mad at me. *(No one will be because you won't make anyone any promises or commitments.)*
- I can't make payments. *(You won't have any to make.)*
- I'm afraid I'll lose. *(Lose what? If you have nothing invested and no promises to break, how can you lose?)*
- But I don't know how to sell houses. *(Maybe this would be a good place to learn, as there is no way to lose.)*
- I just don't know; even though I can't lose, I'm scared. *(It's better to be scared and moving than afraid and frozen.)*

Let's talk about why you would want to retail houses in the first place. Actually, there's only one good reason I can think of from my 22 years in the business and retailing about 700 houses. When I say *retail,* I mean all cash to qualified buyers who paid full price and need new financing. I'm not counting all the owner-financing deals in this number or the 500-plus wholesale deals.

The reason I elected to go the retail route on these 700 houses was because the payoff was large enough to make it worth the effort it takes to find a qualified buyer and get that buyer to the closing table. Even in the beginning, that represented a minimum of $10,000 per house. Now, I just won't retail a house unless it has a minimum of $30,000 net—not gross—profit.

If I lived in a higher-priced market where the cheapest "bread-and-butter" houses started at $200,000, for example, I wouldn't settle for $30,000. I want a minimum of 20 percent of the sales price as a profit, and the truth is that I usually get closer to 30 to 40 percent. In fact, that net profit figure is the biggest factor in determining whether to wholesale or to retail the house.

Now, don't go off the deep end on me when I start talking about a 30 to 40 percent profit. If you're new, you won't believe it. If you've been around a while and aren't doing the same, you need some fine-tuning. I went back and figured out my last six houses for this book. I was rather shocked myself to find out my average net profit on those six deals was a whopping 33 percent. That's one-third of the sales price in my pocket.

I actually bought, repaired, and maintained all six of these houses until they were sold. In the technique I discuss here, you won't buy or maintain or repair. Therefore, I think it's reasonable for you to be will-

They made $30,290 on a vacant land option and have purchased 130 properties since!!
Jack and Michelle Bosch, *Phoenix, Arizona*

Dear Ron,

My wife and I wanted to thank you for all the GREAT material you are providing for real estate investors like us. We finally made it and have our first success story to share.

Last year around August, we had just finished going through all of your 3 courses and were eager to get the first deal done. With the newly gained motivation and knowledge, we decided to finally get serious about this real estate investing business. And what a deal we were able to make happen!!!

At that time I got in contact with a lady in California who owned a 16 acre vacant lot in a beautiful and scenic Northern California area and who offered to sell it for $100,000.00. After a little negotiating (using your techniques) she agreed to a sale price of $70,000.00. My research showed the property being worth about $130,000.00 perhaps even more. Because at the time we did not have $70,000.00 I offered her an option for 90 days. We paid $50.00 for the option. Within a week we had found a buyer for the property who was willing to pay $104,000.00 CASH and 5 days later we did a simultaneous closing and walked away with a check over $30,290.00 (after all expenses).

We were nervous and did about everything wrong that anyone could do wrong. We did not know anything about the disclosures necessary in California, and we even failed to put in a time frame for closing in the contract with our buyer. But because all parties wanted to make this deal happen, everything worked out. We learned a ton and made a GREAT profit.

We were just starting to get into real estate and did not have any prior experience. As a matter of fact I am a first generation immigrant from Germany and at the time was a software consultant. I had never purchased a piece of property in my life. But since then we have bought and sold over 130 (one hundred thirty) properties (mostly vacant lots but also some houses) in the last 15 months and we have made money on every single one of them. And of course I have quit my job earlier this year and am now a 100% full time real estate investor with my wife making 3 times as much as I did as an IT Consultant.

Everything included we spent about $800. If I calculate that correctly this represents a return on investment of 3780% in one month. Not bad for the very first deal and an investment in an option that cost us $50 on a property that didn't even have a house on it.

Thanks again for supplying us with such easy to follow directions to Real Estate Investment.

Sincerely,

J. Bosch & Michelle Bosch

Jack and Michelle Bosch
Phoenix, AZ

ing to work for less than 33 percent, because you'll have no money invested and no risk at all.

Once you learn the system involved in the business of retailing, I think you'll agree with me that it's a business well worth your time to learn. Once you learn how to do it with options instead of ownership, I think you'll agree it just doesn't get better than this. No risk, no money, no credit, and no way to lose. Of course, some people prefer to actually buy and fix because they just like to make pretty something that's ugly. I can understand that; somebody's got to fix those junkers.

But now let's explore an alternative plan. How many houses can you find that fit the following descriptions?

- Vacant or soon to be
- Great neighborhood in any price range (in fact, the higher the better)
- Owner will sell for 20 percent or more below market for all cash
- A house in excellent condition and ready to occupy

You think maybe there might be a few of these sitting around? The answer is absolutely! More than you'll ever be able to handle, so point number one is: *Spend your time on prime prospects only.* A prime prospect is a well-located house in a fast-moving area that's in excellent condition. No projects wanted here. No hurdles to overcome, like smelly carpet, poor landscaping, or other deferred maintenance. No war zones where qualified people don't want to live and no trashy neighborhoods.

OK, Ron, I'm waiting to learn what I'm supposed to do with these gorgeous houses and how I make money if I'm not going to buy them. *The answer in a word is options.*

You see, you don't need to own a house to profit from it. Suppose you own a home worth $200,000 and owe $148,000 to a bank. You work for a large corporation and just got transferred out of state effective in 60 days. Your house payment is $1,285 per month and you're doing OK as long as that's your only payment. But when you move, making a payment on both houses will be a crippling blow. You're thinking about listing with a Realtor and see my ad in the paper:

I'll Buy Your Home & Pay You Cash, Any Price Range, 555-1212

She made $55,000 with a $10 Investment on an option deal!!

Faye Levow, *Exeter, New Hampshire*

Dear Ron,

Here is an update on my progress since the Las Vegas Shindig in July (which was a great time, by the way):

I just closed my second option deal. On another classic LeGrand deal, my business partner and I made $55,000 out of $10!

We were supposed to purchase and rehab a duplex a few months before, but we had problems with the lender and things took too long, so we lost the deal. BUT...

The same owner had a house and 26 acres that we got an Option to Purchase on for a whopping $10.

A few days later, a developer called me from one of my ugly yellow signs with some land to sell me. I was interested in his land and he was interested in the house and 26 acres.

In the end, he decided to keep the land and buy my deal. We got $10,000, non-refundable, up front and the other $45,000 just before the closing. Since it was an assignment of contract, we just took the money and ran...all the way to the bank!

Last week, my offer got accepted on a flea-ridden, stinky, ugly house. $145,000. Fix-up will be about $50,00 and resale range is $280,000 to $300,000 depending what happens in our market over the next few months. We are currently seeking financing.

I also have a possible deal with some people who are moving to their great-grandmother's house the end of September and need to get out from under their mortgage payments. They accepted an offer of $160,000. It needs about $10,000 to $15,000 of work and will resell for $190,000 to $200,000. It's not a big spread, but this one is a creative financing deal:

Here are the options I offered: I will either take over their payments in December and pay them the balance when I resell the house OR pay $80,000 at closing and $80,000 when I resell the house. They will let me know which option they prefer. My exit strategy is to immediately put it on the market both as a "handy-man special" for $180,000 and just walk away with $20,000 and not do any work AND at the same time, advertise it as a fixed up house for $200,000 and get the work done. Whichever comes first is ok with me.

I also met with a guy who got transferred to New Orleans for his job after only a year in his house. The house is all fixed up and has a new above-ground pool, which I encouraged him to take to New Orleans. He had it on the market since March with no offers.

There's a possible "subject to" deal in there with an exit strategy of selling with owner financing or on a lease option, just to bring in some cash flow. The guy is upside down, so that would be the only way I could help him out. Either way, he'll lose money because the market is showing similar houses sold this summer for $6,000 less than he paid for it. He wanted to get his down payment of $45,000, but he'll be lucky just to get rid of his payments. I told him I would give him $5000 over what he owes and split 50/50 anything above a selling price of $246,000. I showed him the comps, so he would know I wasn't trying to cheat him. His only other option is to rent it as a long distance landlord and I tried to discourage him from that potential fiasco.

I am also getting a lot of calls from people who just figure it might be easier and quicker to work with me than going through a Realtor or some other way to sell. They have pretty houses or houses that need light fix-up and are looking for close to top dollar. I've told them that regular buyers don't put up ugly yellow signs to buy houses. I'm an investor and if I work with them, I have to make a profit. If they're not interested, I tell them to call me back if it doesn't sell. As option deals, there's no risk; I just need to find a buyer. If I can make at least $20,000 on those deals, that works for me. On the other hand, if I have to get the work done, a more creative situation will be in order. Next stop will be an ad in the paper to build a buyers list...and a list of people looking to get more than 2% on their savings.

I have enclosed a copy of the two checks we got for the assignment on the house and 26 acres.

Thanks for your courses and your support. The education I have gotten from you has turned my life around!

Sincerely,

Faye Levow

You call my ad and quickly learn the only way I can help you is to offer you my lease option program, giving you two choices. The first choice is that I'll lease option your home, make your payments, and eventually sell the home for cash. I'll need an agreed-on strike price equaling your loan balance when I sell and the right to sublease to a tenant/buyer.

You quickly make me aware that your house is too pretty to allow me to rent it out. You just won't sleep at night knowing a tenant lives in your beautiful home. OK, I say. I understand that. So here's plan two: I'll simply option your house for $148,000 all cash. No terms! No long-term option and no right to sublease.

All I want from you is a key so I can show it and the right for me or my assigns to buy it. I need only a six-month option. I'll advertise your house at my own expense. I'll think about it every day when I get up and when I go to bed and personally work on it until it's sold or the six months expire.

Heck, since you're leaving town, I'll even keep your lawn mowed at my expense for the whole time. The downside is that because you won't let me sublease the house, I can't make any of your monthly payments while I'm selling your house.

OK, that's your offer. Now let's go through all the objections a seller could come up with to our plan two proposal:

Q. *Why should I let you tie up my house?*

A. Good question, but what if I don't tie up your house? Let's do this: I'll put it in the agreement that if you sell your house before I do, I'll cancel the agreement and go on my merry way. You'll owe me nothing. Is that fair?

Q. *Does this mean you will try to sell my house for me, but I'm still free to sell it myself?*

A. Yes, that's exactly what I mean.

Q. *Don't you need a license to do this?*

A. *No!* Not as long as you have a written option agreement. When the seller signs the agreement, you have been given an equitable interest in the house that gives you every right to sell, especially because your

Implementing ONE of Ron's tips netted them an extra $6,000.

Brian and Kristine Lambrecht, *Lake Orion, Michigan*

Greetings Ron, Ray and gang!

When we bought your course and boot camp in July 2003 from a real estate convention here in Michigan, we immediately started listening to your many CDs. We had a house that we were lease optioning to a tenant, who had to relocate in August and so the home needed a NEW optionee. The prior residents were supposed to buy it for $152,000—we figured we would increase the price to $159,900—but on your CD (the timing of when we listened to that particular one couldn't have been better!) you said to make sure we "research" market values BEFORE we put a price on a home—not to assume we are experts at knowing our market!! Thank goodness we took that tip to heart. Because we took the extra few hours to drive the neighborhood and get a CMA done by an agent friend, we ended up asking $168,900 on a "No Bank Qualifying" ad (attached) and had a family MOVE IN within 2 weeks of the ad! (They actually moved in the day after the other residents moved out!) The new optionees gave me a $5,000 option fee (the prior residents had forfeited $4,000) and are paying an extra $50/month over what the prior residents paid. They agreed to the $165,900 without hesitation!!! That GREAT tip paid for our Millionaire Maker Bootcamp alone (and then some!!)! It proves that knowledge IS power and NEVER stop learning!!

We can't wait to get our really "huge" deal, so we can apply part of those proceeds to the MIS bootcamp—we were one number away from winning it for free at the Millionaire bootcamp—we were crushed when the last number was not ours—but we will get there, and soon!! I hope the guy that won realizes what a truly wonderful, prosperous gift he received!!

Congratulations on your book and show—Best of luck on both!!

Brian and Kristine Lambrecht

Happy Holidays Ron, Ray and gang!

A motivated seller called us on our "Home Debt Relief" ad (i.e., we buy/lease houses, make your payments, etc.). We lease optioned her home for $144,000 (market value $155,000), 3.5 year term, making her mortgage (PITI) payments of $1042/month, zero down, and we do not start taking over her payments for 3 months! After 45 days of advertising (cold, snow, Christmas—aaaahhhh!!), we have finally found a great family who will be lease optioning the home from us as follows: $165,900 on a 2-year lease option, $4,000 down, $1,095/month with no rental credit!! Yeah!! It does feel wonderful (and safe) getting in with nothing down in addition to one month of "free" rental income to boot! The $500 deposit check is above and the remainder of the $4,000 option fee plus 1st month's rent will come before we hand over the keys and sign the final contracts next week!

Thank you!

Brian and Kristine Lambrecht

seller has granted that right as well. When you have an equitable interest in a property, in most states you don't need a license to sell it.

Q. *How large a deposit will you give me?*

A. Well, Mr. Seller, let me ask you this: When you list with your Realtor, how large a deposit does the Realtor give you? None, of course. Then why should I? All I'm asking for is the right to buy and a key to show the house. As I'm not even taking the house off the market or occupying it, how can you lose, so why do you need a deposit?

Q. *How long an option do you want?*

A. Well, let's see. How long do you want to give me, considering I'll go away anytime you sell, and you have no risk and nothing to lose? Frankly, all I need is six months. If I haven't sold it by then, I'm "gonna" move on anyway.

This is by no means a full-fledged course on options, but it certainly gets you thinking, doesn't it? Let's see what we've accomplished with our make-believe deal. We've taken control of a $200,000 house in good condition with no money, no credit, no promises to keep, and no risk. If we sell the house, we make about $50,000. If we don't, we lose nothing except the cost of an ad. We didn't deal with any contractors or rehabbers. No monthly payments to worry about and no tenants.

What's more, the seller decided which plan we used: Plan one, whereby we leased with the right to sublease; or plan two, whereby we don't have the right to occupy but do get paid if we sell it.

Looks to me like this just might be the perfect business. The only downside is that you must know how to retail houses for cash. When you put together a system for doing so, I think you'll agree with me, based on this discussion, that optioning houses is by far the best way to acquire maximum short-term cash profits.

Incidentally, don't get hung up on my $200,000 example. You can work with any price range you like—no minimum and no maximum. But remember, it doesn't take any longer to get a buyer through the system whether you net $200,000 or $100,000 or, like my hero Marco, $2,450,000.

Be careful not to spend your time walking over the dollars to get the dimes. If I were you, I'd work on the highest-priced houses in your area

This truck driver has grown to like the option business!

Todd Nelson, *Union Grove, Wisconsin*

Ron,

Thought I should write you to say thanks! Since I attended MMBC in May, I have done a few deals. I got the deed on a $180,000 home, for loan balance of $138,000. I lease optioned it for $189,900 getting a $10,000 deposit and $1,600 a month rent. I also did a short sale. Here are the numbers: First mortgage of $194,000 discounted to $122,000 and second mortgage of $78,000 discounted to $7,800. I sold this property for $240,000 cash. I had $10 in this deal and (maybe) 6 hours. I netted $95,000. Not a bad hourly wage and a real good return on an investment.

I also lease optioned a $145,000 home for $112,000 loan balance. I then lease optioned it out for $6,000 down and $990 per month rent. I recently wholesaled a property for $6,500 net profit, I had $10 invested in it and maybe 1 hour. I also got an option on a $1.2 million dollar home for $780,000. I sold it for $780,000. Now, this doesn't sound too good. But, this house was on the market for 2 years and did not sell. The owner was so impressed that she referred me to a friend of hers who has a $1.8 million dollar home and is going to give me an option for $900,000. I think that might work.

For anyone reading this, I was a farmer and a full-time truck driver. I'm also married with 3 kids. If I can do this, anyone can. They just need to do what you tell them and go to any event you offer no matter what the case.

I had to borrow money to go to your event. I tried other courses and got into a lot of trouble. I had 11 rental properties in foreclosure at the same time. Everyone said, "Haven't you learned your lesson about buying courses off TV?"

Thank God I didn't listen to them and didn't give up. I'm not out of the hole yet. But, at least there is light at the end of the tunnel. Thanks to you.

Thank You,
Todd Nelson
Union Grove, WI

that are moving quickly. It's common sense: The higher the values, the better chance you have of negotiating a larger profit. That's contrary to those junkers, isn't it? When you actually have to buy the house and pay holding, repair, and sales costs, I'd be concerned if you dealt with anything other than the cheap houses.

> *When you have nothing at risk,*
> *you can play for higher stakes.*

All right, I know I said in the beginning you didn't need a cent to do this and then I talked about advertising. OK, you need a few bucks. But wouldn't you feel more comfortable if advertising money was all you had to risk? Or would you prefer having to buy a house; come up with the repair money; hire contractors; pay property taxes, insurance, and utilities; and then get stuck if the house didn't sell quickly? Sounds like a no-brainer to me. Options are a lot safer than owning.

Besides, if you'll allow your mind to go beyond my $200,000 example for a minute, you'll realize this will work on million-dollar houses as well. Wherever you live, there are executive homes worth several hundred thousand dollars more than the seller would accept for a cash sell. Yes, this means you can make $100,000 per house or more. It's your choice. If the numbers scare you, ask yourself. . . .

"What have I got to lose?"

I promise when you get a check in your hands for $100,000, you'll discover options are not only worth your time to learn but they pay better than any job where you swap hours for dollars. If you agree and want to learn more, I have a training event called **Massive Income Strategies** where I cover many little-known techniques, including options, lease options, owner financing, structuring offers, answering objections, agreements, defaulted paper, and a lot more. Call my office for more information at **800-567-6128** or go to **http://www.ronlegrand.com.**

PRETTY HOUSES AND UGLY HOUSES

The real estate investing business is actually divided into only two parts: pretty houses and ugly houses. Retailing and wholesaling involve finding houses that need to be rehabbed. They're ugly. Some need more than $20,000 in work and others need less, but all need repairs. That's why you can buy them at deeply discounted prices.

Lease options, options, and get-the-deed houses are pretty houses needing little or no work. They're in gorgeous areas and in all price ranges from $75,000 to $5 million.

The focus for ugly houses is to buy them cheap. Price is king. Usually it's an all-cash offer. The focus for pretty houses is to take over debt and get some free equity or option and resell. Because little or no cash is required to buy, you usually get less equity than you do in an all-cash offer on junkers, but it's easy in and out because you don't have to raise cash or hire contractors.

Both types of houses have advantages and disadvantages; you may have already formed an opinion about what you'd like to do to create big checks in real estate, but don't be too hasty. All of these techniques work, and all should be in your toolbox. We'll discuss each in this book.

Some people ask me what they should look for first, pretty houses or ugly houses. My answer is always this: "Find a seller who needs to sell and help out that seller whether the house is pretty or ugly." When you get a check from the closing agent, it won't have a note on it anywhere saying this money came from a pretty or ugly house.

I'd like you to learn the whole business, not just a little piece of it as some do. When you can take whatever comes to you—pretty or ugly—and profit from it, you have become what I call a "transaction engineer" and have joined the elite in our business who truly understand it. You can't find pretty houses without finding ugly ones too, and vice versa. Don't go through a whole career as a real estate entrepreneur with blinders on and throw away a dollar for every dime you harvest. Spend a little time and money to learn your craft correctly, and you'll need only a few prospects a month to make a fortune.

The only other alternative is to learn and work only one type of deal and spend all your time looking for a needle in a haystack. Remember *"the less I do, the more I make."* That starts with recognizing opportunity when it's thrown at you and being savvy enough to grab it.

"Leverage your brain, not your wallet or credit."

Ron LeGrand

This Canadian couple have done 30 deals and are going strong!!

Carol and Floyd Torpe, *St. Albert, Alberta, Canada*

Dear Ron:

After attending your course we played the tapes over and over again. We have implemented so many of your strategies I'm not sure where to begin thanking you. We have increased our marketing and the answering service asks the 9 important questions and faxes them to us. We now spend our time on the motivated sellers. Enclosed is a picture of the advertising on our Honda.

When one motivated seller indicated that she was packing up and leaving town and wanted $5000.00 plus assume her mortgage, I asked her what I learned from you, Ron. "Will you sell the house for what you owe on it"? She replied by saying, "Oh, no I would like at least $1000.00". We faxed her the paperwork for the Deed transfer and she had it back to us within days.

We have now accumulated 30 properties and are on the way to financial freedom. We have lease optioned 6 properties. On the most recent one the couple gave us $5000.00 down and we are receiving $1195.00 a month; our expenses are $900.00 giving us a positive cash flow of $295.00 per month. On our first wholesale deal we bought a house for $20,000.00 and sold it for $45,000.00.

We are now making money. Thank you again.

Carol & Floyd Torpe
St. Albert, Alberta, Canada

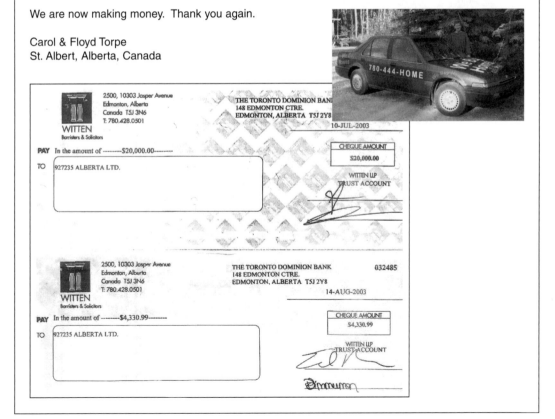

5

FIVE STEPS TO SUCCESS

This business and all others have five steps that must be followed to succeed. If any one is eliminated, the business will suffer or fail outright. If you currently run a business or have in the past and it had problems, I'd suggest you take a good hard look at my five steps, and I'll bet you'll spot the problem.

I spend a major portion of the book covering these steps and incorporate a mini-real-estate-training school in the art of buying and selling houses. The information in the next chapters took a lot of years to learn and is the foundation for all my millionaires and will remain so for future generations.

CAUTION, CAUTION, CAUTION

No book on any shelf can give you a complete education on anything. This one is no exception. The purpose of this book is to awaken the financial genius inside you and make you aware of the fabulous opportunity out there in real estate.

To assume this book is all you'll ever need to know is naive and borders on insanity. I could take any one chapter on subjects covered here and create an entire book or course on it. In fact, I've done that for most of the content.

You have available to you complete home study courses called "Cash Flow Systems," which contain 37 CDs and systems manuals on both the pretty and the ugly house business. In addition, we a have four-day live trainings on both pretty and ugly houses. They're taught about 20 times a year all over the country and Canada. Then we have personal mentoring by phone and in person on a one-on-one basis.

In fact, we have a whole curriculum of live training events to cover every need in real estate and marketing so our clients can move up as far and fast as they choose. It's all on **http://www.ronlegrand.com** or **http://www.globalpublishinginc.com** for you to check out and is called Financial Freedom Academy.

Yes, that was a shameless commercial but I hope it clearly illustrates that no book can ever make you an expert on anything. I'd prefer you didn't take the information in this book and implement it with no further training. I know that's not what you may want to hear but it's the truth.

This business can make you wealthy very quickly, so please give it the time and attention it deserves if you enter it, and do yourself a favor and don't expect miracles from a book. I'm sure glad the doctor who did surgery on me recently didn't get all his training from a book.

OK, my disclaimer is over, so let's get back to the five steps of success. Each is covered in the next five chapters and is applied to both the pretty and the ugly houses as we go. I said earlier that the pretty and ugly house business is actually two different businesses within one. There are a few similarities but, by and large, they're quite different. Even so, the steps to success are the same. Here they are:

Step 1. Locate prospects
Step 2. Prescreen prospects
Step 3. Construct and present offers
Step 4. Follow up
Step 5. Sell quickly

Now, let's see how to apply these steps to buying and selling a house with no money or credit and getting a big fat check quickly.

"Focus on the few, not the many. It matters not how many deals you do, only how much money you make."

Ron LeGrand

This turnaround specialist now specializes in real estate turnaround.

Jill Shepard, *Fenton, Michigan*

Dear Ron,

After reading your book, Quick Turn Real Estate and buying your courses; Wholesale/Retail, Lease/Option, FSBO Workbooks, I decided this was the next business for me. I've been a turn around specialist for the last 10 years, which means I go into troubled or fast growth companies and re-engineer their processes and systems to position their business for the future. This has saved/made hundreds of thousands for the companies I've worked for. However, I was getting tired of trading hours for dollars.

In my first year, I have put 12 properties under contract. I flipped three to investors for quick cash and have nine I still manage. The total property value through my hands in the last twelve months was $2,253,300. The total deposits taken was $22,295, the cash flow was $18,816 for a combined total of $41,111. This number is not exciting, but I worked full time in my consulting business until two months ago. The back end profits yet to be made are $160,000. The grand total for the year in Cash/Equity results are $201,111. This is a net number after all expenses, advertising, utilities, holding costs are taken out! Pretty great for someone who only heard of you last October, and did her first four deals from the workbooks! See the attached worksheet for proof!

I will quadruple the numbers this year. The information from your boot camps and seminars will be utilized to make sure my goals happen. The one major factor in my success was focusing on one system and being coachable throughout the process. Your direct, simple, easy to follow instructions in workbooks, boot camps and seminars have made my success possible.

Sincerely,

Jill M. Shepard
Fenton, MI

C h a p t e r

6

STEP 1—
LOCATING PROSPECTS

Every business must locate people to buy its products and services or it'll soon be out of business. In our case we must locate people who have houses for sale so we can buy their product, a house.

That's not a hard process, but it's deadly if it doesn't get done. In fact, when I converse with students who aren't doing well, it usually comes down to one of two reasons: Either they haven't done much to find deals or they're finding them and letting them get by because they don't recognize what a deal looks like. I'll fix that in the next chapter.

Before I go any further we should discuss the use of Realtors. It's easy to pin all your hopes on them and assume they'll do most of the work for you. Sorry! Bad news! The only time you'll use Realtors is to make offers on listed junkers. Realtors won't be used in the pretty house business for two reasons.

First, they want to get paid; and most pretty house deals are debt takeovers or options, and there's no money to pay Realtors. The seller gets little or nothing, so the deals are cashless.

The second reason Realtors won't be used in the pretty house business is the biggest roadblock: Realtors won't advise their clients to sell the way you want to buy. They'll block the sale and destroy the deal if it involves taking over debt without liability (get the deed) or involves options, usually lease options—all buying techniques in the pretty home business.

Your only market therefore for pretty houses to buy is through FSBOs (for sale by owners). Here you must deal with the seller directly, and all listed properties are off-limits unless the seller can convince the Realtor to drop the listing. Note that I said the seller, not you, must contact the Realtor; if *you* do, the Realtor will most likely want to be paid if you buy the house. Realtors have a contract (listing agreement), and you mustn't interfere with it unless the Realtor chooses to cancel it to help the seller. Violate this rule and you may learn the meaning of the term *tortious interference with a contract.*

Ugly house offers are usually all cash, so it's easy to see how in the case of an ugly house the Realtor gets paid from the seller's proceeds. However, if your entire ugly house business revolves around buying listed houses, you'll have a tough road ahead. Here's a strong word of advice:

Your business must not depend on Realtors to do anything.

Are Realtors useful? Yes, in some cases, such as for buying listed junkers. But don't forget, they control the deal and you're not their only customer. This buffer (the Realtor) between you and the seller will drive up the price and make listed houses tougher to buy.

Your best market will always be unlisted houses; best of the best are houses the rest of the world doesn't know are for sale because they're not on the market until you plant the bug in the seller's ear you're a buyer. Here's a simple rule that separates the real players from beginners:

The easier a deal is to find, the more it costs.

Listed houses and FHA and VA repos are easy to find; therefore, they cost more, and less profit is made. It's always better to have sellers calling you, but here we'll discuss ways to find deals where you make the first contact. Stick to the FSBOs, and I promise it'll be easier to make a lot more money when you discover who wants to deal with you, discussed in the next chapter on prescreening.

THE THREE BEST WAYS I KNOW TO FIND UGLY HOUSES

The first step to a successful business, any business, is to locate prospects who are predisposed to do business with you. The good thing about finding ugly houses is they're easy to spot. They just sit there and glare at you. Anyone can see they need repairs, and we assume if they're ugly, there's a reason to contact the owner to see if you can buy an ugly house at wholesale price.

Obviously, it's a numbers game. You'll buy some and some you won't. In fact, you won't get most of them, especially the ones you think ought to be the easiest to buy because they're the ugliest.

As I write this, I have just seen my Roth IRA grow $80,000 from two checks on two ugly houses I bought, rehabbed, and resold. I made $43,230 on one and $37,233 on the other—tax free for life . . . *and that was only my half!*

Both were partnered deals with people I know, so I only got half of the profits. Of course, I didn't touch the houses. In fact, I've never seen a picture of one of them! Perhaps I should go look at it. Well . . . maybe not. The check seemed to clear OK.

Ugly houses are very profitable—too profitable for you to ignore. Nonetheless, I'm hearing too many students say they'd rather do pretty houses and not mess with the uglies. But that would be a mistake. A big mistake. Sure, pretty houses are easy in, easy out. No contractors and little or no costly entanglements. So what? Does that excuse you from harvesting the gold on the uglies? I think not! The two examples I just told you about should make my case.

You can't find pretty houses without finding ugly ones!

Turn your back if you will, but it'd be a shame to trash a couple of hundred grand a year because you have blinders on. Not only that, but ugly houses are easier to find than pretties simply because they *are* ugly. Usually you find the house first and then see if the seller's needs and the existing financing make sense for you to buy. Besides, buying ugly houses requires very little communication and people skills. You don't have to

Bought for $12,350; sold for $97,500!!

Bill and Lily Wright, *Tacoma, Washington*

Real Estate Investment Success

Ron–

Thanks for asking about my progress as a Real Estate Investor. I have many experiences over the last six years since I first met you. Lily & I have really been working at this on a part-time basis and have found real estate investing to be rewarding, satisfying and profitable. As in any venture, there are many observations, lessons and stories that make up each investor's portfolio, however, the most successful venture that we have had over these six years was not the most profitable, yet it was the single most successful venture that had so many of hurdles of real estate investing that you had talked about and yet we still were able to call this a positive learning experience and make money.

This project was an **Uglllllyyyyyy** house that had been boarded up by the City of Tacoma for over seven years (and these fees were liened to the property that had to be cleared prior to our closing), condemned by the Health Department, lived in by the homeless and scheduled to be razed by the City within three months of our closing ("Fix it or We will level it!!").

Well, what did we learn and why do we think this was a success? We NEVER would have tackled this project without taking your course on ugly houses, improving the neighborhood and how a "rehab" would bring up the property values of all the other houses in the neighborhood. In a short recap, we did WELL & achieved all objectives!!!

We bought the house and property well below the appraised value of the land that the house was sitting on. We negotiated the purchase price based on the half of the MAO ($12,350) since the homeowner was motivated by the city's condemnation process and the lack of interest to fix up the house.

Here's a couple of pictures of progress of the repair and some of the issues that we overcame:

It took us three meetings with the city to approve our rehab plans.

We learned about contractors and had to fire two after materials were missing from the project, some building codes were "ignored", the staircase was built three times, the wrong size window was installed in the upstairs bedroom...to mention some of the issues.

The final city inspection also identified structural & electrical issues.

"DIY" kitchen cabinets saved 80% of the material costs while the assembly of these cabinets cost almost 20 hours to assemble; and

We had no money – we used the "hard money" lender!

Everyone says "It can't be done!"

The total project (from offer to closing) took almost eleven months, but we had & accepted an offer for $97,500 three weeks before the final City inspection which was two days before the buyer moved in and on the Friday night / Saturday morning that our team was installing the wall-to-wall carpet and kitchen cabinets, the **new owner was moving in!!!**

This project would have never been even started without having known that we could overcome our lessons and knowing how to avoid those "knuckle-busters"!!

The "Dream Team" does make a project work!!

We knew what to expect to "overcome"!! Thanks so much for sharing your successes! Yours truly, Bill & Lily Wright meet anyone because most of the uglies are vacant, so buying is an easy process.

If rehabbing turns you off, you have several choices. You can get someone else to handle it (as I did), or you can wholesale your uglies.

Here are my best three methods for finding junkers: the ant farm, Realtors, and direct mail. If you implement one correctly, you should easily do a couple of deals a month. Do them all and who knows! The key word is *correctly*. Not a slap shot attempt so you can make excuses for your failure; serious people do what it takes.

Method One: The Ant Farm

This is by far the most productive way to find junkers. I call it the ant farm because it involves a couple of people (ants) running around looking for ugly houses and bringing them to me. I pay $5 per lead if the leads meet my criteria of being ugly and in neighborhoods I assign.

You should be your own ant for some time. Simply drive around through low-priced neighborhoods and write down all the addresses of ugly, vacant houses. Then come home and track down the owners and call them to see if you can strike a deal.

There are complete details about my ant farm in several sources—my Wholesale/Retail Cash Flow system and at our live ugly house training event.

Here are five key points that explain where most people fail at the ant farm. Like anything else, do it right or don't whine when it doesn't work:

1. Ugly houses are in low-priced areas. You won't find them in gated communities. If you're having trouble locating them, you're in the wrong neighborhood.
2. You must look up all the addresses on the tax rolls and determine if the mailing address is different from the address of the vacant home. If so, get the phone number from Information at 411 and call the seller. No letters. Get on the phone and talk to the seller. You can usually get to your local tax rolls online by going to [your county name.org].
3. If you don't make contact with the seller, the rest is a waste of time. Do what you have to do to make it happen.

4. You must hire a skip tracer to find the ones you can't find. This is where most people quit, yet it's where the real money is to be made.

The harder they are to find, the bigger the profit!

I'm sick of telling people this and watching them go cheap here. If you're not going to do this, the ant farm ain't for you. A skip tracer is **http://www.findtheseller.com,** where you can get it done for as little as $9 each. Tell them I sent you for the best price.

5. You must understand it's a numbers game. You can't get upset after the first 20 houses don't produce a deal.

Let's assume you send a batch of 20 houses to the skip tracer. He'll find 70 percent, or 14 sellers, which means you'll pay about $200. Suppose you get one deal out of 14 that wholesales for a $10,000 profit. Do we need to run a spreadsheet on this? It's a no-brainer.

If you don't get a deal from the first 20 leads …go find 20 more!

If they don't produce . . . get another 20 more! Could you spend $400 to make $10,000? Why is this so difficult for sensible people to understand?

If you do what I just said, you can't fail with the ant farm unless you just totally screw up the offers. It won't fail you. Only you can fail *it.* Doesn't it stand to reason that some of the owners of ugly houses would love to sell them to you for cash? Go find them!

Method Two: Realtors

Realtors have always been a good source of ugly houses, even though it's been a little tougher the last couple of years to get at the deals. The real estate market has been good, which produces easier sales for the banks and brings the wannabe investors out of the woodwork. However, I've been getting listed deals all along as have many of my students. In fact, the one I mentioned earlier that made me $43,000 for my half was real estate owned (REO) by a bank and listed with a Realtor.

Issues to consider on listed houses:

- You'll probably need some proof of funds to submit an offer. This can be the bank statement of anyone you know, a letter from a mortgage broker, a letter from anyone who says he or she will fund the deal, someone's mutual fund or IRA statement, or even your own credit card statement showing cash available to cover the purchase. Proof of funds doesn't mean the funds must come from the source of proof you provide. Just because you show a Realtor your mother's IRA statement doesn't mean Mom is obligated to put up the money. Also remember that the only time you'll ever need proof of funds is when you use Realtors, and not all of them will request it.
- Expect to put up a $500 deposit or more when buying listed houses.
- Keep your offers clean with no contingencies not already covered in the contract.
- You'll use the Realtor's contract or you won't get the offer presented. Realtors will *not* use your contract.
- The first time a Realtor believes you can't close, game's over. The last thing you tell a Realtor is that you want to wholesale the house. Keep your mouth shut!
- If a letter of intent is acceptable to the Realtor, use it. You can fill out the contract when you have a seller in the game. Follow the Realtor's lead here.
- Find the ugly houses that are listed first; then call the listing agent to make an offer. Don't try to get Realtors who deal in pretty houses to help you buy ugly ones. That's like trying to get me into a size 28 pants! It would involve excruciating pain!

Method Three: Direct Mail

Direct mail will produce results if you do it correctly and stick to it. There are numerous targets to mail to, so your best bet is to pick two or three and focus on them. I'd suggest mailings to out-of-town owners of vacant, ugly houses in your own city. They're good and proven targets that yield results.

Another target is the list of condemned houses you can get from your code compliance officer. Of course, there are preforeclosures, probably the highest-paying segment of the business. These are easy to find because in these cases a lawsuit has been filed and is on the public record; but it's difficult to get a response from these owners. So if you're going to work preforeclosures, you'd better get some training.

Frankly, it takes two or three things properly implemented to get several houses a month. Don't get carried away trying to do too much. Choose your weapons and put them to work. In fact, the ant farm will be instrumental in everything I mention here. It will locate the house you buy from Realtors and produce a list of out-of-town owners to mail to if you can't get a phone number. It's cheap and effective, and you can crank it up or slow it down as you see fit. I'd make an ant farm a part of your buying machine.

THREE GOOD WAYS TO FIND PRETTY HOUSE DEALS

I discussed three ways to find ugly houses so it's only fitting I now cover the other side of the business. We should start with defining what a pretty house really is. It's not the price that produces the definition. The house could be high priced, but most people in the pretty house business work in the range of $70,000 to $200,000. If you're in a high-priced market such as San Francisco, where a $200,000 house is rare, your range will be higher.

The point is that pretty houses start at the bottom and go up; they're not just expensive houses, as I've noted. My definition of a pretty house is any house requiring less than $5,000 in work to get it in a good, salable condition. An ugly house is one that needs rehab or a lot of repairs.

I'd want you to work both sides of the business and become a transaction engineer who can recognize a deal when you see it, whether it's pretty or ugly. Don't fall into the trap of trying to get so specialized that you turn your back on lots of other profits—there's gold in both ugly houses and pretty houses.

Most people start with the ugly houses, because they're easy to find and understand, and they either wholesale or rehab and retail. That's OK, but it's only a start. Pretty houses are easy in, easy out. Usually it's a

This Phoenix couple discovered there's a lot more money in buying houses than in listing them.

Brian and Lynette Wolff, *Phoenix, Arizona*

Dear Ron,

I feel so fortunate to be writing you this testimonial letter. It's been just over 3 months since your first ever Millionaire-Maker Boot Camp, which was the first event we attended. It's taken a little while, but now I really believe we will be one of the great success stories arising from those intense days in rainy Atlanta. I told my wife Lynette that our results in August would be the first true test of how well this business really works. On the very first day of August we signed 2 deals with a combined profit of $36,800!

I have been in real estate as an agent, and I've also been a mortgage broker like yourself. My wife Lynette is one of the top "new home" sales agents in town, with over $75 million in homes sold. I've always been grateful for the huge paychecks she was earning except that now since I met you, they don't seem all that huge anymore! As for me, I eventually worked myself up to manage an office for Ameriquest Mortgage. I really thought I was making good money then, but it didn't take long for the bosses to clamp down on my commissions. That is the beauty of this real estate business–it's totally up to you how much money you make. It all comes down to how much time, energy, knowledge, creativity, and salesmanship you deliver on a daily basis. Fortunately for us, a great education in the last 3 can be purchased from you!

Even with all my previous experience in real estate and mortgages, Ron, I have to confess I had my share of doubts along the way. But I just kept listening to your CDs, and I stuck with it! If you allow yourself enough time to figure this stuff out (and I certainly don't have it all figured out yet), no business will ever reward you and your family with the money and time that real estate will. The secret is to just keep trying stuff until something works, and never, never quit.

Ron, it's only been with your help that I've been able to feel so good about myself and my ability to provide the big bucks for my family's future. I haven't felt this proud or excited in years...maybe in my whole life. Ron, I'll never be able to thank you enough for that. And now I have one last thing for which I need to thank you. Lynette and I have always fantasized about working together. Well, Lynette just informed me that she is officially leaving the new home sales business in September and hopping on board the Ron Express with me! YAY!

We now have 8 houses, including 2 short sales (thank goodness for your course on that!) The net profit from the deals we've found in the last 2 months will be well over $100,000, and we are just getting started. Ron, I'm looking forward to an extremely positive and prosperous association with you for many years to come. Take care of yourself!

Brian Wolff
Lynette Wolff

Brian & Lynette Wolff
Phoenix, AZ

P.S. I'm telling everyone to get the Millionaire Maker Boot Camp disc set and listen to CD #18, track 5. It's very educational, and pretty funny too. See you in Las Vegas, Jacksonville, and points beyond!

"get-the-deed" and lease option transaction to a tenant-buyer, which takes a few days, eliminates contractors, and reduces holding costs—plus producing a few thousand dollars in front-end profit. A person could get used to this part of the business and easily make the decision to ignore the uglies.

So how do you find pretty houses? Well, there are a number of ways, but we'll focus on three good ones here.

Method Number One: Signs

Signs never fail to get calls—usually before you get home. I'm referring to stick signs you place on the side of the road. They can be put up with a pointed 1 × 2 foot stake that you can buy at Home Depot in bundles or with a wire rack.

The good news is you'll get calls. The bad news is some calls might be from the city asking you to remove one or two because someone has complained about them. If a call from the city would give you a heart attack, use other methods. Most cities have ordinances against signs, but some don't. You'll have to check into that, but the bottom line is that all cities have signs, and a lot of students elect to take their chances.

I've heard of some investors who were subjected to a fine as repeat offenders, and every once in a while I hear of a city that gets nasty. I once received a letter from a city office in Oregon asking me to advise my students that it has ordinances against these signs. So there, you've been advised!

Many students put up signs on Friday afternoon and pick them up on Sunday night to avoid aggravation from the city, which may sound foolish until you look at the numbers. The signs cost about $3 each, so if you put out 50, you've got $150 invested. Pick up the remaining 40 on Sunday night and the cost is $30 for the 10 signs that come up missing . . . and I promise, they will.

If you get 10 to 15 calls over the weekend and buy one house (as you should) with a $20,000 profit, it's a no-brainer. All of a sudden, it's worth the risk of city heat. In some areas, the city couldn't care less, and your signs have a long life. Don't be scared off by my warning here. Do your own diligence and make the best decision for you.

Most signs are on fiberboard, around 18 × 24 inches. I like black letters on yellow but have used other colors successfully. Be careful when you make up the sign—you don't want to put too much detail on it. Remember, people are moving when they see it, so make the phone number large and don't forget your Web site address if you have one set up.

The signs can simply say:

> I BUY HOUSES
> [YOUR PHONE #]
> [YOUR WEB SITE]

Don't complicate the signs and make them hard to read. You can also have your car or truck lettered with vinyl letters in bright colors. It costs about $300 for the whole job; you only pay once, the vehicle signs won't come up missing, and you shouldn't get a call from the city.

I have students doing 10 to 15 deals a year simply from their vehicle signs. Let the world know you buy houses.

Method Two: Direct Mail Campaigns

This can be a full marketing machine all in one if you do nothing else. Not only does it work well for many people, but the list of targets is so big that you can target your chosen prospects and never run out of prospects. Even though signs work well, the best target you can hope for is an area you like. With direct mail, you use a rifle approach.

Kathy Kennebrook, student turned teacher, has developed a great course on direct mail campaigns that work well for her. She gives you all the letters, step-by-step instructions, and the results she's getting with each campaign. I'd suggest you get her stuff to make your job a lot easier. The few hundred dollars you'll spend is easily wasted in printing and postage by an untrained beginner mailing the wrong thing to the wrong list. You can contact my office for details at **800-567-6128.** By the way, she made $805,000 last year by mailing 12,000 letters throughout the year and never stuffed the first envelope. When I met Kathy, she was working as a field rep for some company paying her peanuts, spending most of her life away from home, and hating her job. You should see her now: only 4½ feet tall with an income larger than most corporate CEOs'.

Here's a list of some possible targets for direct mail that Kathy covers, most of which I've used and that work well for me:

- Preforeclosures are a gold mine if worked correctly—an entire business within the business—and are worth the time and expense to learn. Another student, Jeff Kaller, has mastered the art of preforeclosures and turned it into a three-day boot camp. If you need details, e-mail us at **http://www.globalpublishinginc.com** or **http://www.ronlegrand.com.**

- Out-of-town owners almost always work. The list is easy to get from a Realtor or your local records office. This is one Kathy specializes in (with a 12 percent response rate if I remember correctly). Be sure to mention the property address in the letter and include a response card to make it easy for owners to reach you without calling. Some people simply *won't* call. You must call them after they return your response card! You'll find a good sample in Appendix E.

- New homeowners who've been in their house less than two years. I've heard that more than 70 percent of foreclosures occur within the first two years of ownership, and a large percentage of those occur in the first year. Any list broker can get you the list; you'll find brokers in your yellow pages or go to **http://www.Melissadata .com.** You're looking for pretty houses so you can get the deed.

- Zip codes where you want to buy. Just pick an area, rent the list of homeowners from a list broker, and mail a postcard.

- Divorces. A sale is usually imminent, so get the list from public records and contact the owners.

- Estate sales. Mail to the trustee, who almost always needs to sell.

- FSBO (for sale by owner) ads. You can download the ads from the online classifieds in your local paper or from an FSBO magazine.

- VA (Veterans Administration) homeowners. You can get a list from a list broker and select by zip code or other factors such as property value, length of ownership, and age of the veteran.

- Bankruptcies are a matter of public record, and many of those filing for bankruptcy are looking to sell a home. You can pay cash for the junkers or get the deed on pretty houses and petition the bankruptcy trustee to release the house from bankruptcy. Go to **http://www.pacer.com** for a national list of bankruptcies. If a seller is getting little or no money, it's usually not a problem unless the house has a lot of equity and the trustee blocks the sale, but that's the exception, not the rule. Your mail should be directed to the owner, not the trustee, and your letter should mention you specialize in bankruptcy purchases. OK, I know you don't, but you'll learn after you've done a few! You'll learn the rules, and they won't scare you anymore. You'll become an expert in bankruptcy buys, especially when you learn the art of short sales from Jeff Kaller's boot camp or from my home study course.

Short sales are nothing more than discounting defaulted loans on properties in foreclosure or about to be after you get the deed. My students are making huge fortunes with short sales all over America and I'm not doing badly myself. I've made an *extra* $256,000 from short sale discounts alone in the past six months. It's worth learning.

Method Number Three: Call Ads

I know this doesn't sound appealing, but if you'll do it my way, you'll probably grow to love it. You see, I don't want *you* to call ads; I want you to get others to do it for you—others who'll do it because it's their job and you're paying them. It's so simple that you'll probably try to complicate it, but here goes.

Get the Property Information Sheet from Appendix D and have your helper call all of the Sunday FSBO ads every Monday night between 6 and 9 PM in areas where you want to work. Have your employee-helper fill out the basic information you need to determine if you want to call the seller back. The only info I need is the asking price, the estimated value, the loan balance, the condition of the property, the address, and whether it's listed with a Realtor. With this information, I can prescreen the prospect sheet in five seconds and make my decision to follow up or not, as I discuss in the next chapter. If you pay your helper $2 per script, the helper will make $10 to $20 an hour, and you can avoid talking to a bunch of dead-end leads who don't want, or need, to sell.

Your job is to take the big pile of ads and reduce it to a little pile of prospects that appear motivated and willing to give you equity. That's it! You can make a few calls a week to good prospects that have been sifted

This attorney made $8,700 on his first deal!

Jeffery S. Watson, *Conneaut, Ohio*

AZAZA HOMEBUYERS, LLC.

Dear Ron,

After over 12 years of practicing law at the same law firm, I believed that my Christmas bonus was a sure thing. Not in 2003. Fortunately, I knew how to make my own bonus. I bought this house for $58,000 and wholesaled it for $69,000. After closing costs, I netted over $8,700. It did turn out to be a Merry Christmas!

After the double closing, the seller's attorney called me to talk about other possible deals.

Thanks for all of your help!

Best Regards,

Jeffery S. Watson

Guardian Title & Guaranty Agency, Inc.
Cleveland Escrow Account
1370 West 6th Street, Suite 300
Cleveland, Ohio 44113

THE HUNTINGTON NATIONAL BANK
CLEVELAND, OHIO 44115
4-15
410

PAY TO THE ORDER OF   Azaza Homebuyers, LLC

December 17, 2003

$67,267.28

Sixty Seven Thousand Two Hundred Sixty Seven and 28/100 Dollars   Dollars

Memo   0321569 Property 1601 Elmwood Avenue

and sorted out before you talk to them. This method alone could easily make you half a million a year! It's really that simple if you can recognize a deal and follow up to get it done.

TWENTY-TWO MORE WAYS TO FIND DEALS

When I started, I knew that, as sure as pushing the gas pedal makes a car go faster, investing more in my buying machine would increase my income. The first several months were the toughest because I needed every dime just to keep the lights on and the roof over my head. If money is tight for you, hang in there. It *will* pay off. Think of your business as an airplane. For a plane to take off, the pilot must give it more power; the plane goes faster and faster until it finally becomes airborne. At that point, does the pilot decrease power to the engine? No! He continues to give it full throttle as the plane climbs rapidly up to cruising altitude; then it's full speed ahead. Likewise, you should keep feeding fuel to your buying machine even if you're flying high, and you'll keep speeding toward your financial goals. Don't do what the so-called competition does and start cruising before you're even in the sky. Keep the buying machine cranked to full throttle.

Now let's look at the 22 more ways to find motivated sellers:

1. **Credibility kit.** This item is a must for every serious real estate investor. Its purpose is to identify you as someone who can be trusted. With that in mind, what do you suppose should be included?
   - *Presentation folder.* This doesn't have to be expensive, especially if you're going to mail it out, but it should be neat and professional. You can and should spend a little more on the folders you carry in your briefcase and hand out personally, as their effect on a customer will be crucial and immediate. You might even have these professionally bound at your neighborhood print shop.
   - *Cover letter.* This is how you'll establish yourself with someone who doesn't know you, so it's very important. It's somewhat like a résumé because it'll include personal as well as professional information, such as the number of your years in business, how long you've lived in the area, schools you've graduated from

(local only), college degrees, organizations you belong to, and so on. Your credibility kit should also include either a picture of yourself or a picture of you and your family.

- *Letters of recommendation.* Get these from people who are relevant to your business—for instance, your closing agent and real estate attorney. While you're at it, see if your attorney will write a letter stating that the lease/purchase agreements, lease options, and the like are perfectly legal. A letter from your bank will also add credibility. This letter does not have to include your credit worthiness or your financial statement; a simple statement will do, such as "John Smith is a good customer in good standing with First National Bank and has been since 1999."

- *Better business bureau membership.* Join the BBB and put that in your kit. Sellers will call to check you out, and your BBB membership will go a long way toward your credibility. Being a BBB member has gotten several deals for me.

- *Additional items.* Include anything that will add to your credibility as a businessperson. References from local community leaders would be good. A letter from your insurance agent and CPA could also be included.

- *Pictures.* Finally, pictures of yourself with local celebrities make for great conversational pieces as well as more credibility reinforcement. As time goes by, you'll have more and better items to add to your kit, so never consider it finished. Once you have a good prototype, however, it's time to use it. What follows is a short list of reliable sources for motivated sellers; you'll want to use as many of these as possible, but never stop looking for other ideas. And don't forget to track your results.

2. **Running your own ads.** All investors run ads, and many of them are the same. Your challenge is to be different without losing the simplicity and effectiveness you want. Don't be afraid to test new ideas constantly and track your results. When you get a call, whether from a classified ad or the other ideas I'm sharing with you, ask where the caller saw your ad. Here are a couple of ads that work for me:

I Buy Houses
Any Condition–Price–Area
Walk Away Today—555-5555

Or how about:

I Buy Houses When Others Say No. Call 287-5244

Be innovative and try your own ideas. Run your ads in the major daily newspaper and run it 7 days a week, 365 days a year. Another great place to run your ad is on cable TV. I run mine on the electronic program guide. It runs at least once every hour for 20 seconds. I get more than an acceptable response from this ad. Definitely check it out.

3. **Radio spots.** You can run a 30-second or a 60-second commercial. The longer format is preferable because it allows time to fully explain your program and costs roughly the same. You can get a professional station announcer to read it for you, usually for free. The cost of air time can be very affordable, about $10 to $20 per spot if you use talk radio or business stations. I don't recommend a music station because it is cost prohibitive.

4. **Home shows.** I'm referring to live events held in exhibit halls where you rent a booth, hand out your fliers, and talk to attendees. For better results, offer some kind of a freebie, such as a plastic visor, rule, or Frisbee, with your company name on it. You can save money on these shows by hooking up with another exhibitor for just a small space to display your fliers and entry forms for your *free gift drawing*. Entry forms ask the entrant's name, address, and phone number—and give you a valuable potential lead. You might also have a questionnaire asking such things as these: Are you thinking about selling your home? Do you know anyone selling their home? Are you looking to buy a home in the near future?

5. **Magnetic signs.** A magnetic sign for all your vehicles is a very affordable idea. Keep it simple. For example: I Buy Houses, Cash, 555-5555, and [Web site].

6. **Door hangers.** A door hanger is simply a flier designed to be put on a door knob. This is a great idea for targeting a specific neighborhood where you would like to buy. On one side of the door hanger is your ad "I Buy Houses When Others Say NO" and the other side offers some kind of incentive such as free pizza. When you place the door hanger, make sure your offer is facing toward the front. Print on a bright, neon-colored paper.

7. **Shirts.** Have your message printed on T-shirts. You might even print it on small T-shirts for your children to wear to school. If you do this, consider printing *"My Daddy Buys Houses."* Cute, huh?

8. **Sponsor a Little League team or bowling league.** With a modest donation, you can have your company name and phone number on team uniforms and prominently display team programs—even on the playing field or bowling alley.

9. **Moving billboards.** These include billboards and signs on city buses, taxi cabs, and the like, an idea I like a lot. City buses are great for targeting particular areas of town. Remember to keep your ads simple and easy to read.

10. **Bus benches.** Many bus stops have park benches with space available for advertisements. Again, keep your ad simple.

11. **Golf courses.** Many golf courses, both public and private, offer display advertising in various ways around each hole. Check it out.

12. **Business cards.** This is another one of those obvious things. Business cards are very affordable; just remember to use both sides of the card. I like to use the back of my cards. Place business cards on bulletin boards at grocery stores or leave them at restaurants or anywhere you think people might see them.

13. **Direct mail packs.** Some of the trade names are Val Pak, Money Mailer, and Paper Mint. If you use one of these, you'll get the best response by offering a free giveaway or some kind of genuine discount, such as a free pizza or $5 off. You can have your bonus offer printed on the reverse side of your ad. Test different ideas and track your results.

14. **Builders.** Builders can be a great source for deals. Your lease option offer gives them cash flow, top dollar. Don't ignore this idea.

15. **Corporate communications.** Many large companies have their own in-house newsletter and/or bulletin boards. These are good places to reach employees who are being transferred out, laid off, divorced, or undergoing other lifestyle changes that requires them to sell.

16. **Tax rolls.** You can locate and access property owners who are out of town through tax rolls. Mail owners a letter along with your credibility kit. Don't do just one mailing either. Mail them

He made $27,460 with $100 the easy way.

Manuel Coelho, *Artesia, California*

Dear Ron The Millionaire Maker,

Thank you for sharing your wisdom with me at the Las Vegas Seminar. One month after that seminar I got a response from one of my out of state letters. I made an offer for $240,000 on a house that was worth $320,000 and got it accepted over the phone. My mouth dropped when the seller said let's open escrow. Well I had to keep my cool being a Realtor in the past and it's challenging to believe someone would accept that offer on a house in good condition, but they did and I had a smile from ear to ear. A few days later I put the same house in contract with another investor for all cash for $270,000 and closed 2 weeks later and received a check for $27,460.05 for taking action on your education. I thought I needed money to fund deals, but I only needed 100 bucks after learning a simple strategy called wholesaling.

After this deal I have done 3 more in which I got paid $10,100 on one and I am going to get paid around $60,000 on the other two in January. Thank you for showing me how to become a millionaire. The more I listen and take action on your education, the closer I am to becoming a multimillionaire.

Earlier, I had purchased a huge Janitorial Business that had 83 employees and thought I was going to make a lot of money but soon found that it was a non-profit organization. The only people making money were the employees and that transaction set me back over $300,000. When I discovered your education I quickly got your message that says, "Stop crying over spilled milk and go milk another cow". Thank you Ron I have always wanted to be a Real Estate Investor and you showed me how with little or no risk. Ron, you are definitely someone who makes a huge difference in this world.

Kind Regards and Happy New Year!!

Manuel Coelho
Artesia, CA

at least five times, each time about three weeks apart. Track your records.

17. **Ads in FSBO magazines.** This is a great place to run your ad that reads "I Buy or Lease Houses." If you're cold-calling as I mentioned earlier, you can reference your ad when you cold-call sellers from the magazine.

18. **Foreclosure service.** This is a service that provides you with the names and addresses of people in your county who are in foreclosure. This by itself can be a very lucrative market. It does require a special kind of knowledge, but it is easy to learn and well worth doing.

19. **Vacant houses.** Great place to leave a flier or business card. You may try direct mailing along with your credibility kit. If the residents have left a forwarding address, the post office will deliver a solution to a problem they may be looking to solve.

20. **Ads in homeowner association newsletters.** Most neighborhood homeowners associations have newsletters and welcome advertisers. These newsletters are mailed to every homeowner in a particular neighborhood. The ads are cheap, so you can afford to keep your ad there forever. When you have a house to sell in that neighborhood, why not advertise it for sale there also?

21. **Yellow pages.** Some of my best leads came from a dollar-bill-sized ad under *Real Estate* in the yellow pages. You won't get a lot of calls, but those you do seem to be of good quality; and this seems to be the result my students report. The downside is it's a yearlong commitment of several hundred dollars a month, so probably not the place for a beginner to start.

22. **Real estate agents (continued).** When you're dealing with real estate agents, keep in mind they aren't in business to make money for you. They are in the business to make money for themselves. So you need to approach them with a game plan outlining the several ways they will make money by helping you find deals.

I target small independent real estate offices and the top listing agents with big-name firms. I tell them the kinds of properties I'm interested in buying, what I expect from our relationship, and what they can expect from me. My goal (and yours) is to develop a working relationship with an agent that will be profitable for both of you.

It's important to show real estate agents that you're professional and serious about buying a lot of properties. Show them your credibility kit. Explain that money is not a problem, that you can close fast, and you rarely have contingencies. If meetings go well, arrange future meetings at regular times when you'll exchange information. Agents will give you the new properties they've found, and you will bring them up-to-date on the progress you've made with each property they've previously given you. Don't depend on only one or two agents, however; always be on the lookout for new agents to work with.

More on Real Estate Agents

The following is what I want agents to do for me and what I will do for them:

- *Find properties that can't get listed.* The listing agent gets a commission even if another agent or agency sells the house. For that reason, real estate agents are always looking for properties to list. In their search, they may run across sellers who can't list because they have no equity and can't afford to pay commissions. I ask them to simply refer me to these sellers. If I'm able to put together a deal, I'll pay $500 as a referral fee. I choose $500 because it's enough to get their attention and make it worth their while. Sometimes their fee will be higher if the deal has a lot of equity.
- *Find sellers that are in preforeclosure.* Most real estate agents aren't interested in a property in preforeclosure because of time pressure—but I am. If they refer these properties to me and I'm able to put together a deal, I will again pay them a $500 finder's fee. In some cases, where it makes sense, agents will make $500 and also make the commission if they find a buyer first.
- *Find vacant properties in nice neighborhoods.* Vacant, unlisted properties usually represent a problem you can solve at a profit. The property may be vacant for any number of reasons, including preforeclosure, a divorce, transfer, and so on. There is no way for agents to make money on a vacant house unless they can find the

seller and get the listing. The effort is usually not worth agents' time, so I ask them to give me addresses and other particulars. If I can put together a deal, I'll pay them my $500 finder's fee. What could be easier?

- *Find cheap, ugly properties listed below market value and in need of repairs.* Granted, it may be a little difficult finding a good real estate agent who'll continue to find you these properties. They know most of your offers won't be accepted, and those that are will be low offers that pay only small commissions. However, if you haven't limited agents to just cheap properties, they'll be glad to find these for you because it is one of the several ways they can make money working for you.

- *Bring me any deal that might be profitable, where the seller is motivated and open to terms.* This could lead me to get the deed or owner-financing deals as long as it's not listed yet and a full commission is not expected. The deal will determine how I pay my agent. When you're just beginning your relationship, you may want to pay agents a little more. Remember, if an agent didn't bring you the deal, you wouldn't have made the profit. So why should I mind paying agents? I don't!

Another benefit I offer real estate agents is to refer buyers to them— that is, people who have called me about houses I have advertised but, for some reason or another, didn't want the property. This potential benefit gives an agent a strong incentive to work hard at finding deals for me. If you work hard to make money for your agents, they'll work hard for you. If they don't, find other agents.

> *"No man ever achieved worthwhile success who did not at one time or other find himself with at least one foot hanging well over the brink of failure"*
>
> Napoleon Hill

He turned $100 into $24,000 and never owned the house.

Kyle Bush, *Atlanta, Georgia*

Dear Ron,

I am sending this letter to thank you for the invaluable education and knowledge that you provided in your boot camp and to let you know that I closed my first deal.

Using what you taught me, I was able to make **$24,000.00** with only $100.00 of my own money and absolutely NO risk. I put a house under contract with a purchase price of $226,000.00 with a $100.00 binder deposit. I sold the house for $250,000.00 a few weeks later by assigning the contract. At the closing, I walked away with a check for $24,000.00!

I have a few other deals that are currently in the works that should net at least as much as my first deal. I am so glad that I decided to attend the boot camp and make the up-front investment to learn the correct way to invest in real estate.

I have enclosed a copy of the check.

Many thanks,

Kyle Bush
Bush Realty Group, LLC
Atlanta, GA

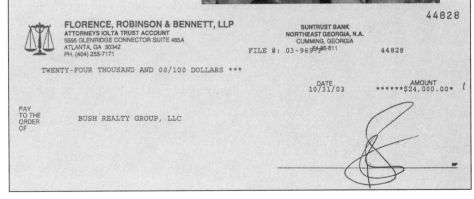

FLORENCE, ROBINSON & BENNETT, LLP
ATTORNEYS IOLTA TRUST ACCOUNT
5555 GLENRIDGE CONNECTOR SUITE 485A
ATLANTA, GA 30342
PH. (404) 255-7171

SUNTRUST BANK
NORTHEAST GEORGIA, N.A.
CUMMING, GEORGIA

FILE #: 03-969   64-86-611   44828

44828

TWENTY-FOUR THOUSAND AND 00/100 DOLLARS ***

DATE
10/31/03

AMOUNT
******$24,000.00*

PAY
TO THE
ORDER
OF   BUSH REALTY GROUP, LLC

7

STEP 2—
PRESCREENING PROSPECTS

This may very well be the most important chapter in this entire book because the ability to tell the difference between a deal and a dud is the difference between success and failure. It's also the only way you can ever implement my credo: *"The less I do, the more I make."*

Some investors spend their time driving around looking at dozens of properties a month, even hundreds. This is not only a gross waste of time but it's downright stupid. Chasing dead-end leads is similar to dealing with unmotivated sellers and can be a tremendous waste of time and energy. Unfortunately, many people never really learn how to avoid it. Well, I can solve this problem very simply: *prequalify every prospect that comes your way.*

I've found if you spend as little as five minutes getting prequalifying information from a prospect, you may avoid spending hours and hours gathering details about a property you never had a chance of buying. And any time you can spend minutes to save hours, it's like putting money in the bank.

Some investors have a tendency to take a phone call from a prospect and rush right out to look at a house in hopes something will develop—especially if business has been slow. They'll be out there measuring for carpet and gathering useless facts before they even know if they have a chance to put the house under contract. What a crazy waste of time, especially when you know you should never leave your desk without a solid reason.

Properly prequalifying a prospect helps you determine if further action is warranted. When making the initial contact with a prospect, you should ask yourself these three questions to determine where you can make the deal:

1. Can I buy the house wholesale?
2. Can I create a "subject to" deal?
3. Can I option or lease option the house?

If the situation doesn't result in a positive—yes—answer to one of these three questions, you don't have a deal. It's that simple. There is no reason for you to waste any further time on the conversation, much less travel across town to look at a house you'll never own.

Five minutes is all it should take to determine if you can create a deal with a prospective seller. Of course, you'll have to take the seller's word on things like the condition of the house, mortgage balances, liens, judgments, and so on. However, if the information seems reliable, and you feel the seller is motivated to pursue one of the money-producing models stemming from the three questions presented above, then you should arrange a meeting to verify your assumptions about the viability of the deal.

When I leave my desk, my chances of putting a house under contract are about 80 percent. By the time I ease the Mercedes out of the driveway, I've fully qualified my prospect, and I know I won't be just collecting a lot of useless facts.

Instead of being professional fact finders, we should get into the business of being professional offer makers. If you follow this prequalifying procedure on every lead, you'll save yourself a lot of wasted, unproductive hours, and you'll start to find the business really coming together for you.

PRESCREENING JUNKERS

This is really a simple matter of math after you've collected four key items:

1. After repair value (ARV)
2. Asking price
3. Loan balance
4. Estimated repair costs

I'll give you a magic formula to use when buying ugly houses that took me ten years to create, and then I'll cover the four key items above. This formula will never fail you no matter where you live or what price the house you buy; it works in any city. If you stick to it, buying junkers is easy. If you sway from it and use the SWAG theory (scientific wild ass guess), it'll be only a matter of time before your next seminar in Hard Knocks University.

Here's the magic formula when making *all-cash offers only:*

$$ARV \times 70\% - Repairs = MAO$$

That's after repair value (ARV) times 70 percent minus total repair estimate equals maximum allowable offer (MAO). However, MAO is not what you'll pay. Your offer should always be at least $5,000 below MAO, or don't buy the house. If you do, you'll pay too much; that's not a guess, it's simple math.

Forgoing a long drawn-out explanation of what went into the creation of my formula, here's the simple realty. Your net profit should be at least 20 percent of the sales price if you were to buy, fix up, and sell. Your other costs will eat up another 10 to 15 percent, which is at least 30 percent off the top for expenses and profit, not including repairs.

Using the 30 percent number automatically adjusts the dollars as the value of the house goes up or down, although the percentages won't change. However, the cost of repairs is considered case-by-case, varying with every deal, so you can't put a percentage number in a formula that's reliable.

So ARV times 70 percent means you've taken 30 percent off the top for profit and costs except for repairs. That ensures at least 20 percent going to the net column, so you factor in your *minimum* profit before you make an offer.

If you intend to wholesale this house to an investor, you can expect him or her to pay at or about MAO for the house. Don't expect the investor to pay more; you must leave enough of a reason for the investor to want your house. So if you intend to sell at MAO, you must buy the house more cheaply so you build in a profit for yourself of at least $5,000. The further below MAO you can buy, the bigger your wholesale profit.

You may be wondering how you can buy a house this far below ARV. The answer is simple: It must be ugly—filthy, stinking ugly—the kind of ugly that repulses most people. A lot of rotten wood, termite damage, leaking roofs, overgrown shrubs and lawns, rats, roaches, dead animals, toilets overflowing with human feces, and on and on. The house should smell so bad when you open the front door that the odor drives you backward.

The uglier the house, the bigger the profit.

Houses you can fix over a weekend with a little sweat and a paintbrush are usually not the kind you can buy below MAO. *You'll spin your wheels on the wrong prospects if you miss this point and get no offers accepted.*

The next most important item when prescreening ugly houses to determine whether they're prospects worth chasing or instantly passed over is this:

There must be a big spread between the ARV and asking price or the deal is dead.

AN IMPORTANT PRESCREENING LESSON

Whether you're buying a pretty house or an ugly one, there is one universal truth you must never violate or you're a goner. This is a principle that many do violate in their early days of investing, most of them messing up and growing to hate real estate—even though real estate investing wasn't the problem. The real problem was the investor who didn't take time to learn this principle:

Never buy a property unless you can get free
equity the day you buy it or know how to
create free equity shortly thereafter.

People who pay retail price for real estate don't understand this rule and usually live in the property. They're not in it for the money, but you are. Your profit can come only from free equity in the quick turn business. You must get it with the deal or you shouldn't buy the house. That's why a house where the seller is asking at or about ARV is not a house worth chasing. It's a dead horse, so bury it now; you can't motivate an unmotivated seller. Move on quickly and find the people who want to deal with you.

Whether it's a pretty house or an ugly house, your objective is to find sellers who *need* to sell, not *want* to sell.

Sellers who need to sell will make you rich.
Sellers who want to sell will make you old
and tired and will put you out of business.

Find the people who want to deal with you and lose the rest at lightning speed. If you do, you should succeed; if you don't, you'll most certainly fail. I've been at this for well over 20 years, 1,500 houses, and over 300,000 students. Not one thing creates failure more than trying to deal with the wrong people. It can only lead to rejection, discouragement, and failure.

And that's why the *spread* is the big key when processing whether a junker is a prospect. The bigger the spread, the better the prospect. That's also why the ugliest of houses are usually the ones with the biggest spread. The seller is more motivated, therefore driving down the asking price and increasing the gap between the after repair value and the asking price.

Many times you'll discover the asking is close to, or even below, MAO. When this happens, you have a hot prospect, and nothing should stop you from coming to terms. This usually occurs on only the *really* ugly houses.

Now, let's discuss how to find the ARV and estimate repairs. Before we do, remember you must know the ARV, the asking price, the loan balance, and needed repairs before you can make an offer. Never make an offer before you find out what a seller wants. If you let sellers speak first, you may discover they'll take less than you're willing to pay. You speak first, and you'll never get lower. You instantly lost the negotiating process.

> *What comes out of your mouth will
> determine what goes into your
> bank account.*

You must know the loan balance, and the only way to know is to ask. If a seller owes more than the amount you're willing to pay, a cash offer is out of the question—unless it's in default and you understand short sales. For you to not know what's owed but then to make an offer for less makes you look foolish and may end the relationship.

Knowing the loan balance instantly tells us whether this deal is a good prospect or is better suited for a "subject to" deal (get the deed). Many times you can get a house for free by simply taking over the debt and putting up no cash but still get a lot of equity because the house needs repairs.

Here's an example of one I did recently. The house was worth $115,000 after repairs. The dad had died and left the son the house with a $52,000 mortgage and needing $15,000 in repairs. Of course, that looked like $30,000 to the untrained seller, who was a pharmacist. The seller called on the basis of our ad and said he just wanted out. He was sick of the house after devoting several weekends to it and had simply lost interest. We went to the house, met the seller, got the deed, and left owning the house. The seller even agreed to make the next three payments simply because we asked.

We spent $15,000 on repairs and cashed out at $114,900. Not bad for a free ugly house, huh?

How to Determine the ARV (After Repair Value)

These are several ways you can make a determination of the ARV:

- You're licensed and have access to the Multiple Listing Service (MLS).
- You know or will find a real estate agent who can do a market analysis for you. Because you'll be making offers on some listed

houses, the listing agent should provide the after repair value (ARV) on these. This can also lead to a relationship that allows you to find comparable sales completed on nonlisted houses.

- You subscribe to a database service that allows you to tap into tax rolls so you can pull up your own market analysis. You should investigate a service of this type in your area. We use First American Real Estate Solutions, which you can locate on the Internet and is also referred to as Win 2 Data.

- Look for similar houses in good condition on the market in the subject area. Call agents and FSBOs (houses for sale by the owner) from yard signs to determine asking prices.

- If you're contacting the seller directly, you should always ask what he or she thinks the house would be worth if it were in excellent condition. This may or may not be a real number, but it's something to go by until you can do a more diligent investigation. Always ask how the seller arrived at the value. If it came from an agent's analysis or an appraisal, remember that it's probably the "as is" value if the house is ugly. You're looking for the after repair value, so it should be higher. If the seller's figures came from the tax assessment, it's usually well below the real market value.

- There are numerous Web sites you can go to for comps (see Glossary). Type in search words like "comparable market value" or "comps" or "real estate value," and you'll get plenty to choose from. Some charge and some are free.

Estimating Repairs

This one scares most people with no background in repairs. I guess we should be glad it does, because the public's lack of knowledge in this area is what creates the opportunity in junkers. Most people think it costs twice what it really does to repair a house. It won't take long to get a handle on this; in fact, it's one of the easiest things to learn if you realize you don't have to be that close to make a deal work—all you have to do is get in the ballpark.

I've renovated between 400 and 500 houses and here's a shocker for you:

I have never been correct on my repair estimates—not even once.

Repairs always cost more or less than I anticipated, usually more. But it never killed the deal or caused me to lose money. I've always made a handsome profit on every rehab. You see, if you use the MAO formula I gave you, there's a margin for error already built in. Besides, it's your buyer's opinion of repairs that counts, not yours, if you intend to wholesale the house. Usually, wholesale buyers underestimate repairs anyway, so you can be way off and still wholesale the house.

If your repair estimate seems to kill your deal, the problem isn't your estimate. The real problem is that you got away from my formula, used SWAG (scientific wild ass guess), and paid too much. Once that happens, it's downhill the rest of the way. Pay too much and there's not much you can do to make it up. Buy it right, and you can mess up everything afterward and still make a profit.

But don't worry, I'll make it easy for you to estimate repairs; you'll soon be doing it by walking around a house or looking at photos as I do. Here's my simple system. Most houses you find to wholesale or retail will be in the lower end of the market, ranging from 1,000 to 2,000 square feet and one or two stories. After a while, they all start to look alike. Your renovation costs will run between $10,000 and $25,000 on these houses 95 percent of the time. So the system for estimating becomes simple:

Your repair cost will be $10,000, $15,000, $20,000, or $25,000 . . . pick one.

Yep! It's that simple. Just trust your instincts, and you'll be in the ballpark with an estimate that's good enough to arrive at a repair cost for making an offer. But what if you're wrong? In fact, I'll guarantee you're wrong. So what? If you're wholesaling, it won't matter. If you were retailing, I'd expect you to get a "real" estimate from a contractor or two before you close the purchase. If you're too far off, you can change your offer, back out, or wholesale the house. It doesn't matter.

Of course, if you are one of those analytical personalities, you'll ignore my suggestion and dot every *i* and cross every *t* before you can make a decision. While you're doing all that and warming up your repair software program, my trained students and I will have made an offer, gotten it accepted, sold the house, cashed the check, and spent the money. But, hey, at least you'll feel good about your repair estimate on a house you'll never buy.

UGLY HOUSE EXIT STRATEGIES

Most investors buy ugly houses to either wholesale quickly or rehab and retail to an owner-occupant. Some investors keep them for rentals after rehabbing, but I don't like this plan because it involves long-term debt to raise the money to buy and repair, requiring a payment low enough for a positive cash flow. This debt is usually personally guaranteed—a cardinal sin to me. There are other, much better ways to buy keepers. The most common is just getting the deal on not-so-ugly houses and taking over nonpersonally guaranteed debt.

Whether you intend to wholesale, retail, or rent, the buying process is the same on ugly houses. Your exit doesn't change the MAO formula *if you're paying cash*. If you're new to the business, I'd strongly suggest you stick to wholesaling and get some checks before venturing into the world of rehabbing and contractors. For that reason I won't be covering that part of the business in this book, but it's covered in my Wholesale/Retail Cash Flow System you get on my Web site at **http://www.ronlegrand.com.** In fact, it took an all-day seminar on 6 CDs to cover from the time you purchase to the time you sell; the art of wholesaling is covered in the first 5 CDs. There are 12 CDs altogether, so you can see why I can't do the subject justice in a book aimed at exposing you to the whole business.

Now let's move into the world of prescreening pretty houses to see how we can make some more fast money without rehabbing.

PRESCREENING PRETTY HOUSES

There's no MAO formula that applies to pretty houses, but the rule about getting free equity stands. If you can't get free equity, why would you want the house? Fortunately, you don't have to have a lot of equity to make quick easy money. Because you don't have to raise cash to buy a house or repair it, you can operate with less equity and costly entanglements. However, the same principle applies to the spread between the ARV and the asking price: Whether a house is pretty or ugly, the best prospects are those with the most free equity.

The bad news is that most people who call you to sell their pretty house will want close to the ARV. They are not prospects—they're "suspects." You can't work with them, and you should know it immediately on learning the ARV and the asking price are close. Remember, you can't make unmotivated sellers motivated—they either need to sell or they don't.

The good news is that some sellers who call are willing to give up a substantial amount of equity in exchange for debt relief and peace of mind. You'll know it as soon as you ask their opinion of the market value and the ARV, and then ask what they want. If the spread is big, you may have a prospect who needs to sell.

How big is *big?*

Good question! The answer depends on your knowledge of your planned exit strategy and your personal financial situation. Here are your choices of exit strategies on pretty houses that you lease option from a seller or to which you get the deed:

- Immediately install a lease option tenant-buyer and get a nonrefundable option deposit of at least 3 percent of the ARV. This is the most common and most profitable exit and also the easiest and quickest.
- Sell for cash to a qualified buyer.
- Move in yourself.

If you choose to sell with a lease option, your monthly payments on the "subject to" debt you took over must be low enough to be covered by the incoming rent, or this choice is not available. (The same applies if you lease option from the seller.) Therefore, your only choice is to cash out now if the payment is high. In that case, you'll want more equity so you can make a decent profit; the minimum should be 20 percent of the sales price.

You can live with less equity if the payment is low because you can lease option the house to a tenant-buyer quickly and pick up several thousand dollars from the option deposit. I'd suggest you get at least 10 percent of the value in *free* equity before considering to take the house. Too many deals are out there to take less. Here's an example to help you understand this a little better.

A seller calls you with a three-bedroom, two-bath house (a 3/2) in good condition worth $150,000. She owes $138,000, and the loan is current. On asking her the magic words, "Will you sell the house for what you owe on it?" you learn all she wants is debt relief and a quick exit. Her monthly payment is $1,182, which includes taxes and insurances. You figure it would rent for at least $1,200 a month and maybe more. Armed with this information you collected in just a few minutes, the best plan is to get the deed, immediately put a lease option tenant in the house for about $159,000, and get a $5,000 to $10,000 option deposit within a few days.

You didn't get a lot of equity, but you'll make a quick $5,000 to $10,000 up front and still have a back-end payday if your tenant gets financing to buy in the future. The payment is covered by rent, and you acquired a nice asset with no money or credit at risk while at the same time helping out the seller. She got her life back, you got a house, and your tenant-buyer got a home.

The deal I just described is common and widely available in your city. I'll bet there's one waiting for you within a mile or two from where you live. Even if the numbers are different, the technique is the same.

This deal would work the same way whether you got the deed or you lease optioned from the seller. The exit is still to lease option to a tenant-buyer, made possible because you got some free equity and took over a reasonable monthly payment that could be covered by rent. Even if you want to move in to the house yourself, you'll want a reasonable monthly payment and some free equity.

If you intend to option the house and resell it without the right to install a tenant-buyer, *free equity is the ruling factor.* The more you can get, the more you'll want the deal. I'd suggest at least 20 percent, and I'd work hard to get more.

Earlier I mentioned my student Marco, who made $2,450,000 on one house. He did this by optioning an $8,500,000 house for $4,000,000 with a $100 deposit and selling it at auction 43 days later for $5,600,000. He also sold some furnishings and a yacht belonging to the same seller and got a percentage of these items. (This house had been listed with a Realtor for four years with no sale.) Marco moved it in 43 days. And some people think the cost of education is expensive—ignorance costs a lot more.

The point here is that on luxury homes you must get a much bigger spread than 20 percent. Most of the time you'll be selling well below market to move a house quickly, so don't back yourself into a corner by agreeing to pay too much.

Any time you deal in houses above the $300,000 range, a 20 percent spread in most markets doesn't excite me. After all, a Realtor and closing costs would eat up 10 percent. A seller who won't give up a lot of so-called equity is a seller who *wants* to sell, not *needs* to sell. Move on.

The *loan balance* is another key element in prescreening. A good sign the seller needs debt relief more than cash to sell is when the asking price and the loan are not far apart. If the loan and the asking price are far apart, on the other hand, the seller is looking for cash and debt relief.

Good news: Most of the houses you lease option or get the deed for will be for the loan amount or sometimes a little cash to move. This type of deal will make up 80 to 90 percent of your pretty house deals and are easy to find.

This week I have purchased two houses "subject to." The first house is in excellent condition and is worth $185,000. The seller owes $142,000 with a payment of $1,165 a month. He was asking $10,000 but accepted $2,000 and deeded me the house. That's $43,000 of free equity for $2,000. You don't need a computer to figure this is a good deal. The second house is worth $95,000 and needs about $3,000 in clean-up work. The seller owes $62,000 and wanted no money because she was behind two payments of $485. I got the deed and will make up the payments as soon as I lease option the house to a tenant-buyer. I'll do so "as is" on a work-for-equity program and let the buyer do the repairs in exchange for a little equity. I expect to sell the house for $90,000 "as is" with a minimum deposit of $3,000 from the buyer from which I'll make up the payments. That's $28,000 in free equity that cost me nothing.

To me this deal is barely worth doing. To you it may be a home run, especially if it's your first deal. I bought another house this week at a foreclosure auction for $310,000 that was appraised for $460,000 and needs no work. What a fun business!

> *"Dealing with unmotivated sellers is like kissing a toad with warts . . . it'll give you a bad taste for toads."*
>
> Ron LeGrand

60 homes in six years and going strong.

Larry and Kimberlee Frank, *Mt. Morris, Michigan*

ASAP INVESTMENTS, INC.
Mt. Morris, Michigan 48458

Dear Ron,

Larry and Kimberlee Frank started their real estate career in May of 1998 at the age of 35 and 45. We had to overcome a problem before we could start real estate. We had no money, living pay check to pay check like everyone else until we learned different ways of acquiring real estate without money. Larry worked for Ford Motor Company since 1972 and retired in April of 2002 (30 years) only because of real estate. Kimberlee worked 18 years as a legal secretary for an Attorney, Builder and Real Estate Broker. Kimberlee and Larry are full time investors now. Kimberlee is also a Real Estate Agent just for investing purposes. We reside in Fenton, Michigan. We have three children. Jason is 25 who is involved in our business, Hollee 11 and Taylor 7 (boy). We had a burning desire to succeed in real estate because of the money that can be made. In May we attended the first of many of Ron LeGrand's boot camp and that is when things really started happening. We believe that education is the key to becoming successful in any business.

We have purchased over 60 homes in the past 6 years worth millions of dollars. We presently have 26 houses and a 7 unit in our portfolio totaling 2.5 Million Dollars (purchased cash, subject to, pre-foreclosure, foreclosure, wholesale, land contract, etc.) with a net worth of 1.2 Million Dollars. We make a minimum of $15,000 per deal, usually more. These numbers are changing all the time. We purchased every property using many of Ron's techniques. Our most recent deal was we bought a bank owned under MAO using a private lender for $37,900.00 after rehab and six months we sold it for $119,400 after expenses giving us a check at closing for $31,060.47 (see check). To stimulate the slow market, we offered our 91 Mercedes Benz 420 SEL with the purchase of the home. The house sold that weekend after being on Channel 12 News because of the Mercedes but the Buyer used the money towards closing costs and we kept the car. Thank goodness. We love our Mercedes, Ron. (See attached picture of us with our vehicles – notice license plates "Buy Homz" & "By Homes")

Ron, we also want to mention we believe there are a lot of seminar speakers out there just selling their courses and not really telling all the facts. We believe your courses are very detailed and straight forward which allows anyone to follow it. Of course, we came up with our own niche (rent to own) thanks to your training.

Sincerely,

Larry and Kimberlee Frank
Mt. Morris, MI

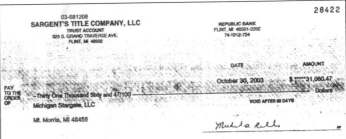

8

STEP 3—CONSTRUCTING AND PRESENTING OFFERS

There are only two types of houses on which you can construct and present offers: pretty houses and ugly houses. If you'll remember, most pretty house offers involve getting the deed, an option, or a lease option. Most ugly house offers are simple all-cash offers.

In the last chapter I covered the process of constructing offers, but I'll do a quick recap before I get into using a few magic words for talks with sellers. Ugly house offers are easy to construct. Find the ARV, estimate repairs quickly, ask if there's a loan balance, and apply the MAO formula:

$$ARV \times 70\% - Repairs = MAO$$

Now, back off the MAO by at least $5,000—more if it's really ugly or in a war zone. No science, all math.

Pretty house offers are also easy to construct once you understand your objective is to get the deed for little or no money, lease option for little or no money, or option. All require free equity or it's a no go. Try to get in with little or no money, and don't guarantee debt. Make sure you're dealing with sellers who need to sell and you'll find all of this much easier than you think. This advice covers 75 percent of the deals you do. The rest can be covered in our training and really can't be done here without causing you more harm than good.

MAGIC WORDS THAT MAKE MILLIONS FOR THE REAL ESTATE ENTREPRENEUR

I've just finished reading (for the second time) a book called *Magic Words That Bring You Riches,* authored by my good friend Ted Nicholas. Ted has sold over $200 million of information products worldwide by direct marketing. Over the years he put together a collection of "magic words" to persuade people to do things they ordinarily wouldn't do.

In *Magic Words,* Ted discusses how to do such things as get the best table in a restaurant and first-class seats on airplanes. He talks about how to slash the cost of a room at first-class hotels and attract all the money you need for any business venture. Want to approach a member of the opposite sex and immediately elicit interest? How about renting a Mercedes for the price of a Ford or buying jewelry at below wholesale prices?

Ted can tell you how to attract the best employees to make your business prosper, as well as how to get capable people to work for free. He even discusses ways to gain financial interests in other people's companies without investing one red cent. Pretty cool stuff, huh? And that's just the first few chapters. This book is also a masterful direct marketing bible covering every aspect of the business by a consummate professional. As I said, I read it twice.

Then it hit me! Like Ted, I've got a collection of magic words I've accumulated over the years, most designed to help me get into or out of a real estate deal. All of them work. The words you are about to read have made me millions of dollars and, if used properly, could do the same for you. The truth is that students have been trying to get me to do this for years, but it was Ted Nicholas's book that pulled the trigger.

Here's a set of magic words you should use daily to buy junkers:

"If I pay you all cash and close quickly, what's the least you would accept?"

And that's always followed by:

"Is that the best you can do?"

These words cut to the chase and save you a lot of time otherwise spent beating around the bush. Of course, if you're naming the price you'll pay before you ask what the seller wants, I'll have to take you out behind the woodshed.

Ye who speak first have big mouth and will pay handsome price for house.

Those words aren't exactly magic, but they speak the truth nonetheless. Never, *never* name the price you'll pay or the down payment or monthly payment you'll pay or accept when selling.

OK, let's say you've asked, "Is that the best you can do?" and the seller says yes. A good follow-up line that works for me is:

"So you're saying if I don't give you $_____, you won't sell the house?"

Now if the answer is still yes, you won't be buying today unless you're willing to change the focus to a terms deal rather than a price deal.

A good icebreaker to use when you want to make it clear that you're not happy with the number you've been quoted is:

"What's your second choice?"

I usually chuckle or use a hint of humor when I ask this. It's better than simply saying "I won't pay the asking price."

Let's say you're trying to get a seller to name the asking price and the seller just won't. You know better than to pressure, but you can't get the seller to break. Try this:

"How about a dollar?"

This will get through and probably produce an answer. If so, you're back in the screening process and know where you stand. If not, you can come back with this:

"I simply have too many prospects to work with to waste time on those I can't buy. If you'll tell me what you're asking, I'll know quickly if we can do business. Is that fair?"

By this time, the seller's usually in or out. You can't buy houses from uncooperative sellers. By the way, did you notice some powerful magic words hidden in there? Take note of how I tend to answer a question with a question. "Is that fair?" turned my response into a question and put the responsibility to answer back on the seller. It also softened the blow and made me seem warmer and fuzzier. "Is that fair?" is a powerful set of magic words that should become a part of your everyday vocabulary with almost everything you negotiate.

Let's say you're prescreening a seller who has a house with a mortgage balance. First, you want to know what's owed on the property or you can't possibly determine whether it's a deal. These aren't magic words, but they are critical ones:

"What do you owe on the house?"

What if the seller responds that it's none of your business? You then say:

"I buy _____ houses per year and use many different methods. I'm probably the most serious buyer you've talked to yet. However, I'll need the facts to be able to present you with an intelligent offer. Will this be a problem for you?"

Again, a question in an answer's clothing. Did I not sock it to them on that one? Frankly, anyone who won't give you the facts is not ready to sell yet. You got your answer . . . move on. You can't make unmotivated sellers motivated.

Now you have your answer. You know the loan balance. Now it's time to find out where you're headed with this deal, so ask:

"Will you sell the house for what you owe on it?"

Those magic words can make you $500,000 a year if you ask them on all your deals. With just those 12 little words, you'll know instantly whether you'll be getting a free house by taking over the debt or an almost-free house with debt plus a little cash thrown in. Of course, you may also learn that the seller wants full price and isn't flexible. Again, you found out what you needed to know with 12 words. Now you know whether to proceed with the deal or move on.

Now let's say you can't get a deed because of the due-on-sale clause or the seller won't trust you with his or her credit. But you see opportunity there and a lease option makes sense. Here's the opening line for presenting the offer:

"I will lease your house with the right to buy it for the loan balance when I purchase. I'll guarantee your payment and maintenance until the loan is paid off and the house is out of your life. How does that sound?"

Notice how all the benefits come before the question. The seller has enough information to encourage a positive response. Isn't that better than asking "Will you lease option your home to me?"? Another good question that will ease the seller's mind and make you seem genuine is this:

"If it doesn't work for both of us, then we don't want to do it, do we?"

That makes it pretty clear that you're not desperate to make the deal. Another version is:

"If this will cause you to lose sleep at night, I'd rather not do it. Is it going to be a problem?"

Here's a good one to break a stalemate and get you back in negotiation as well as collect more facts that might lead to different offers:

"If you and I can't do business today, what will you do with the house?"

This also gets the seller thinking, particularly about all the ugly answers to that question. The answer may be, "I'll put it on the market or list with a Realtor until it sells."
Your response:

"And what if it doesn't sell?"

At least you'll get a feel for whether this seller is worthy of your follow-up list. I hope you know by now that . . .

All sellers' minds will change with time and circumstance.

Here's one you'll love if you're a beginner and worried about the seller finding out that you don't exactly know what you're doing. First, don't sweat it. You don't have to appear to be an expert. You can try to fake it, but if you're confronting intelligent sellers, many times they'll see through you and try to ask you embarrassing questions. So if you're asked if you've ever done this before, use these words:

"Well actually, no. This is my first deal after graduating from some rather intense training. I was hoping you'd help me do it right. OK?"

Asking for help brings you down to the seller's skill level and you've built trust by answering truthfully. Don't worry about the seller's expecting you to be an expert. If you seem sincere and excited, you'll usually get the deal. In fact, being too smart or seeming too confident will often turn off more people than if you appear to be a novice. They'll think you're too green to cheat them.

Now let's say you're talking to a seller about carrying a mortgage and the subject of interest comes up. Your goal is zero interest, so you shouldn't be the one to initiate conversation on this topic. If the seller doesn't mention interest, you shouldn't either.

When presenting an installment offer, the magic words are:

"I'll pay $_____ per month until you're paid in full."

Of course, this means you've divided the loan amount by the monthly principal payment you want to pay, excluding interest. If the seller comes back with "What interest rate is that?" your response is:

"Why do you need interest?"

Then if you get more argument and it becomes a sticking issue, you could respond by saying:

"What's more important—getting interest or the house being sold now?"

If that doesn't get the job done, say:

"If I give you interest, how much can we lower the price?"

Or:

"Will you sell to me with no down payment?"

Or:

"Would you wait six months (or a year) for your first payment?"

Or:

"Would you take 25 percent off the balance I owe you if I agree to pay you off within _____ years?"

Of course, these same tactics can be used if the seller is asking you to raise your offer. You'll notice it all comes down to some very powerful magic words that can be adapted to many uses (If I. . . . Would you. . . .)

Here are some magic words that you can use when optioning a house:

"If we can agree on a price I will option your house and use all my resources to get it sold. All I need is a key to show it and a written option agreement to get started. Is that fair?"

If the seller balks or starts coming up with objections you can defuse them with this:

"Mr. Seller, I'm spending my money and my time on getting this house sold, and if I don't succeed, I lose, not you."

Obviously, these aren't all the magic words you can use, and they don't cover every possible use, but I'll tell you from experience that they're worth a fortune if you use them.

PRESENTING OFFERS

Dealing with an FSBO is a simple matter of coming to an oral agreement and then converting it to writing with a purchase and sale (P&S) agreement, a lease option agreement, an option agreement, or an actual deed transferring ownership on the spot. Until you have a written agreement, you have nothing but words. An oral agreement "ain't" worth the paper it's written on. Get it in writing quickly.

Use a P&S agreement when a formal closing will take place later, such as in an all-cash purchase. Usually a lease option, an option, and a deed transfer are done on the spot with a tabletop closing in the seller's kitchen. Some get a P&S agreement and have the seller meet at an attorney's office within a few days to have the documents signed. I prefer you do the latter but will admit hundreds of tabletop closings are done daily all over the country.

A good practice is to get all the paperwork you think you'd possibly need signed ASAP. You can always have them re-signed in front of an attorney later. Get a commitment while the seller is willing and ready. Postponing that commitment might give your competition a window of opportunity.

If this process scares you, I understand. In the beginning it's scary walking into someone's home with a file folder and leaving as the owner of the home. It defies all your senses and previous training. It shouldn't be that easy. Why would people leave a loan in their name and trust you with their credit and just give you a house with free equity?

That's a hard one to grasp while you're reading a book, but the first time you go to see a seller who *needs* to get out now, you'll begin to understand that all the stuff that bothers you isn't bothering the seller. Remember this:

> *It's not your job to think for other people.*
> *It's your job to give them choices and let*
> *them decide what's best for themselves.*

If your prospects have been prescreened properly and want to do business with you, the best thing you can do is give the prospects what they want—a quick exit, not a couch and a psych exam.

EARNEST MONEY DEPOSITS

You'll either be buying from FSBO houses or through Realtors. If it's an FSBO, you'll use a purchase and sales agreement and put up a very small deposit, usually $10. In deals with motivated sellers, a deposit isn't an issue; sellers couldn't care less. You're only giving a deposit to show a monetary consideration.

Contrary to common belief, a deposit isn't even required. Consideration doesn't have to be in the form of money (it can be love and affection), but why risk a challenge? Just give up the $10 and get the seller to sign it's been received. My contract has a place at the end for sellers to sign confirmation of receiving a deposit. My cash flow systems contain all the documents you'll need if you can't find them on your own; go to http://www.ronlegrand.com.

Dealing with Realtors is a wholly different ball game. All Realtors use their contract, which is OK, and they'll want a much larger deposit—from a minimum of $500 depending on the size of the deal. But don't forget you're in control here. You decide how much you're willing to put up; if it's not reasonable, the Realtor may not present your offer or you'll look foolish if the Realtor does.

If you know you'll take the deal—you should if you use my MAO formula on junkers—and you have the deposit, you'll look like a professional with a decent deposit. However, the deal's at risk if you don't buy—that is, unless the seller can't deliver good title. So if you're gonna deal with Realtors, you can expect to put up a deposit. I've put as much as $50,000 as earnest money. Of course, it was on a $5 million house, which may be scary to you but . . .

*If you're going to run with the big dogs
and pee in the tall grass . . . you got to
get off the porch.*

CONTINGENCY CLAUSES

These are commonly referred to as "weasel" clauses—ways to get out if you change your mind. Most real estate courses tell you to load up your contract with them to protect yourself—but from what? The most you can lose is your deposit if you back out. No one can force you to buy. They don't put you in jail. They simply keep your deposit—all of $10 if it's an FSBO.

Contingency clauses could fill up this book if I chose to write them. But some good news for you is that weasel clauses are for people who aren't serious about buying property. The clauses are unprofessional, unnecessary, and cost you deals.

However, it means I'm using a Realtor if my deposit is more than a few hundred dollars, and then I *will* protect myself. But I only need one clause to do it in most cases; it's common and acceptable to institutional sellers, who expect it. In fact, it's built into a lot of contracts on bank-owned property. When I made the offer on the $5 million house, I used a contingency clause and got my $50,000 deposit back when the value came in lower than represented by the Realtor. Here's the clause:

> This offer is subject to a property inspection and appraisal suitable to and paid by buyer to be done within 30 days.

That pretty much covers everything and anything you want it to and gives you time to verify your assumptions, including a home inspection, contractor estimate, and appraisal for the after repair value. If you don't buy after that, you *should* lose your deposit. It's only fair.

"If the offers aren't getting made . . . you aren't getting paid."

Ron LeGrand

Tom Lyons, a skeptic, has seen the light!!

Tom Lyons, *Dayton, Ohio*

RAELYN PROPERTY MANAGEMENT

OUR SERVICE REVOLVES AROUND YOU

Dear Ron,

I apologize for the delay in providing you this testimonial; however, I have been very busy diligently applying many of the techniques that I learned as a result of purchasing your cash flow system. I must admit I was extremely skeptical that a $1500 system could generate any significant amount of financial security. I believed the so-called "financial gurus" that preached about achieving long-term growth and appreciation by applying dollar cost averaging and diversifying my investments in the stock market. Unfortunately, I soon realized it would take a lifetime to build my retirement nest egg and it also meant I would have to work at my J-O-B until I was too old to enjoy what I had saved. I was definitely on the slow and risky train to obtaining wealth. Another "handicap" I have is that I earn a salary of $70,000 a year working as a civil engineering design consultant. When I first started it was hard for me to expand my reality and believe I could make a monthly cash flow from real estate investments that would replace what I earn at my job. I have been struggling to rid myself of the "golden handcuffs" of job security.

Enter Ron LeGrand's Fast Cash with Quick-Turn Real Estate. I absorbed the information contained within the book like a dry sponge soaks up water. That's when I decided to purchase your cash flow system. Since acquiring your easy to follow system and applying several of the techniques you teach, my real estate investing has started to gain momentum. I now have a total of sixteen units and approximately $2,000 a month net cash flow.

I must admit, prior to studying your courses, I did not understand the importance of finding motivated sellers. Then I ran an "I Buy Houses" ad and had individuals calling me, hoping I could help them solve their real estate problems. One such deal sticks out in my mind as a good example of what you instruct your students to work towards. There was a seller who needed to get rid of his home that he no longer lived in. It had been listed with a realtor for six-months and he was getting desperate. He was not behind in payments and was not comfortable with signing the deed over. Therefore, I purchased it on land contract with $200. It took me two weeks to lease option it out to a tenant buyer. I have a $100 a month net cash flow and a potential $12,000 back end.

On another occasion, I purchased a bank owned property for $45,000 and put $1,500 into it for repairs. Three months later it appraised at $87,000, I refinanced it and walked away from closing with $19,302 in my pocket. Ultimately no money invested and a $125 per month net cash flow and a potential back end of $10,000. I have enclosed a picture of the property and a copy of the HUD statement that I received at the closing.

It is still hard for me to believe that it can be this easy to make money and I thank you for your assistance in leading me towards a brighter more secure future.

Investing in Ohio,

Thomas R. Lyons

Thomas R. Lyons, P.E.

PROPERTY MANAGEMENT • LEASE OPTIONS • HOME BUYERS • INVESTMENT PROPERTIES

9

STEP 4—FOLLOWING UP

The most violated rule in business is the lack of follow-up. Most businesses are one-hit wonders whose owners quit immediately after a prospect says no.

Your job is to stay in the loop with sellers *who pass the prescreening test* until they've sold the house or you've bought it. This applies to prospects now, not suspects. Get rid of the unmotivated sellers immediately and follow up with only the good prospects you can't quite come to terms with now. It'll pay handsome dividends. Remember: All sellers' minds will change with time and circumstance.

When a seller says no, it doesn't always mean no; it usually means please keep bugging me until the time is right for me to say yes. Here's an old marketing axiom that's true in all businesses, including real estate:

*Eighty-two percent of all sales are made
on the second through the seventh contact
with a prospect.*

When you give up too quickly you may be taking an 82 percent pay cut without even knowing it.

Have you ever said to yourself, "This is the way it's going to be, by golly, and I'm not changing my mind"? Then a while later you did a 180-degree reversal. Things happen, attitudes change. Sellers make payments on vacant houses, miss their loved ones who've already "moved on," are forced to leave town quickly, get into financial trouble, realize their house is not the only one available on the planet, get tired of "lookie loos," and are confronted with numerous other motivations for acting immediately. Hang in there until the time is right, and keep a communication link.

The next part of following up is to get a title check done immediately after getting a signed contract or deed. You can't lease or sell a property unless you know you can deliver good title to a buyer. All kinds of things can cloud title and create problems, some even unknown to the seller. Here are examples of some but definitely not all:

- An incorrect deed in the past chain of title
- Missing signatures
- Undisclosed marital status
- Forged checks
- Liens and judgments attached to the property
- Unfinished bankruptcy or even a current bankruptcy seller didn't disclose
- Unnotified creditors in past foreclosure proceedings
- Pending foreclosure

Heck, you don't even know for sure you're dealing with the right owner until you have a title search done. Have you heard about the fellow who waited until a couple of owners went on vacation and, while they were gone, had a fire sale of their homes at a dirt cheap price to five different buyers? All he did was take big earnest money deposits all weekend, sign contracts, and then skip town before the owners returned. Now he's getting free room and board, but he almost got away with it.

All you must do to have your title checked is call in a title search to a title company or to your attorney, who'll want the address, the seller's name, and a legal description if you have it. A few days later you'll get a report if you request it and know if you have any problems. The cost for a title search ranges from $65 to $150, but many times you can get it done free if you develop a relationship with the title company and do constant business.

If a problem arises, you have four choices: (1) Ask the title company if it can fix the problem; (2) fix it yourself after the company tells you how; (3) make the seller handle it; or (4) back out of the deal. Any real estate contract will provide for the return of your deposit if there's a title problem.

If no problem exists—which is usually the case—you can move to step five, which is to sell quickly and is the subject of the next chapter.

"You may not get rich quick, but if you never get started,
you'll never get rich."

Ron LeGrand

A commercial real estate broker sees the light!!

F. Scott Tonges, *Pagosa Springs, Colorado*

Southwest Property Trust Inc.

Ron, I've been in the commercial real estate brokerage business for 26 years. I've handled the sale of office buildings, shopping centers, medical buildings, industrial properties, apartments and hotels with my largest single transaction at $22 million. I spent 15 years collectively with the two largest commercial real estate brokerage firms in the country. What I can tell you first hand is that I see big shots every week and they've got no cash!

I must have read most every book and taken loads of courses on making money in real estate. Through my commercial work in several states, I've seen investors make money and lose money. It has become an increasingly complex and difficult business and I'm seeing more lose money than make it these days. I was looking for a better way myself and did not want to deal with banks who are tougher than ever. I'd even owned some rental homes in the past and lost money on each one. Then I read your book and took some of your courses. I realized you had perfected a completely different method to make money in real estate.

In truth, I've not seen anything to compare with your approach. For my first transaction I placed a classified advertisement as you suggested and was seeking lease option opportunities. A woman called with a vacant home here in the southwest. I was soon to learn she was 4 months behind in payments with her first and second lien holder, facing foreclosure, and living out of state. Now what? Deciding to proceed to offer it as a lease option and see what might happen, I went ahead and put photos on my web site and began advertising. I quickly got interest from a couple who saw my unusual ad which I'd learned from your course too. The wife was in Washington DC and the husband in Albania. They were retiring but knew this area, having lived there in the past and they liked the web photos. We arranged for a purchase by mail and fax, I got a lender to work, and they first saw the home in person the week of the all cash closing. In a simultaneous closing, I purchased then resold it; I got a check for $8,200. The lender was paid off, a second lien holder got something (rather than nothing) and I even got some money to the owner. Except for one visit to see the home and take pictures, I did all this from 200 miles away from the market I work.

What's really great about your approach is that it's low to no risk and the rewards are substantial. Also, unlike my commercial activity, there are far more opportunities with homes. Keep up the good work, Ron. I will!

Sincerely,

F. Scott Tonges

10

STEP 5—
SELLING HOUSES FAST

One of the most common fears people have about getting into real estate is the fear of being unable to sell a house and somehow getting stuck with it. I can understand why this fear would create anxiety for beginners because they simply don't have enough facts to overcome the fear. However, if you're not a beginner and the fear remains a problem, you have no excuse. So let's get it fixed right now.

The truth is that selling should be
the easiest part of your business.

Are you not buying because you're waiting to sell what you have? Is your income suffering because you haven't plugged the hole in the back end? Are you so afraid of selling that you quit (or never started) buying?

In this chapter, I discuss the reasons why some people have trouble selling, how to dispose of the reasons, and a step-by-step process for selling wholesale deals, lease options, and cash-out buyers. I've identified 14 reasons here why people have trouble selling houses. Pay close attention to reason numbers 4 through 7 because, when combined, they amount to about 80 percent of the reasons that houses don't get sold quickly.

Most of the time it's a people problem, not a house problem.

These are the 14 main reasons why houses don't sell quickly:

1. Not ready to sell
2. Poor area
3. Overpriced
4. Salesperson's personality problems
5. Inflexibility of seller
6. Salesperson's lack of knowledge about available financing programs
7. Salesperson's lack of knowledge about attracting and prescreening leads
8. No follow-up system in place
9. Functional obsolescence
10. House very small
11. Salesperson losing control of loan process
12. House too far from city
13. House in price range too high for most buyers
14. Only one bath

Notice that the majority of these problems are directly related to the person in charge of making the sale; the rest should be fixed before you buy. Now let's examine some of these reasons for problems more carefully.

NOT READY TO SELL

- Front appearance—Would you want to see the inside?
- Roof—Does it need to be replaced?
- Exterior paint—Is it at least two colors and does it look fresh? Are the colors pleasing or gaudy?
- Interior paint—Is it two colors or does it look like a white tornado went through?
- Interior trim—Is there color, paper borders, blinds, bath and kitchen accessories, lever door handles, shower curtain or door, and so on?

- Carpet—Same old lifeless, ugly brown or have you tried hunter green? Would you want this carpet installed in your home?
- Central heat and air—If you're in the southern two-thirds of the country, it's not an option. Do it.
- Kitchen—Does it have plenty of cabinets or just enough to get by?

Customers won't complain about shoddy repairs. They just won't buy.

If it doesn't look good enough to satisfy your wife, your buyers won't like it either. Spend a few more dollars and make it a house you can be proud to sell and one you know your buyer will rave to others about. If you do, amazing things will happen:

- It will sell quickly.
- It will appraise for more.
- You'll sleep better at night.
- Your buyers will send you customers.
- Your good reputation will spread quickly.
- The neighbors will send you customers or sell their houses to you.
- Your attitude will improve, and you'll enjoy dealing with buyers more because you know you have a great product.
- You'll save the extra money you spent in holding costs. So in reality all these benefits are free.

POOR AREA

- Is it a war zone? If so, you must learn to sell low-income houses, or else don't buy there if you intend to retail.
- In low-income areas it's critical you master the art of financing. You won't survive if all your sales must be to a qualified buyer or sold for 100 percent cash out. Get educated or get out of the war zones.

Here is the *good* news:

- You can make some large spreads on these houses because you can buy them dirt cheap.
- Most of your competition won't touch them.
- They're easy to find and easy to buy.

- At today's interest rates, buyers can qualify with small incomes.
- Financing is plentiful, some even with no down payment.
- You can always wholesale if rehabbing isn't feasible for you.

And the *bad* news:

- Vandalism is normal.
- You'll have to screen out a lot of buyers.
- You'll be tempted to break the law by falsifying down payments because most of your buyers are broke. But don't do it.
- You'll have to take back a lot of seconds, and 50 percent or more will default. So what? It's all free money anyway.

If you're going to work the low-income or war zone areas, just be sure your exit is clear and you don't get into any traps. Don't rehab in a war zone unless you know where to get the buyer financed and you can live with vandalism.

In addition, you must be flexible on terms, not expect to get cashed out 100 percent, and clearly understand you will be prescreening one of the most uneducated segments of our society. It will take patience and practice.

OVERPRICED

Overpriced is not what you think. Just for the record, all my houses are overpriced. And I'm proud of it in case anyone asks. You should always set your sales price higher than the amount the house appraised for. If you don't ask for more, I can assure you that you won't get more.

But there *is* a limit. Putting a $125,000 price on a $100,000 house is pushing the envelope, although putting a $109,900, or maybe even a $114,900, price on it may work fine.

Your market will tell you quickly. If all the buyers complain about the price, you know you have a problem and may want to lower the price a little.

Warning! Make sure the price is the problem before you start fixing what "ain't" broke. Only your buyers can tell you the price is too high—

not your spouse, your neighbor, your brother-in-law, or especially your Realtor. You can always lower the price, but you can't raise it once it leaves your lips. I don't know for sure, but I'd bet I haven't lowered the price on more than 15 percent of all the houses I've sold. As a rule, 10 percent above the appraised value or good comps is the upper limit. You'll have to decide the price based on the area, condition and salability of the house, and the heat of the market. Just don't give away money because you're listening to morons.

SALESPERSON'S PERSONALITY PROBLEMS

Have you every talked to a seller or a Realtor you didn't like—a mean-spirited, grouchy personality perhaps? How about someone who just won't shut up long enough for you to ask a question? Maybe you've encountered the prescreener type, who treats you like the enemy until you pass his or her qualification test.

How about all those times you got a wife on the phone, and she was afraid to speak without her husband's permission (or vice versa). That doesn't even count the ones who do talk but never say anything. Then there's the clueless spouse who can't even tell you the asking price, much less the other details. How about the couple in the middle of a divorce—and the wife talks to you as though you're the one who just cheated on her?

Then there are the know-it-alls who want to do a seminar for you on the phone to impress you with their knowledge about the art of real estate. They can't sell their own house but can certainly tell you how to do it. Of course, we can't forget all the "thinker" brains trying to sell to the reptile brains and vice-versa. Or the sellers so in love with their house that it takes them 30 minutes to describe every little detail while you're trying to stay awake.

The key for you is to not become like one of those people I just described. If you already are, you can resolve the problem once it's identified. Here's a hot tip: Record your calls and listen to yourself selling your house. If there was a moron on the call, you'll probably recognize his or her voice. Every time you talk to a buyer, you must sound *friendly, flexible,* and *excited.* If you can't, then get someone else to sell your houses.

INFLEXIBILITY OF SELLER

This means that most sellers can see only one way to sell a house, and if that doesn't happen, the house will sit and sit until that perfect buyer comes along. Finding an A-credit buyer to cash you out isn't the only answer, especially true for low-income houses, where A+ buyers are scarce.

The more you know about different exits, the easier it will be for you to become flexible. If you don't have your money in the deal and can live another week without the cash from the sale, you are freed up to get creative and look at other alternatives.

> *Here's a news flash for you: It's your job*
> *to find a buyer who loves your house . . .*
> *then make it work!*

This means that sometimes you must be flexible. It's not a perfect world; bend a little. Here's a short list of selling methods:

- Sell to a qualified buyer and cash out now.
- Lease option to your tenant-buyer and cash out later.
- Sell with owner financing and help the buyer get refinanced later.
- Sell with owner financing and sell the note at closing for 93 percent of its face value. We spend a whole day on this in the Paper Power class, which is part of our curriculum at Financial Freedom Academy.
- Get the buyer an 80 to 90 percent loan with a secondary lender at a higher rate and take back a second mortgage or deed of trust for the difference.

There's always another way.

SALESPERSON'S LACK OF KNOWLEDGE
ABOUT AVAILABLE FINANCING PROGRAMS

If you're going to master your craft of selling houses, you must learn a lot about financing programs. What will kill loans? What programs require little or no down payment? What credit can be fixed and what can't? What will the lender want fixed before closing? Who will let you take back a second and who won't? And add 40 or 50 other questions you'll get the answers to as you go. You don't have to know all there is to know about financing to sell a house, but the quicker you learn certain basics, the easier it gets. Make an appointment with three or four mortgage lenders and pick their brains. Let them help with what will work and what won't. Then when you get an interested prospect, it's simply a matter of getting the buyer's information to the lender of your choice and letting the lender tell you what will work.

That's the best way I know to learn the ropes about financing. But a lot of veterans won't even take time to do this. I guess they feel they're too good or too smart to ask for help. My friend, what you knew about financing a year ago is not what you should know today. It changes monthly. You must stay on top to be the best. That will happen automatically if you're selling houses regularly, so don't worry about it.

SALESPERSON'S LACK OF KNOWLEDGE ABOUT ATTRACTING AND PRESCREENING LEADS

The first step to success in buying and selling is locating prospects; without potential buyers, it's very hard to sell houses. Frankly, an ad in the newspaper should be enough to attract plenty of prospects if you know how to write the ad and where to put it.

I can't turn this into an ad-writing course, but any ad that gets prospects to call is a good one. Any ad that doesn't is a bad one, or it's in the wrong publication. Make sure your ad gives the prospect a reason to call. Try to include a USP (unique selling proposition): What are you offering that everyone else isn't?

For example:

Lease Purchase
No Qualifying Owner Financing
No Bank Qualification
No Money Needed
Easy Terms
Owner Will Help
Will Accept Anything on Trade
No Down Payment
You Get a Car with the House, and on and on

Some students use flyers distributed in newspapers and don't run ads. Others use a lot of signs, referrals, mailouts, the Internet, and electronic voice broadcasts.

The key is to make sure you keep a good flow of leads coming in until the house is sold. Where most people fail is in the way they handle leads once they come in. That, my friend, is by far the weakest link in the chain. Leads must be prescreened properly and the good ones worked daily. Out of any batch of leads will usually come some qualified ones—maybe not with A credit but qualified if you're flexible, as I discussed earlier. What I look for most are people who love the house and are excited about owning it. Give me that and a little something to work with, and I'll get them in it.

NO FOLLOW-UP SYSTEM IN PLACE

The easiest way to sell houses is to work a buyers' list you built from the last house you sold. If you have more buyers than houses, you don't run ads, send flyers, mail letters, or any of that other stuff. You pick up the phone and call the prospects you've prescreened from the last time and tell them about your new house.

It's easier to suffer the pain of creating a buyer's list once rather than talking to dozens of prospects from ads every time you get ready to sell. You don't have to be an organizational wizard to do a little follow-up. Hey, a pile of prescreened buyers on the corner of your desk with no separation or filing system is better than nothing. Sounds a little like my system, but at least I put them in a file folder. Then I misplace the folder, but I always know it's close (somewhere).

FUNCTIONAL OBSOLESCENCE

This one is a house problem, not a people problem. You usually can't fix it so shouldn't buy if it's present. That way you won't have trouble selling.

Here are some things that come to mind:

- Extremely small rooms
- Bathroom off the kitchen

- Walk through bedroom to get to the only bath
- Low ceilings (under seven feet)
- House add-ons done unprofessionally
- Strange layout that can't be fixed
- House adjacent to odors, commercial property, school, or anything else that makes location undesirable
- Bad (or no) foundation

Those are just a few of the things I can think of now. Note: Sometimes you can correct them and sometimes you can't. If you don't see a way, simply pass.

HOUSE VERY SMALL

I guess this is also functional obsolescence, but it's very common. Any time a house has less than 1,000 square feet I get cautious. I've learned that houses under 1,000 square foot are usually hard to sell, and there's not much you can do but keep looking for a small family of one or two people. I'm not saying such houses won't sell. I'm just saying they're harder to sell. I've probably done 200 houses with areas of less than 1,000 square feet.

I think I own three or four now. I guess that verifies there is a buyer for every house. If I can buy such houses cheap enough, I'll still do so today. But I know going in they may take a little longer to sell.

SALESPERSON LOSING CONTROL OF LOAN PROCESS

You must remain in control from the moment you buy the house until you get a check. That includes the loan process. You decide who does the loan, who appraises the house, who gets the survey and termite report, and who closes. You are also in charge of speeding up the loan. Yep! You, not your lender.

You should check in every few days, push for results, and round up missing paperwork. If you don't, the close will drag on forever. Would you allow your boss to hold your paycheck for two to three weeks until she decides to pay you? That's exactly what you're doing when you let a loan processor jerk your chain. So the next time you lose a buyer because a loan processor didn't close quickly enough, go to your bathroom mirror and cuss out the person responsible.

The last time I lost a buyer two days before closing was because God told him not to buy. Had I been two days earlier, maybe I wouldn't have been competing with God. Oh well. Six weeks later I sold the house for $3,000 more than the first buyer. Maybe I wasn't competing with God after all.

HOUSE TOO FAR FROM CITY

That's an easy one. Don't buy it unless you want to create a lot of driving time so you can listen to more of my tapes. Frankly, I don't buy anything I intend to retail that's more than 30 minutes from my office. Of course, I know for some in big cities that's about three blocks away. Hey, you can always move.

HOUSE IN PRICE RANGE TOO HIGH FOR MOST BUYERS

Sometimes the price has no bearing because the upper market is hot. If it is, the high value is not an excuse for a slow sale. The problem is elsewhere on this list. But in smaller cities, where a $500,000 house is a mansion, you can certainly expect selling to take much longer.

But that just makes a case for you to not guarantee monthly payments on big loans. Unless you're a sadist and looking for pain, you shouldn't try to outguess the market. Don't count on a high-priced house selling quickly just because *you* like it. Remove the risk, give yourself time, and you'll discover the big ones sell just like the little ones, but I hope with a lot more profit.

Caution. You'd better make sure you have a large spread on those big babies. Buyers of $500,000 homes are more sophisticated and more apt to ask for a price reduction. The good news is these folks can usually qualify for a loan, and the majority of the sales are all cash. Owner financing and lease purchase just don't have the sizzle they do on the lower end. That doesn't mean it's not used, only not as often.

ONLY ONE BATH

I've sold hundreds of houses with only one bath, but it's not my preference. Cheap houses—not a problem. Houses above $80,000 to $100,000—very difficult. And for houses much above $100,000, it's almost impossible. People who can pay more want more. If you can't add a bath, you may wish to consider not buying if you feel it's important to a sale.

I have never added a room on a house to add a bath. The only time I *have* added a bath, I've used the existing structure, which should cost you no more than $2,000 to $3,000. Trying to sell a four bedroom, one bath house ain't easy. Selling a three bedroom, one bath house is OK as long as the house is small. Selling a two bedroom, one bath house is the norm that buyers expect.

I won't guarantee that every problem you'll run into is on my list, but chances are that if you take a good look at this list the next time you're having trouble selling a house, I bet you'll find the problem on it. If you do run into something out of the ordinary that I've not discussed here, drop me a line. In the meantime, remember there are no real problems, just solutions. And very often when you do run across a problem property, there's hidden profit there for someone who knows the answers and can create a solution.

A STEP-BY-STEP PROCESS FOR SELLING

Here you are with your first deal under contract to buy, lease option, or option and only a few days or weeks from cashing in. That's great, but before we start the process of selling junkers to a bargain hunter or lease optioning a house to a family or finding a qualified cash buyer, we must complete a very important step.

Either a title company or an attorney must do a title search to verify no liens are on the property other than those disclosed by the seller. The title company or attorney will also verify that the current owner is the only owner and there are no other parties of interest. Until this process is complete, you're not ready to sell or lease the house. Most states allow title companies to close real estate transactions, although some require attorneys to close. A call to a local title company will provide the answer.

Ugly Houses to Wholesale

If the property you're buying is an ugly house that was listed with an agent, the agent will want to handle this for you. Simply ask who he or she intends to call for the title work and say you'd like to handle the title yourself. If no agent is involved, you'll need to call a title company from the phone book, from a referral, or from a real estate agent. You'll need the legal description of the property to order a title search. If the house is listed, your real estate agent will provide it. If not, you can get the legal description from the seller's deed of mortgage or from public records with your database service.

If you're wholesaling a junker, either call or visit the title company or attorney or choose another company or attorney. Hold a short conversation with the one you choose about an assignment of contract, making sure your closing agent won't be a problem when it comes time to close. This is important to ensure the continuity of your deal. Agree on a price for this service (closing) before you order a search. The cost should not exceed $100; if it does, shop around.

If you're checking the title on a pretty house you intend to lease option to a tenant-buyer, you should make it clear you won't be closing right away but will be leasing the house. In such a case, you won't need a title policy at this time, only a search. Therefore, the fee you negotiate will come out of your pocket and be a cost of doing business.

Don't let your Realtor get wind you are doing an assignment of contract. Make certain your title agent doesn't divulge this information either. When you're satisfied the closing agent will perform without becoming an obstacle, you may order a title check and deliver a copy of your purchase agreement and assignment of contract if you're doing a closing on a wholesale deal. In the case of a lease option, your title agent won't need an agreement because you're not closing at this time.

If you don't feel comfortable with your conversation with the closing agent, find another agent. This whole process should take place within three days after you get an agreement to buy, lease, or option in your possession.

Step 1. Getting Ready to Sell

Once you know the title is clear, the next move is to prepare the house for sale. This won't be difficult because in most cases you're selling it in its "as is" condition as an ugly house. If it's a pretty house deal, the house should be in good condition so the only concern is when it can be occupied. When wholesaling a house, you won't need to put up a For Sale sign; and, in fact, you shouldn't put one up in most cases as you don't own the house.

A sign isn't necessary and may attract attention from the seller or agent if placed without permission. If you're using an agent and buying an institutionally owned house, you'll find it difficult to get possession of the property during escrow or permission to clean it up and get a key. It becomes a liability issue.

If the seller is not an institution, it's much easier. You can do pretty much what you can get permission to do. If the yard needs cleaning or the house is trashed and you don't mind getting it cleaned up, simply ask. You should be able to get a key as well. However, you are not to spend much money or make any alterations to a house you don't own. Remember, you are selling "as is" for a wholesale price; your buyer is getting a good deal because of the condition of the house. The most you'll do is clean up the premises and secure the doors and windows—usually you won't even do that.

If you're doing a lease option, there shouldn't be anything for you to do to the house except wait until it's vacant and ready to rent. When the house is vacated or about to be, it's time to start attracting tenant-buyers. If you're forced to do some minor cleaning up or carpet shampooing, make sure this gets done before showing the house. Again, this should involve a little work at most—not an expenditure of more than $100 or $200.

Once you have possession, place a Lease/Purchase or For Sale by Owner sign in the front yard. You can have it made at any sign shop, or you might find a sign in a supply store; you can also go to http://www.banditsigns.com.

Step 2. Attracting Buyers

It's now time to run an ad whether you're wholesaling, leasing, or cashing out. I'll start with the wholesaling process. Run an ad in the daily paper under "Investment Properties" or a similar column; a three-day ad should be sufficient and should read:

Handyman special, cheap, cash
[Your phone number]

Don't add anything to the ad. If the paper insists you put in anything else, fight hard to not allow it, although changing the word *handyman* to *handyperson* is acceptable if the paper insists. Make sure you or someone working with you is available to take or return calls.

Don't volunteer information. Answer only what you're asked and send the prospects to the house you have advertised. Tell them to get in if they can and just look if they can't. When asked what you want for the house, be prepared with your answer and don't sound wishy-washy. If you've used my formula for making an offer and are reasonably close on your ARV and repairs, your asking price should be at or about the MAO, which should be at least $5,000 more than you agreed to pay.

Be sure to build a buyers' list in the process. It will become your most important asset as a wholesaler. Keep track of the number of calls you receive. You are not to visit the house with your callers. They'll call you back if they're interested; if they don't, you call them. If a prospect who wants to buy hasn't contacted you within five days after your placing the ad, extend the ad for five days. Continue this process until you get a buyer who wants to meet and give you a $500 deposit.

If you're dealing with a tenant-buyer for a pretty house, you want to run an ad in your daily paper in the area that matches the location of the house. Make sure the words *lease* and *purchase* are in the ad.

Running an ad for ten days at a time is sufficient. You can always cancel or extend as needed. Don't put the required deposit or monthly rent requested in the ad. As the calls come in, be sure to capture information from the prospects who sound interested. Send the prospects to see the house. Make certain they can look into all the windows, but you are not to show the house until the prospect calls you back and expresses an interest. Let the house show itself. In fact, most of my successful students, as well as myself, buy a lockbox from Home Depot to install on the front door with a key inside it. Now, instead of meeting prospects at the house, you can give them the lockbox code and let them look on their own. If they like what they see, you'll get a call if you leave flyers on the counter with all the facts about the house and your phone number.

I know this sounds scary at first, but you'll quickly discover the risk of buyers' stealing something (from a vacant house) is far easier to deal with than making numerous trips to show houses to people who frequently don't show up. "The Less I Do, the More I Make."

Never tell the callers what you want for a deposit. Always ask what they have to work with first. Those with the most cash will rise to the top of your list. Those with little or no money should be quickly discarded unless they have good credit, in which case they become buyers you get financed now with the numerous no-money-down, first-time home buyers' programs available.

Step 3. Prescreening Buyers

Again, let's start by prescreening calls on houses you wish to wholesale to bargain hunters. You've run a handyman special ad and getting calls from prospective buyers. You've sent several to the property and now one who shows serious interest calls you back and says he or she wants the house.

Ask your buyer when he or she would like to close. If the answer is ASAP, you have a real prospect. Any other answer is not acceptable unless you're convinced your buyer is real and can perform. If the buyer needs to see the inside and couldn't gain entry on his or her own, you'll have to make arrangements for getting in. If no agent is involved, this can be done easily by getting a key from the owner if you haven't already done so.

If an agent is involved, ask the agent if you can get a key to show the house to prospective contractors. Most will cooperate, but some won't. If this presents a problem, you may be forced to have an agent meet you at the property with the buyer, or tell the buyer you don't have a key and can't get in at this time.

You'll be surprised to learn that when you leave enough profit on the table for your buyer, the buyer will usually find a way in or agree to buy without entry. Your common sense applied to the circumstances surrounding the deal will guide you to the right choice here. Use your own judgment.

Meet with your buyer at a mutually agreeable time and location. Or meet at your office if applicable. Ask the buyer to bring a check made out to you for $500. Have the assignment of contract prepared and ready to sign. If you have set a fair sales price, don't come off that price; just tell your buyer that's the least you can accept. Show no flexibility. Once you have a signed contract to sell along with a deposit, you may move to the next step.

Now let's move to prescreening tenant-buyers for lease purchase or cash-out deals. When prospects who have inspected the house call back to see the inside, prescreen them before setting an appointment. If they have no money, have no credit, or can't afford the monthly payment, you don't need to meet them. Make an appointment only if you feel good about the chances of the prospects' buying. Good credit may or may not be necessary; this will depend on the situation. However, a substantial earnest money deposit is always necessary for you to install a lease option tenant. No exceptions!

Meet prospects at the house or let them go through the house by themselves and leave some sample applications on the counter. The application must state they're granting you permission to check their credit. Tell them you'll let them know within two days and secure their deposit. The bigger the deposit, the better. Get at least $500 at this point and more if you can.

Make the prospects aware that this deposit is refundable if you can't accept them. Let them know when they can expect to meet you or your mortgage broker to complete the paperwork if they're approved. When you meet again, obtain the remainder of the deposit and have your mortgage broker run a credit report and tell you what kind of loan the broker can get your prospect.

If your intent is to lease option, you simply need to know what you're dealing with. Credit may not be your main criterion for selecting a tenant-buyer, but you should always know with whom you're dealing before accepting a prospect.

If you're looking for a qualified buyer to cash you out now, it's simply a matter of letting your mortgage broker or loan processor guide you on what kind of loan is available for your buyer. If you like what you hear, pass it on to your buyer and let the processor take it from there, arranging a meeting to get an application. You bow out and let the processor get a loan completed.

If you don't like what you hear, simply return the deposit and move on.

More Magic Words When Selling

Now let's look at the selling side and discuss a few choice words I use to find good buyers. When wholesaling, I want to know my buyer will come to closing with the money and isn't simply trying to jerk my chain. In this case, the magic words are "When do you want to close?" If the buyer needs more than ten days, he or she is a time waster and I'm at risk. If the buyer says "ASAP," I know the buyer's serious.

So many magic words are available when prescreening prospective buyers for pretty houses that it's easier to simply use the whole script—all these words are magic. I can't tell you how many hundreds, maybe thousands, of buyers I talked to before I developed the words and the order in which I use them. Here we go:

"Do you want to buy or rent?"

If the answer is rent and you want to sell, the rest is worthless conversation. But before giving up, use one more line:

"If I can show you how to buy and get financed, would you rather own than rent?"

If yes, continue. If no, save your breath. Next:

"Have you ever tried to buy before?" "Yes." "What stopped you?"

This lets you know immediately what you're dealing with.

"Is your credit good, fair, or ugly?"

Don't ask, "How's your credit?" Some people are ashamed to tell you it's ugly and will simply lie. Give them a multiple-choice question so they know you won't be shocked if they have poor credit. If it's bad:

"What's on it a bank wouldn't like?"

This breaks the ice and gets the customer to open up. Now the big question:

"How much money can you raise for a down payment?"

Whatever the answer:

"Can you get any more?"
"Can you borrow more from relatives?"
"Do you have credit cards?"
"Do you have something you could sell or trade to me?"
"Can you repair houses or have other skills to earn more?"

Now let's assume you see someone you can work with and you want that prospect to get excited and realize that you are his or her solution to home ownership. Here are the words that will glue that person to you:

"If you can convince me you want the house and make a commitment to buy, I'll get you financed one way or another. Even if I have to be the bank. If I can't get you in a home of your own, no one in this city can."

These words have sold a lot of real estate for me. They really make an impact on your buyer's level of hope. Follow them up with assurance that you are easy to work with and very flexible and the prospect will be putty in your hands:

"We can do whatever you and I agree. I own the house and I'll do what it takes if you will. Is that fair?"

Well, that ought to be enough magic to keep you practicing a while. Of course, these words aren't really magical until you begin to actually use them and make them work.

Step 4. Closing the Sale

If you're wholesaling a junker, deliver both contracts to your closing agent by fax or in person to set up a closing. If a Realtor is involved, you must notify him or her of the time and place, but remember that you should be in control of the process. Simply call the agent and coordinate a time suitable to your buyer and the seller.

Call the buyer with the time and place as well as the closing agent's telephone number. A cashier's check is normally required to close so the buyer will need a little time to acquire it. If the seller isn't present, it means the closing package has been completed by mail prior to your closing.

Attend the closing. While there, your job is to sit back, be quiet, and let your closer do his or her job. You'll be surprised how quickly it will happen. Once the buyer has come and gone, all that's left for you to do is get a copy of the file and your check. Make a copy of your check and submit it to me with a short letter discussing your success.

Now let's move on to our lease option buyer. If you like your prospect, set an appointment to meet. Go over the terms of the agreement and meet on all issues, including the length of the lease, the late penalty, repairs, pets, the purchase price, the option deposit, and the monthly rent.

While you're together, call your attorney and set an appointment for your buyer to sign a lease and an option agreement. *Do not prepare these documents yourself. Let your attorney handle it.*

Make certain tenant-buyers know they need to bring with them the balance of the deposit money as well as the first month's rent and the attorney's fee.

It's important you don't practice law here. There are several reasons why I strongly suggest you let your attorney handle the signing party:

- The attorney will prepare the agreements so you don't have to.
- It's free for you; your buyer will pay the $200 to $300 cost.
- Your buyer will know the agreements are professionally done and will feel more comfortable with the deal after the excitement wears off.
- There is less chance of the buyer demanding the return of the option deposit later when he or she decides to move. This is non-

refundable money, as your attorney (and the agreement) will clearly spell out and receive acknowledgment.

- If you ever do get into a dispute, there's no better witness than the attorney who closed the lease, explained the rules, and prepared the documents.

If you want an excellent lease option agreement, whether the houses are pretty or you're installing a work-for-equity tenant, you can go to http://www.goffn.com and join our Financial Freedom Network. It has three Web sites—one for buying, one for selling, and one that's an intranet site loaded with hundreds of forms and agreements. The lease option agreements I spent $6,000 to have prepared are on the site along with a list of benefits as long as your arm.

OK! The only kind of buyer left is one who's applying for a loan and closing the deal before moving in. The old-fashioned way: cash out now.

At this point you've already talked to your loan processor and determined if your prospect will get a loan for an amount you can live with. If it's a go, simply have the processor call the prospect to take the long form application and check in from time to time on the progress. When all the documents are in, you go to the closing and pick up a big check. The last step is to take your family out to the finest restaurant in town and celebrate. Don't forget to tell them why and to make an announcement every time you close a deal you're celebrating. Watch how fast they get interested in your business. A few trips to fun places would also help to increase the excitement level.

Here are the steps in a line-by-line format with some additions I didn't mention above:

Wholesaling a Junker

1. Get a contract to buy.
2. Check the title.
3. Run an ad.
4. Send callers to the house.
5. Get an assignment of contract and a deposit from the buyer.
6. Send the assignment of contract to the closing agent with an agreement to buy after you have a clarifying conversation. Have the agent notify the buyer and the seller.

7. Attend the closing and pick up the check.
8. Celebrate and do it again.

Selling to a Tenant-Buyer

1. Get the deed or lease option agreement from the seller.
2. Check the title.
3. Get ready to sell if the house needs work.
4. Run ads and place signs.
5. Send callers to the house with lock box code. Leave info on the counter.
6. Get credit application over the phone or in person and send to the mortgage broker or loan processor if either has at least a 3 percent deposit.
7. Determine your next move based on the report from processor. If it's a go, move to the next step.
8. Set up a meeting and get the money.
9. Set up an appointment with your attorney.
10. Send attorney the facts to fill out the lease and option.
11. Let attorney close and send you the lease agreement and remaining funds from the deposit and/or first month's rent.
12. Celebrate and do it again.

Selling Houses to Buyers with New Financing Now—Cash Out

1. Get a deed, lease option, or option signed by the seller or purchase all cash with a private lender.
2. Check the title.
3. Renovate the house and get it ready to sell.
4. Run ads and place signs.
5. Send callers to the house with lock box code. Leave info on the counter.
6. Get the credit application on the phone or in person if prospect states his or her credit is good or fair.
7. Determine your next move based on the report from processor. If a loan is available, you can accept move to the next step.
8. Let processor set up a meeting to get application and deposit if you haven't done so already.
9. Check in from time to time.

10. Go to the closing and pick up check.
11. Celebrate.

I know this doesn't cover everything you'll ever need to know to sell houses. In fact, I could write a book on any process I just described that we do in a three-day training event called Selling Houses Fast. Then there's the auction method, the round-robin method, staging houses, how to sell high-dollar houses, problem houses, getting weak borrowers qualified, autopilot systems using technology, marketing tools, and numerous other subjects to fill an entire book.

I know I sound like a broken record but if all this stuff interests you, do yourself and your family a favor and get some quality training from the pros who walk the walk. Go to **http://www.ronlegrand.com** or call **800-567-6128** and ask about our training.

Here's a free offer for you. I recently did an interview with my student turned teacher, Kris Kirschner, from Atlanta. Kris used to work for UPS at a pretty decent salary until he met me and got his life back. Today he buys and sells six to ten houses a month in Atlanta and has created an auto-pilot system whereby he never talks to a buyer or shows a house. He has truly mastered my credo of "The less I do, the more I make." By the way, his average profit per house is $30,000. If you'd like the CD where Kris goes through his system with me, simply complete the order form at the back of the book and my staff will send it free of charge as a small token of my appreciation for buying this book.

> *"Most people give up just when they're about to achieve success; they quit on the one-yard line. They give up at the last minute of the game, one foot from a winning touchdown."*
>
> H. Ross Perot

Slow Start to $275,000 a Year!!

Michele and Naveen Khurana, *Gainesville, Florida*

Florida Property Solutions LLC
"Serving the Needs of the Greater Gainesville Community"

Dear Ron,

Here's your long overdue testimonial. Sorry it took so long... we've just been too busy to stop!

It took us a while to get going with this business. We had other things on our plate. I also didn't know anything about real estate and my husband's self-esteem was almost non-existent due to some bad business decisions that had left us in the sub-basement of financial security. After about 9 months of part time effort we finally landed our first deal: a bank REO in a questionable neighborhood that we outbid 12 other investors for! We were in bliss! (It didn't matter that if we'd been on top of things we could have purchased it at the courthouse steps for less than half of what we paid for it!) We put too much time and money into the house, it took too long to sell and then to close, but we finally came out of the deal with $12,000 in our hot little hands. It wasn't enough, but we paid for our education with this one too.

That first house was practically all we did in our first year in the business. Since that time (one more year) we've done another 13 houses: 5 REO's (rehabs), 4 "get the deeds" (my husband negotiated significant short sales on two of these!), 2 out of town owners responding to a letter campaign and 2 houses from our yellow page ad from owners in various stages of distress. Those houses have meant around $275,000 in cash and equity to us. That's a big step up from the basement for us!

Ron, we can't thank you enough for all that you've done for us. We were getting pretty desperate and had no idea where to turn for help. Your kindness in sharing your experience and expertise with us as well as thousands of others around the country will never be forgotten. You've definitely made a difference in our lives, a difference that will continue in the years to come. Thank you again!

Sincerely,

Michele and Naveen Khurana

11

WHERE TO GET THE MONEY WITH NO CREDIT OR PARTNERS

Back in the early 1980s, I got this notion that I wanted to be a real estate investor. I had seen an ad that read: "Come learn to buy real estate with no money down." The thought appealed to me, especially as I was struggling to make a living, and the one thing I didn't have was cash or credit. My whole focus, from morning to night, was how to get enough money coming in so I could keep my old beat-up jalopy running and pay my bills. I worked long hours, doing everything I could to stay ahead of the rat race, because I was brought up to believe that all it takes to get rich is working hard and keeping your nose clean. Boy, wasn't that a load of baloney?

I wasn't concerned then that my family and I could lose everything because, frankly, we didn't have a whole lot to lose. We had already filed for bankruptcy a few years earlier, which was devastating to my confidence and my ego. All the assets we owned were stuffed into a 1,000-square-foot house that my dad had helped me buy by loaning me the money to assume a VA loan. The one thing I hadn't lost—and by far the most important—was my burning desire to get more out of this life than a job and mere survival. I knew there had to be more out there than making a living. I just didn't know what it was. I can remember times when my will to win in these circumstances caused me so much anxiety that I hated to get out of bed in the morning. Each day was just as boring and uneventful as the last, and I didn't have any answers to how to change things, let alone improve them.

I was broke and bankrupt, felt worthless, and was headed nowhere. How could a guy like me ever expect to make any real money? I had nothing to work with. At least, that's what I thought at the time, but that burning desire just wouldn't rest until I found a way . . . and that's what compelled me to attend my first real estate seminar, even though I had to borrow the money to go. The difference between me and many others is that burning desire. Without it, you don't stand a chance of making any real money. You see, the same desire that compelled me to attend that seminar also compelled me to use what I learned there and to stick with it. It would have been so much easier to quit when the first obstacle arose.

But I didn't quit, and the rest is history. I believe the main reason I can communicate so well with beginning investors lies within my humble beginnings. In a nutshell, *I've never forgotten the gut-wrenching anxiety that comes with being broke . . . and I never will!* Now you may be asking yourself what all this has to do with raising money to do deals. Just bear with me, and you'll see my reason for telling you this tear-jerking story. In fact, there are three:

1. I want you to get a feel for where I was when I began as an entrepreneur so that the next time a stupid thought such as "You gotta have money to make money" enters your head, you'll think of me and immediately come to your senses.
2. I want you to understand that no success comes without sleepless nights and plenty of anxiety.
3. When you start using what I'm about to teach you, you'll experience rejection, which may bring some anxiety. With time and success, that anxiety will go away—especially if you persist until you win. If you quit, however, the anxiety of being a loser never goes away.

WHERE TO GET THE MONEY

Not knowing where to get the money to do deals keeps a lot of people out of the business and, unfortunately, costs them financial freedom.

And that saddens me because it's the easiest hurdle to overcome. Before we talk about where to get the money, let's discuss what we could do with it if we had it. I wouldn't use it to buy pretty houses—you simply don't buy attractive houses in nice neighborhoods priced at retail value and pay cash for them. And you won't get them at wholesale price because there is no reason for the seller to discount.

Because the only time I'd pay cash for a house is when I buy at wholesale price, cash isn't necessary to deal in houses needing no repairs. For those houses I use lease options, options, owner financing, or debt take-over, all of which require little or no cash when done properly. When we're in the wholesaling business, our job is to find houses that can be bought at wholesale price and quickly flip them to retailers.

We find the bargains and pass them on to the bargain hunters quickly. This doesn't require cash because the buyer brings the money to purchase from you. Then the closing agent subtracts what you agreed to pay and cuts you a check for the difference. The only cash you need is for an earnest money deposit. That's almost never more than a few hundred dollars and usually less than $100 when dealing with sellers directly.

So we don't need to raise money to do 90 percent of the business. The money comes from our buyer at a simultaneous closing or we simply don't need it to do the deal if we're properly trained. That leaves only one type of deal that does require money: buying a house and re-habbing it. This requires money but certainly not yours. So let's discuss how I solved the money problem when I began.

My first seminar taught me a few techniques about how to find deals, so the first thing I did was start looking. I found a Realtor to help me find junkers from the MLS book, and it wasn't long before my offer on a small fixer-upper was accepted.

I remember my Realtor asking me several times if I had the money. I simply gave her the answer I had learned in class: "The money's on the way." Now I didn't have a clue where it was coming from, but I knew if I could find a good deal, I shouldn't have too much trouble finding a money partner. As it turned out, I was right.

I took the deal to my ex-boss and he liked it. He put up some of the money and went to the bank to borrow the rest. That was the beginning of a partnership that lasted six months and 23 deals until I found a source of funds that eliminated my having to share 50 percent of every deal. This source supplied all the money I needed to buy junkers as long as I bought them cheaply enough—which launched me into a whole new career. My new source was a mortgage broker, who I promised I'd make famous; his name is Al Coplan, hereafter referred to as Al.

Al's job as a one-man brokerage company was to pair private lenders, who had money to invest, with borrowers like me, who could bring him safe loans. Al didn't care about my credit or my income. His only concern was the collateral for the loan. When he put out money for his friends, relatives, and other private lenders, he had a simple system: If the loan went bad, he was responsible for doing whatever it took to make sure the lender didn't lose money . . . even if that meant coming out-of-pocket. Throughout our relationship, Al was adamant about his loan requirements. Put simply, his entire system revolved around one basic rule: *If I can't take the property back for the loan amount plus costs and make money, I won't do the loan.*

You see, Al didn't care about credit or income because it was, and still is, totally irrelevant to the safety of the loan. The only real insurance then was, and still is now, a low loan-to-value ratio. He simply wouldn't make a loan for more than 50 percent of the value of the property based on his appraiser's report. Of course, the downside was that these loans were high priced. The rate was 18 percent and Al got ten points off every loan (that's an extra 10 percent, just for his services!). If that wasn't bad enough, his lenders got six additional months of interest every time I paid a loan off early, as I always did. Yes, the price was high, but it didn't take me long to figure out it was still cheaper than 50 percent to a partner plus I kept total control.

The upside was that Al would loan on the after-repair value, not the purchase price. This was critically important to an investor who was buying houses for 20 to 40 percent of their value because the houses needed work. He would escrow for repairs, but I became good at buying houses cheap enough for his loans to cover all the costs and the repairs, even when he withheld money until the work was finished. This meant that in every case I was borrowing much more than the purchase price.

We would close the loans a few days after the appraisal came back. No credit reports, no income verifications, and no other qualifying obstacles. Al provided a readily available source of funds for anyone who could live with a loan no higher than 50 to 60 percent of the appraised value. The cost was high, but as I quickly learned:

*The cost of the money is irrelevant.
It's the availability that's important.*

As a borrower, my association with Al lasted several years. He made a lot of money for me and vice versa. Al is in business to this day and hasn't changed a thing so far as I know. In fact, I'm gonna send him this book when it's finished so he'll know I kept my promise to make him famous!

It took me a few years to figure out that if I could find my own private lenders, I wouldn't have to pay Al 10 percent of every loan to find them for me. It also occurred to me that I too could lend money and collect those 10 percent checks. All I had to do was get a mortgage broker's license, which is exactly what I did. To this day, I still make private loans and collect 5 percent of each, and the same lenders who fund these loans also fund loans on houses I buy and sell personally.

By using money from my own private lenders for deals, I don't pay a brokerage fee. A basic fact of business: When you go directly to the source, you don't have to pay a middleman (broker). Just in case you haven't figured it out by now, here's my point:

*The best source of money you'll ever find
for deals is from people just like you within
50 miles of where you're sitting.
There are more private lenders fitting that
description than you'll ever need.*

They're easy to find, once you learn how, and it's an inexhaustible supply of money. You don't need credit or committees, and you can have the money a few days after finding the deals. You'll be a hero to your lenders because they will be receiving a very high rate of return safely. So let's spend some time learning first how to find these folks and then how to convince them to loan you their money.

As I said earlier, they are all around you. They're people just like you and from all walks of life. You're not looking for huge pools of money from pension plans, banks, or insurance companies. Focus on small amounts of money from everyday folks that will be money in their IRAs or money they have in stocks, bonds, CDs, savings accounts, or other investments. I've found IRAs a very easy source to tap for two reasons: First, making loans is an approved use of a self-directed IRA if it's with the right company as discussed later in the book; second, it's money most people consider off limits until retirement, so it's been sitting there doing nothing but getting low return.

Once you show prospects how much faster their money grows at 12 percent as opposed to 7 percent and point out it's all tax deferred, it's simply not a hard sell. Yes, 12 percent is the rate I offer all my lenders, whether I'm borrowing for my own use or acting as a broker for others.

So the first hurdle you have to overcome is to get your greed glands in check. If you go cheapskate and try to lower the rate, you'll get a lot less cooperation. Just remember that people who invest money do so for one reason only: to *make* money. If you take away the financial gain, you take away the incentive. Better to pay too much than too little. Better to have happy lenders who can't wait to tell their friends than wishy-washy lenders who have to be begged. If you make it worth their while and come through on what you promise, they'll soon be begging you to get rid of their money.

On the other hand, don't spoil them. Offering 18 percent only creates a question of high risk and costs you more money. A 12 to 15 percent return is enough to create excitement, and sometimes you can do better than that with people who know you and trust you. The best way to set a rate is to simply ask a few potential lenders what it will take to get them interested. If they are happy with 10 percent, don't kill the goose.

In order to borrow someone's IRA, it must be set up with a TPA (third-party administrator) who can fund the loan. Most IRAs aren't set up this way. It's no big deal to transfer, but you must help lenders take this preliminary step. Here's how: Go to http://www.trustetc.com and ask for several IRA transfer packages. Once you have them, you can hand one to your new lender when the need arises. Your lender simply fills in the form, attaches a small check, and mails it; Equity Trust—the best company I've found to handle IRAs—does the rest.

It takes about ten days to do the transfer. When it's completed, your lender simply faxes a request for the money to the closing agent, and Equity Trust will promptly reply by wiring money if requested. So you're ready to close as soon as the money arrives.

If an IRA is not involved, you're ready to close as soon as you convince your private lender and get the title checked. One of the great advantages of private borrowing is fast closings. I close almost all my loans the day after I get the funds to the closing agent, which is always the day after my lender commits. We're talking five to seven days after the ink dries on the purchase contract if the seller is ready, and that includes appraisal time.

The question I ask prospective lenders is simple, to the point, and prequalifies them quickly: "Do you have an IRA or other investment capital that's not getting you a 12 percent return safely?" If they answer yes, they're either lying or not a prospective lender. If they answer no, the next thing you must do is find out if they even have an IRA or other money. The easiest way I've found to do this is follow up my first question with "Would you like to?" They'll either say yes or "I'd love to, but I don't have an IRA or other investments." This is where you either explain the program or go on to a qualified prospect.

You won't have to ask too many people before you get positive results if the following three conditions are met:

1. Your prospective lender must be qualified.
2. You must have some semblance of credibility.
3. You must be able to prove your case, not just expect your prospect to accept your word.

We've already discussed how to quickly prequalify your prospective lender with a couple of questions. So what do I mean by a semblance of credibility? I mean that you must look and act like someone who can be trusted and is competent to deal with another person's money. Do you dress professionally? Are your shoes shined and your hair neatly cut? If you feel you lack credibility, ask yourself (or someone who knows you and will be honest) why, and remedy it. More often than not, correcting the problem is as easy as getting a haircut and buying a nice shirt and a new pair of shoes.

If you feel you lack credibility from lack of experience, don't sweat it. Proving your case and acting with enthusiasm will overcome a lack of experience. If you think your young age presents a credibility problem, the same holds true. Act with enthusiasm and confidence and you'll get results.

Your biggest selling tool is the fact that you can protect your lender so well with equity. Point out that in a worst-case scenario the property will pay even if you can't. Talk about high return, safety, and how you want a lasting relationship with people who can mutually profit from your sweat.

Show your prospective lenders exactly what your intentions are for the property. Don't ignore the negatives and don't glorify the positives. Tell it like it is, tell the lenders how they win, convince them you're looking out for their investment and show them how all the proper paperwork will be done. Put them in touch with your closing agent or attorney and answer all their questions truthfully. By going through all these steps like a pro, you'll instill confidence in your prospective lenders and infect them with your enthusiasm. You simply won't have to beg anyone to lend you money. It's just not hard to convince people that 12 percent is better than the 3 or 4 percent that they're probably getting now.

You Won't Have to Beg

As a beginner, you'll have to prove your ability. But once you have a track record and a good reputation, that won't be necessary. Your word and a mortgage or trust deed will be all you'll need.

But for now, let's look at what a lender would like to see to feel at ease with the deal and you. Actually, this package is no different from the one you should compile before you buy a house. Your lender will probably want to see an appraisal and possibly a repair estimate before committing to the loan and may even want to see the house. If so, a complete repair estimate is very important to convince a lender that the cost is near the amount you think it is.

Furnish lenders a list of the closing documents they will receive. Or better yet, have them call your attorney or title company. By proving the value of the house with an appraisal and providing the proper documents after closing, you'll have shown professionalism and built a case for safety. These items should be included in a lender's package:

- Appraisal of the after-repair value
- Title insurance furnished by the closing agent
- Fire insurance naming the lender as mortgagee
- Original note prepared by the closing agent
- A copy of the mortgage or deed of trust—the closing agent will record the original and forward it to your lender
- A list of repairs and possibly an estimate of costs

Remember, the first step is to get moving and start asking. You may have to "kiss some frogs," but that's the price of success. You'll be surprised at how few people you have to ask to get good results.

Just keep in mind how easy your job of buying houses will become once you can stop worrying about where the money will come from. At least 400 of the 1,500 houses I've bought have been financed with private loans through the method I've just shared with you.

I can't tell you how much that means in profit, but I know it beats the heck out of any job I've ever had! I'm sure you'll feel the same way once you do what it takes to get the money flowing. It will get easier each time you ask. Before long, you'll have more funds available than you can use all by yourself. That's when it's time to start making money as a mortgage broker yourself, just like my friend Al and me.

IT TAKES MONEY TO MAKE MONEY AND OTHER *BIG LIES*

Those who've said it takes money to make money were people trying to justify why they're broke. It doesn't take money to make money— at least not your money and frequently none at all. The truth is that if you can't make money without money, you can't make money *with* money!

When I started in 1982, I had no money or credit, as I noted earlier. I was broke. I had no credit cards, no rich relatives, not even a wife working to support me. I'd quit my job and burned the ships behind me. The only way out was to make it or get another job. I had a mortgage and bills just like everyone else, yet somehow I made it happen. I succeeded in spite of the odds stacked against me.

You wanna know why? I succeeded *because* I had no money or credit! Believe it or not, *having* money and credit when you begin your career as a real estate entrepreneur can do you more harm than good. It can ruin you if you're not careful. Having no money keeps you focused on doing the deals that don't require money. If your credit sucks, as mine did, you can't apply for bank loans. Therefore, you inadvertently avoided the two biggest mine fields—not because you were so smart but because you had no choice.

Whether you have money or not, you should learn to leverage your brain, not your wallet. When you do that, having money becomes a non-issue because you don't need it to buy houses. If you write big checks, you're always worried about losing those checks. If you guarantee loans, you risk everything you own. Do neither, and you eliminate your risk. I've said those words a thousand times, and I still see people who should know better doing it anyway.

Don't get me wrong; I'm not saying you shouldn't have money. I'd actually prefer you to be filthy, stinking rich! I'm just saying you'll get there a lot quicker if buying houses doesn't depend on your capital or the number of loans you can borrow. Because if it does, you're a slave to your limited resources, and your business will move at a snail's pace.

How many loans can you get before you get cut off? Only a handful! Then what? How many deals can you buy if you have to write a check for each? You get the drift. On the other hand, how many loans can you take "subject to" before you get cut off? That's right, there is no limit! And no one's counting because it's endless. You can buy 500 houses and never ask permission or fill out an application to submit to a brainless loan officer.

The loans are not on your credit, and you aren't personally liable. If disaster, such as a deep recession, strikes before the loans are paid off, it's now the bank's problem, not yours. ("Subject to" means the loan stays in the seller's name, but title transfers to you.) You can learn more about this from the For Sale by Owner Cash Flow System and the Massive Income Strategies training. See **http://www.ronlegrand.com.**

If you're buying junkers to rehab, how many private loans can you get before you're cut off? All you want! You should always come away from a closing with more than you need to buy and fix the house. So having enough money to buy a junker isn't a problem. The problem is lining up your lender or mortgage broker to get the money for you, which you can do in a coma once you make up your mind to get it done.

How much money do you need to wholesale a house? You guessed it: nada! Well, maybe a $10 deposit to the seller. Can you raise that all by yourself? How much do you need to lease option a house and then sublease it to a tenant-buyer? You know the answer: none!

So let's recap for a minute. Taking over "subject to" loans on pretty houses usually requires no money from you or, at most, a small amount. Yet you can immediately lease option a pretty house or sell with owner financing and pick up $5,000, $10,000, $20,000, or more from a deposit or down payment, all within a few days. You can also buy junkers and rehab them using private loans: getting cash when you buy and sell and never spending a dime of your own money. You can also lease option pretty houses from the sellers and sublease to tenant-buyers, picking up deposits in the thousands within days and huge back-end checks when the buyers cash out.

And don't forget about the bargains! Flip them to bargain hunters and make $5,000, $10,000, or more and never own the house. All of this with none of your own money or credit. I don't know what's stopping you, but what stops a lot of folks is lack of grit! No guts. Afraid of their own shadow. Going through life avoiding confrontation or pain; can't grow because they won't go. You wanna know who seems to do the best in this business? The people without money or credit but lots of grit. And how do you get grit? Simple: You first suffer adversity and get beat up and kicked around a while. Then one day you wake up and realize no one can hurt you anymore and there's only one way to go . . . up.

When you stop worrying about losing, you can start thinking about winning. You see, people with grit have learned to stop playing not to lose and begin playing to win. Does this mean you don't have grit if you haven't been to the bottom? Of course not. Adversity is not a require-ment for grit. It just seems those who are the bloodiest seem to be more fired up and move more quickly, with more passion. They've seen the black hole and they don't want to go back.

It's quite common for those who begin with money to leap before they look and spend money on stuff that doesn't produce revenue—stuff like office furniture, computers, electronics, and foolish advertising that wastes money. Smart entrepreneurs put their money in the bank and start their business on a shoestring. The fancy stuff doesn't put a dime in the bank; to do that, you must make offers, and you should be mak-ing them without using your money or your credit.

"Success seems to be connected with ACTION. Successful men
keep moving. They make mistakes, but they don't quit."

Conrad Hilton

This Restaurant Manager Closed Two Wholesale Deals and Made $13,000…in spite of His Skepticism!!
Bryan Blasband, *Philadelphia, Pennsylvania*

My name is Bryan Blasband. After studying your course, I quit a full-time job as a restaurant manager to start a real estate investing business. Using some of the marketing techniques, I put 2 houses under contract to wholesale. In November I closed both deals back to back, collecting in excess of $13,000. My next goal was to have another ugly house under contract by year's end, and I'm happy to report that I signed one last week.

As a restaurant manager working 6 days a week, I had little time and energy for anything else. The decision to quit was terrifying because I'm still digging out of some other failed business ventures. My wife and I agonized over this, but realized to get ahead we needed to take some risks. Two deals later, we're very excited about the possibilities of this business. We now know that wholesaling is just the tip of the iceberg.

To the skeptics in the audience, I have found all the information in Ron's course to be true in the real world. For example, I was nervous about finding buyers once a house was under contract. Ron, they called left and right after placing your "handyman special" ad. Some of them call every few weeks just to follow up. AND…the investor who bought one of my houses told me to find her 5 more. Believe me, I'm working on it! Another thing I questioned was why anyone would want to buy a house from me when they could find it themselves. Again your information holds true. The rehabbers are busier supervising crews than marketing for ugly houses. They are all too happy to pay the wholesaler for a gem.

Thanks again Ron, for helping me change my life! I am going to be a serious player in this business. Enclosed are copies of checks and my picture. I look forward to thanking you in person in the very near future.

Best regards,

Bryan Blasband

HOW YOU CAN RETIRE WITH AN IRA WORTH $1 MILLION

I know this sounds like another one of those glorified headlines to get your attention but without a lot of truth. I know it's a very strong statement and sounds too good to be true. But what if it *is* true? What if you could have a cool million dollars in your IRA within a few years so you'd never have to worry about retirement income? What if you could do this without writing another check to your IRA? I have some good news and some bad news. The good news: You can! The bad news: It requires work!

Is it too much to ask you to do some work for a few years so you can retire rich? You've got to work at something anyway, so you might as well get rich while doing it. The information you're about to read is unknown to most of the world. Most people think the way to grow your IRA is to make annual contributions and let the manager of the IRA invest it in stocks and mutual funds. Then, over a period of 20 to 40 years, it grows into a large sum of money for your retirement. That's the thinking of conventional wisdom.

Let me tell you how I feel about conventional wisdom. It's almost always wrong! Let's take a look at a better way. Check it out for yourself and see if you agree. I speak to groups of people all over the country and sometimes ask how many in the room have an IRA. I have never had more than a third of the class answer yes. So why don't more people have IRAs? Here's what they tell me:

- They can't let go of the $3,000 maximum contribution. Having the money at hand for immediate usage is a lot more important than retirement.
- They never thought about it.
- They feel they can invest in other financial ventures that can produce more income.
- They know they should but never seem to get around to it.

If you're one of these people, it's probably time for you to wake up and take action before it's too late. You see, an IRA is about all we have left that our Uncle Sam allows us to use to grow filthy rich without paying taxes along the way. I don't have to tell you that money grows a whole lot faster if the IRS isn't taking its 25 to 40 percent share as fast as you can make it. Every dollar you send to the government is money that can't earn anything for you until the day you die. Every dollar you can stash away that's tax deferred or tax free can compound throughout the rest of your life.

For example, let's say you kept an extra $10,000 out of the IRS's hands this year and invested it at 15 percent (which you easily can), and it compounded for 20 years before you started using it. How much do you think it would grow to? How about . . . $197,155? That's about two-hundred grand you could have available for retirement by wising up and keeping the ten grand you're now giving away. This is assuming you don't have to pay taxes as you go, and you don't in your IRA.

"But, Ron, my accountant tells me I can't contribute more than $3,000 each year. Where did you come up with this $10,000 figure?"

Your accountant may be right. There is a limit to how much you can contribute. But wait! Go back and ask your accountant if there is any limit on how much your IRA can make in a year from its investments. He'll scratch his head and tell you no. *There is no cap on how much income your IRA can produce!*

Incidentally, if you have the nerve, ask your accountant what his or her net worth is. I dare you! You probably won't like the answer. I want you to remember that this is the person from whom you're seeking financial advice. Also remember: The broke can't teach you how to be rich . . . they're not qualified.

"OK, Ron, so tell me how I can make my IRA wealthy without making any contributions." If you're a real estate entrepreneur, you're making money from buying and selling or keeping houses. If I've trained you, you're doing this by using little or none of your own money. The objective is to create cash and cash flow by leveraging your brain, not your wallet or credit. And *your IRA can do the same thing.* That's right. Your IRA can buy houses, the same way you do. You have to do the work, but your IRA gets the money, tax-deferred or tax-free. Here's a real life example. A student called me with a house in Atlanta that's worth $575,000 in a gorgeous area. The seller owed $492,000 with a $4,200 per month payment. She was $13,000 in arrears. After some back and forth, she agreed to deed us the house if we made up the $13,000 in back payments.

We did our due diligence, verifying the facts and value with an appraiser. We've closed on the house and currently own it. But instead of taking title in a trust with me as beneficiary, I took title in a trust with my *IRA as beneficiary.* I had my IRA administrator send the check to the closing attorney for the back payments along with instructions on how I wanted to take title. He created the trust; I didn't even have to appear at the closing.

Now in this case, my IRA did have to come up with $13,000 to make this deal work, but normally when I get a deed, it's free or pretty close to it. Keep this in mind and don't get hung up on the down payment. Let's look at the results: We received $83,000 in equity for $13,000. We've obtained a beautiful home in the same area several Atlanta Braves have homes as well as Whitney Houston. We've purchased with no liability and can sell the same way. We simply took over the mortgage "subject to." So what's our exit? It's simple. Sell the same way we bought it. Get as much down as possible, preferably $80,000, and deed it to someone else. Worst-case scenario is we get $40,000 or $50,000 down and take back a second. Or take something in trade. Easy in, easy out.

Let's review: If we get $80,000 and subtract $13,000 before a payment comes due, we'll net about $65,000. That's $32,500 for my partner and $32,500 for me. Whoops, that's not true; that's $32,500 for my IRA! Tax deferred. What if I did three or four of these a year? That's a hundred grand I helped my IRA earn, *tax deferred.* And we're only talking about this year. What if I did this every year until I didn't want to anymore because my IRA had more money than I could spend? You can do eight to ten deals in your IRA on an annual basis without its being called a business.

At least, this is what I've been told by the people who administer IRAs. Of course, there are a few rules and more questions. Perhaps I can't answer these questions for you, and, frankly, many accountants can't either. Seek the best advice you can find and do what you feel is best for you. Your IRA must be self-directed.

The best company I've ever found to handle this is Equity Trust. The people there understand what you're looking for, and they have taught me how to do this. Call them at **440-323-5491** or go to **http://www.trustetc .com** and ask for a self-directed IRA package. Equity Trust will put your money in a money market account until you tell it what to do with the money. When you find a use for the funds, Equity Trust will write the check according to your directions and mail it to the address you provide. It takes less time to carry this out than it's taken me to tell you about it.

Next, you must learn and understand the meaning of self-dealing, which can be deadly to your wealth. You cannot sell your houses to your IRA. You shouldn't get your IRA involved in any deal you or your entity was previously involved in. If your IRA buys a house, the house should go directly from the seller to the IRA and not pass through you. Don't take back notes on houses and give or sell them to your IRA. Keep it clean. Do your homework: Equity Trust has an entire book answering all of your questions.

Now you may be thinking I'm advocating your using your IRA money to buy houses. Not hardly. The last thing I want you to do with your IRA cash is to buy real estate. Why? Because you don't need money to buy real estate . . . and neither does your IRA.

You should buy or option deals in your IRA that don't require cash. Next, take that cash when your houses sell and buy all kinds of neat stuff to increase the yield on the cash—stuff like discounted paper, defaulted paper, mutual funds, hot stocks, and so on. Here's the point: So long as your money is tied up in real estate, it can't be getting a high return on semipassive investments. It can only grow as fast as the real estate allows. So let's get the best of both worlds. Create cash by actively buying and selling houses with little or none of your IRA's money. Next, take those profits and make them grow by at least 15 percent per annum outside of real estate.

Roth IRAs—tax deferred or tax free. Make certain you ask about a Roth IRA and take time to learn its potential. You're never taxed, you can use it for a first-time home, and you never have to take it out. Of course, there are exceptions and rules. So take the time to learn about the Roth and use it. If you qualify I promise it will be a huge return on your time investment. I know! About now you're saying:

"Well Ron, you just told me not to use my IRA's money to buy a house, and yet you did exactly that with your own IRA."

Guilty as charged! In fact, I'm quite often guilty of actually doing the stuff I tell you about, although I actually practice what I preach! I said don't use your IRA to invest in real estate, but what I meant was *not for the long term.*

If my IRA writes a check for $13,000 to buy a house with the expectation of getting back my $13,000 plus $32,500 within 60 days, is that OK? I don't need a spread sheet on this one. That's exactly a 1,500 percent *annual* return on investment. I bet that's better than any money market or CD you currently have. I'll bet that's even better than your stock portfolio's performance last year.

Is it a great deal? Yes! Is it the best you can do? No! The best return on your money is called *infinity*. If you don't invest money, you can't measure the return. That's my kind of deal. But if you've got the cash, you've got to do something with it. So may I be excused because I didn't get an infinity yield this time? Try to tell your accountant and banker you can get a 1,500 percent yield on your money. Watch their eyes glaze over. Remember, all it takes to get a tax-deferred, infinite yield on your IRA is for it to control or buy your real estate without using its money.

Can you option a property without money? *Yes!* Can you wholesale a house without money? *Yes!* Can you take a house "subject to" without money? *Yes!* Can you lease option a house without money? *Yes!*

Wait, here's more! Did you know your children or grandchildren can have an IRA you can start without their knowledge that can become their own when they come of age? What a way for you to provide for your children's educational future. Without writing a check! Without borrowing a dime! And if you open up an IRA for your children or grandchildren, I wouldn't tell them if I were you. Can you guess why?

Let's play with some numbers. Suppose you can set aside enough time away from your job to do three or four deals a year, netting a total of $50,000. Then you decided you were going to do the same thing for the next five years and then quit. You know you can get a 15 percent return in your sleep. Simply make loans to other investors in your city, as I discussed in the last chapter, and charge 15 percent interest. Add two or three points and maybe a prepayment penalty when it's paid off and your yield could easily top 25 percent. What was your total contribution? Zero! Your IRA made money, but you didn't contribute any of it.

What is your IRA worth at 15 percent in:

5 Years?	$387,548
10 Years?	$779,948
15 Years?	$1,567,869

OK, let's now suppose you get a little ambitious and do better deals that make $100,000 each year in your IRA.

What is your IRA worth at 15 percent in:

5 Years?	$775,069
10 Years?	$1,558,996
15 Years?	$3,135,798

Remember, I'll put $32,500 in my IRA on this deal. If you're an active real estate entrepreneur, it's no big thing to let your IRA have a few of your deals. Most people spend more time buying a car, planning a vacation, or taking in a football game than planning for retirement. So what about you? Is this going to be a scanned-over chapter to be quickly cast aside because your favorite TV show is about to air? Or could it be a valuable piece of information that will have a major impact on your future because you decided to take action? Hey! I'm only the messenger boy. My job is done. Yours is next.

Do you remember Marco's big option deal that netted him $2,450,000? His total cash outlay was $100. What if he had let his IRA put up the $100 and do the option instead of him? That means . . . he'd have had $2,450,000 in his Roth IRA tax free for life. Had he simply put that money into mutual funds earning an average annual return of 12 percent (which is easy to get), his IRA would be worth:

- $ 8,085,948 in 10 years
- $14,689,714 in 15 years
- $78,163,529 in 29 years (his retirement age of 59½)

Not bad for a $100 investment, huh? Bad news! Marco didn't use his IRA. Oh well! What's an extra $78 million? Nothing he can do now but make it up on the next one.

Caution. The example I just used involves buying property that comes with debt financing. Even though you or your IRA didn't create the debt, the IRS may still consider the purchase debt related. This could trigger UBIT (unrelated business income tax) and cause the transaction to be taxed on its profit.

UBIT can easily be eliminated by using an option instead of a purchase. Have your IRA option the property from the seller or even from a land trust if done correctly. A little time learning the rules is time well spent. In fact, it's worth a *tax-free* fortune to you.

This subject is of extreme importance to your retirement and peace of mind, and I'm on a mission to educate America about this valuable information.

> *"The secret of success is to be ready for opportunity*
> *when it comes and then take action before it leaves."*
>
> Ron LeGrand

She made $61,000 in her IRA ... Tax Free!!

Marilyn Williams, *Austin, Texas*

Dear Ron,

It was great meeting you in person at the Ron LeGrand event in
Las Vegas in July, and hearing you talk on how to purchase property
with Self-Directed IRA's your company provides.

You asked me to write a letter for others so they can understand how to
purchase with their IRA's. SO HERE'S MY STORY!

I purchased my first property after starting the Ron LeGrand system,
through my Roth IRA at Equity Trust Company. Believe me I knew
nothing about taking deeds to properties much less in the IRA's name.
So what did I do? I called Equity Trust and told them that I had a person
wanting to deed me a house and I wanted it to be purchased in my Roth
IRA. **Equity Trust told me step by step what I needed to do!**

IT WAS AS SIMPLE AS THAT.

**Just to let you know that deal worked out! I did purchase the house
with my Roth IRA. That deal netted me $61,000. YES $61,000,
PURCHASED WITH MY ROTH IRA, TAX FREE!**

Marilyn Williams
Austin, TX

LEGAL CONSIDERATIONS

13

LAND TRUSTS AND
LEGAL CONSIDERATIONS

Are you aware that every time you sign your name on a note, you're risking everything you own to fulfill that debt? Did you know that in most states creditors can sue for default on a mortgage note and come after you personally without even bothering with the house? That's their right. They can look to all your other assets to satisfy your debt in place of, or in addition to, the property you mortgaged.

But don't worry! I have a solution to that problem for some types of financing. This solution also solves several other problems associated with owning real estate. It's simple, yet it's extremely important to all of us who buy houses. Anyone can use it, and it doesn't cost a nickel extra to take advantage of it. This solution is called a *land trust*. First, let's learn what it is and then I'll do a crash course on why and how to use it.

DEFINITION OF A LAND TRUST

It's irrelevant to us, as investors, how land trusts originated or that a lot of history is behind them. Such trusts were first used hundreds of years ago, but we only need to focus on how they can benefit us now.

For simplicity, consider the land trust a method of taking title to property—nothing more, nothing less. It is an agreement between the officer of the trust, called the *trustee,* and the person who actually controls the property, called the *beneficiary.* The trust identifies certain duties that each agrees to perform. The agreement is signed by both parties, and then it becomes the property of the beneficiary. The beneficiary owns the trust, and the trust owns the property. The trustee has only those powers granted to him or her by the beneficiary, and he or she performs minimal duties—usually just signing the documents. The trustee has no personal liability or responsibility to do anything more than those minimal tasks.

A land trust has two main components: The first and most important is the *deed of trust,* which replaces a regular deed and includes the language that both sets up the trust as soon as the deed is recorded and gives the trustee limited powers; the second component is the *trust agreement,* which spells out all the conditions of the trust. This agreement stays with you and is the only document that discloses the beneficial interest. Both documents are easy to complete and not a big deal.

People ask me all the time: *"How do I form a land trust?"* Simple! Fill out the deed of trust and record it. You've just funded the trust with the property so your trust is formed. It exists until the term stated in the trust agreement expires or until you deed the property from the trust to someone else.

REASONS TO USE A LAND TRUST

Savvy investors use land trusts every day. This powerful document offers personal and legal advantages not associated with any other kind of property ownership. I'll discuss each of the benefits briefly in the following sections.

Privacy

Secrecy is an important aspect of a trust. No one knows you are the beneficiary except for you and the trustee. When somebody checks the title to the property, you don't own the property; in fact, you have no interest in the property as far as the rest of the world knows. All they see is that the property is owned by a trust. They don't know the beneficiary's name. The only way they will find that out is by court order—or if your trustee has a big mouth.

A deed is recorded at the courthouse and bears the name of the trustee as grantee. Nowhere does it mention the beneficiary's name. The trust document itself remains in the possession of the beneficiary. It isn't recorded anywhere nor does it become public knowledge. Therefore, you have total privacy.

Loan Liability

The trust can and should be used to create seller carryback financing. There is absolutely no reason for you to ever personally sign a note to a seller. If you fail to heed this advice, you may very well be headed for an expensive real-world "seminar."

The process is simple. The trust takes title to the house, so the trustee signs the note as trustee. Because your name appears nowhere on the document, you are therefore not personally liable. So long as the words *as trustee* appear after the trustee's signature, he or she is not liable either. Presto! You have just created a note that won't ever come back to haunt you. The most the seller can get back is the property because you didn't guarantee the debt—the trust did—and the only asset in the trust is the one house you bought from the seller. So, in effect, the house guarantee is the debt.

Lawsuit Protection

Another key reason to use a land trust is limited lawsuit protection. It's not a foolproof plan to keep you from being sued because your beneficial interest can be attached, but it's a lot better than owning property in your own name. The first thing an attorney does to prepare to sue you is check your assets; all the attorney can do with a land trust is check your name. But if your name doesn't show up, and it won't, the attorney doesn't have a clue you have anything to do with this property.

The only way the attorney can find out is to get wind of the fact that you own properties in trust, call you in for a deposition, and ask you point blank, "Do you own any interest in any trusts?" At that time, you have to either answer yes or commit perjury. Let's assume, however, that you leave your properties titled in your own name or, even worse, jointly with your spouse. Now you get sued, and the plaintiff (the suer) is awarded a large judgment over and above your insurance benefits. The minute that judgment is recorded, it attaches to your properties and prevents any future sale or refinancing until the judgment is satisfied, if ever. In fact, the plaintiff can now start action to attach your assets, and everything you worked for is lost.

On the other hand, let's say your properties were in a land trust before the legal action started. First of all, a name search will produce nothing because you own nothing as far as public records are concerned. This alone will stop most lawsuits in their tracks. If it is obvious a judgment can't be collected if won, it would be fruitless for anyone to pursue a lawsuit and incur the costs unless insurance proceeds were available. Under those circumstances, the case would usually be settled out of court.

But let's assume none of that happens but you are sued anyway, and the suer gets a judgment. It doesn't attach to the properties because you don't own them. The trust owns the house, and you own the trust.

Before we become too smug, be aware that this legal protection doesn't prevent a good attorney from coming after your interest in the trust. But the attorney must first discover you have an interest and then that there's someone willing to pay the high cost of another separate, expensive, and risky legal action. Even though it's not a foolproof lawsuit protector, a trust sure beats owning property in your own name.

Estate Planning

A land trust is a good first step to estate planning, but it is by no means a total plan. Many kinds of trusts and other entities are available—a subject I deal with at our live, three-day Entity Structuring training if you're interested. Go to **http://www.ronlegrand.com** or call **800-567-6128** for more information.

If your property is in a trust and you die, whoever is your beneficiary now owns the trust. He or she now owns whatever interest you owned. To avoid probate, however, in most cases this needs to be taken a step further. The most widely used method is to place the land trust in a living trust or a family limited partnership. And this topic could lead us into a discussion that would fill a book so big you'd have to haul it around in a wheelbarrow.

Attachment of Judgments and Liens

I just discussed lawsuit protection as a result of the privacy created by using a land trust, but consider this:

You just got a huge tax bill from the IRS because you didn't pay all your taxes two years ago, and the IRS didn't agree with your version of the return. Several months go by, but you just can't come up with the money to pay and the IRS issues a tax lien against you. As soon as the lien is recorded, you now have a lien on every piece of property you own in your name. You've just become the "stuckee." You can't sell or refinance until the IRS is paid.

Had your properties been titled in a land trust, as they should be, the lien wouldn't attach to the properties. Remember, you don't own them; the land trust does. *A lien against you can't attach to assets you don't own.* You may sell some properties to get the money, or you may do nothing. Your options are still available because you made a very simple move to never own anything on public record in your own name.

For clarity, I didn't say the IRS can't get your assets; I merely said the lien doesn't automatically attach on recordation. If the IRS wants your beneficial interests in the land trusts, it'll get them. But chances are good they never will. The odds are with you, but don't construe a land trust as some kind of tax-avoidance device. It's a transparent entity so far as the IRS is concerned, which means the IRS will tax you in the entity you report ownership on your return, regardless of whether title is in your name or a land trust.

If I were you, the IRS is one gorilla I wouldn't dance with. The good news about paying taxes is there's plenty left over for you. If you're worried about paying too much in taxes . . . *you ain't makin' enough money.*

Ease of Transfer

When you sell to buyers who understand trusts, quite often they would prefer you assign them the trust rather than having the trust deed the property to them. This action saves closing costs because nothing changes at the courthouse. The trust still owns the house, and you are simply selling the trust. It is done with one sheet of paper called an *assignment of beneficial interest.* It's as simple as your signing it, your trustee signing it, and your handing it to a buyer. That's it! Now, of course, your buyer will want to check the title first and will probably want someone to prepare a closing statement, but all the normal transfer and recording costs have been avoided.

Bank loans. When you go to a bank to borrow money that is secured by property, the bank will require your personal signature on the note. It will not let you take title in the trust because the bank doesn't understand it. If you have intentions of buying a property and refinancing, don't take title in the name of the trust. A bank won't make a loan to a trust. If you are going to refinance, take title in your name, refinance, and *then* place the property in a trust. The lender cannot call the loan due as long as you are the controlling interest in the trust, even if the loan contains a due-on-sale clause. In 1982, the Garn-St. Germain Federal Depository Institution Act made it illegal for a lender to call a loan simply because property has been transferred into a trust.

APPOINTING A TRUSTEE

The trustee must be a person you trust or in many states it can be your corporation or limited liability company (LLC). You could make a family member, friend, or title agent your trustee. The trustee can be someone out of state, but remember that the trustee does the signing for any transactions of the trust. The trustee can close deals for you when you're not in town because of the trust provisions. But the trustee can sign documents only because you, as beneficiary, give him or her permission. The beneficiary has all the control. The trustee has no control, except to do what the beneficiary instructs; the trustee signs all documents at the direction of the beneficiary.

This has been a brief introduction to a few of the key ideas regarding the use of trusts. To use trusts effectively, you need to learn much more, but the subject is too extensive for this book.

I have thousands of students using land trusts nationwide. That's because trusts are simple to use, cost nothing extra, and provide all the benefits previously discussed. Bearing that in mind, please don't let a so-called expert convince you otherwise. Get the facts from the people who know instead of constantly reinventing the wheel.

If you buy real estate, you should be using land trusts! It's just that simple.

IGNORANCE WARNING

You will meet resistance from people about land trusts, especially attorneys who don't understand them. If you need an attorney's blessing before you use one, the chances aren't good you'll find an attorney to give you that blessing.

The problem: Attorneys just don't get it, and they confuse it with other business entities like business trusts that require a tax return, ID number, and bank account. A land trust needs none of those things. It needs:

- No tax ID #
- No tax return
- No annual dues
- No bank account
- No special forms to file
- No permission from untrained advisors or anyone else on earth

Some attorneys attempt to nix its use because there is no state statute covering land trusts. Therefore, attorneys assume it can't be used and come to other erroneous conclusions derived from ignorance or lack of research.

Absence of evidence is not evidence of absence.

No harm will come to you if you use a land trust, but serious harm can come if you don't. Let's look at a worst-case scenario. You put your house in a land trust and someone convinces you you've done an evil thing and must take it back out.

It's simple. Fill out a deed from the trust to you and go to your recorder's office and record it. Voilà! No more land trust. Back to normal with your asset exposed to creditors and predators and a sitting duck for anyone with a smarter lawyer than yours.

If I were you, I'd be very careful listening to anyone who suggests to you that exposing your assets is the right thing to do.

Who are you listening to?

FREE OFFER

I'm sure you have a lot of questions about land trusts. I was interviewed recently by a good friend and student turned teacher, Randy France, all about land trusts. On this free CD, he asked me every question his students had been asking him and I answered all of them. The interview came out very well, and I've found the CD pretty valuable to those who really want to understand land trusts.

It's yours free as a gift from Global Publishing and me for buying this book and reading this far. Simply return the order form at the back of the book. Maybe when you see me at a live seminar somewhere, you can buy me lunch. Is that fair?

I also did an interview recently with an attorney who specializes in asset protection, entity structuring, tax reduction, and estate planning on a nationwide basis. I learned some things I never knew even after years in the business. This free CD is also available at your request on the form in this book.

"Each problem has hidden in it an opportunity so powerful
that it literally dwarfs the problem. The greatest success stories
were created by people who recognized a problem and
turned it into an opportunity."

Joseph Sugarman

He has cerebral palsy and made $37,000 his first month.

Jon Bladel, *Pollock, Louisiana*

Hi Ron,

My name is Jon Bladel, from Pollock, Louisiana. We met at the Millionaire Maker Boot Camp Event. I'm the one that stayed in a motor home in the hotel parking lot. I started the year with a "BANG". We sold three homes the first week of January, with a gross total of $37,000.

January 7th, I sold two, homes on the same day. Both people never thought they had good enough credit to ever buy a home. I was able to get them 100% financed. The first person was a 43 year old, single woman, working three jobs. I sold her a nice brick home, for $60,000 dollars, that I optioned for $42,000, just 5 days prior. I'll profit $18,000 dollars. The bonus is, she works at one of the largest radio stations in our area. She's giving me a very good deal on radio ads.

The second was a couple with four small children living' in a small 3 bedroom home. I sold them a 2,000 sq.ft., 5 bedroom home for $90,000. I optioned for $85,000, with a total profit of $5,000. They also deeded their present home over to me. I'll make $10,000 to $15,000 dollars off that home.

I sold a home with a lease option, on January 10. I received the deed on the home five days prior. The buyer gave me $14,000 down, and I'll have him financed within a year, with another payday of $10,000 dollars. Plus, he has become one of my bird dogs and has already brought me two very sweet deals.

I have two hurdles working against me. The first is, I'm in Louisiana, with all of these, ass backwards coon ass laws. The second is, I have Cerebral Palsy, so this proves, that with your program, any body, anywhere, can do this and make lots of money!
$$$$$$$$$$$$$$$$$$$$$$$$$$$$$$$$$$$$$$

Thanks,

Jon Bladel
Pollock, LA

EDWARD J. SIEJA   10-03
187 DUB BRYANT RD.   PH. 318-765-7267
ATLANTA, LA 71404   84-13/654 148   133

DATE 1-10-03

PAY TO THE ORDER OF Bladel Enterprice $ 14,000.00

four teen thousand dollars and 00/xx   DOLLARS

BANK ONE.
Bank One, NA
Baton Rouge, Louisiana 70801
www.BankOne.com

MEMO For Down payment House

SUCCESS

14

TIGERS ARE THE LAST
TO STARVE IN THE JUNGLE

In light of the 9/11 tragedies in New York and Washington, D.C., I thought it would be good to talk about mental toughness. I got a few letters asking me what I thought would happen to the real estate market after the attack of 9/11. Tons of these letters were written in fear. Folks were afraid that business would take a dive because the market is afraid to buy houses, and everything will change. Here's a news flash: It absolutely has changed!

The world will never be the same. We'll all be more afraid of lunatics now than we were before September 11. Security has tightened, and everyone is talking about it; the news is a 24-hour talk about terrorists, and no one is certain what they'll do next. But one thing is certain: People will always need a place to live. I remember when the prime rate was 18 percent in the early 1980s. Back then I had my hands full buying houses from people who couldn't sell. I spent my time helping people find a way to sell to me!

The Realtors were falling like flies, and everyone was bad mouthing real estate because you couldn't make a living at it . . . at least that was the gossip going around. I was too hungry to listen to that baloney, so I bought about 70 houses that year! I guess everyone forgot to tell me how bad the market was—either that or I wasn't listening. Frankly, back then I did a whole lot less listening than I do now.

Today the prime rate is low. It would seem as if sellers could find buyers as fast as they put a house on the market. Here's another news flash:

Houses don't sell any faster or slower whether the prime rate is 2 percent or 6 percent.

It ain't the rate that sells the houses. It's the person in charge of making the sale. Oh sure, lower payments help . . . but a positive attitude and a friendly voice help a lot more. That was the case in 1982 and it's the case now.

Your attitude will make you wealthy or it will make you a whiner!

If you think anything terrorists can do will destroy the need for Americans to own a home or ruin your business as a real estate entrepreneur, perhaps you should get away from the TV and get back to reality! To be blunt, I'd suggest you grow up and quit listening to all the dream stealers who are looking to blame others for their own failures.

Some people ask me if I am afraid to get on planes now, and my answer is absolutely not. I didn't get where I am today by sticking my head in the sand and letting lunatics run my life! I couldn't wait to get back on a plane. I look at it like this: I've got a better chance of getting killed in my car than on a plane, and that is a proven statistic. So I guess you could say the odds are in my favor. Besides, can you think of a safer time to fly than now? Security is at an all-time high, and no plane full of American men will let terrorists take it down since we can guess their true intentions now. I'd be more afraid of having my lifestyle disrupted because I'm filled with fear or because I lost my freedom or health.

Prostate and colon cancer along with heart disease scare me a whole lot more than a lunatic with a death wish. I fear stagnation, procrastination, laziness, and paralysis and don't give a second thought to the morons. I don't sit around wondering who's going to take my assets. I don't spend more time playing not to lose than playing to win. My assets are protected, and frankly they're not all that important to me anymore. I could lose them all tomorrow, and I would have them back in a year! At least the ones I'd want back!

My biggest asset besides my family is located between my ears and it's not my nose! That asset took 57 years to develop, and as long as I have it, money isn't hard to come by. If you take a look around and ask yourself what really has meaning in your life, I bet you'll discover it isn't anything you've bought. Willie Mays said it best:

"It's not my wife . . . it's not my life . . . why worry?"

I guess it all comes down to your attitude, but far too many people worry about things that don't mean spit! The worse violators worry about things they can't change or control. What good will it do to sit around and fret? Get busy. Do something positive. Go make some offers and sell some houses!

If you're busy enough, you won't have time to worry. Get away from the doom and the gloom and turn off the TV for a while. Get to some of my events and get recharged! Hang around people on the move and get away from those who can't talk about anything but what's on the news. Some suggestions:

- Go make some money!!
- Donate to charities!
- Go back to church if it's been a while!

Do something new, such as buying a car or taking a vacation . . . on a plane! See some new places and make some new friends. Join a new club or volunteer for a political office. Write a speech or a book! Hug your children and take them to a movie. Sit down and talk with them for one hour with no interruptions. Go to a party or, better yet, have one! Invite the neighbors over! Take your spouse to a new restaurant and buy the most expensive thing on the menu, then go home and make love until morning!

Go shopping and get a new wardrobe. Have some of your clothes made by a tailor. Get a massage and a full body treatment. Have the masseuse come to your home every week. Hire someone to mow your lawn so you can sell your lawnmower! Next time you're in the grocery store, look for someone who needs assistance and offer to pay for his or her groceries.

Volunteer to serve food to the homeless on the holidays. Put up the biggest Christmas display in your life! Have a flagpole put in your front yard and fly the biggest American flag it can hold. Forget about all the stuff that can go wrong and think about making things go right.

Focus on what you can control and forget about the things you can't. Develop mental toughness! Picture yourself filthy, stinking rich and work every day to make it happen. Pretty soon it *will* happen. Then you can show someone else how to and become that someone else's hero.

Enjoy every moment of life you have left and don't let others use your time unless you're willing to give it up. Cherish every moment and never stop asking yourself: Is this the best use of my time? If you maintain control, mental toughness will come. If you let others control your emotions, you'll be a weak, mental wreck and no good to yourself or anyone else.

Toughen up, grow up, and move up!

Join the ranks of the mentally tough by making mistakes and living with them, knowing it's all part of learning. You can't get tough without getting beaten up first. That means you must always be moving forward, not standing still.

Find out what's broke and fix it. If you're not making enough money, the only possible reason is looking at you from the other side of the mirror. Accept responsibility for your own actions and toughen up. It's you, baby! All you and nobody else! It isn't me, and it isn't the family or the boss, it's *you!!*

The quicker you accept that fact, the quicker you can begin fixing you. The terrorists didn't make you who you are, and they certainly can't keep you from doing what you want to do.

Sorry to be so brutal, but frankly I have had a bad day listening to whiners looking for excuses, so I'm taking it out on you. Guess I should get a little more mental toughness huh?

"Failure is not an option. It's just the nagging possibility that helps you stay focused."

Anonymous

Lauri and Jeff Giles, *Mechanicsville, Virginia*

Dear Ron,

This is not a letter to tell you how rich we have become by using your system. It is however a note of thanks because you taught us the skills necessary to take our real estate investing career to the next level.

We attended the NAREI conference in Washington DC in October. Up until then we had been investing in Real Estate full time for several years but didn't know how to take the next step. We were making a 6 digit income but had reached a block in the road. We wanted to make the BIG money and do less work!

There were several speakers at this conference, all selling their programs. But when you came on stage we felt a connection with your down to earth style and sense of humor. We had no idea how to do short sales, or lease options. We had only been flipping and wholesaling homes in the past. Once we heard you speak and bought your course we realized the importance of having a well rounded program that includes all aspects of investing.

You said to "just do something, go make a mess of things"! So we did! We listened to your CD's on the way home and realized some of the leads we turned away before, we now could make work somehow. On **Monday** after the weekend seminar we got our first deed on a home and started our first short sale process. Over the next few weeks we started another short sale, and acquired 3 lease option homes. The first two were rented to tenant buyers within a week – just like you said would happen. We didn't know if we were using the right forms or filling everything out properly but we just did it! Only one of the short sales was approved, but we were getting some good experience.

Our favorite deal so far is a sandwich lease on a $350,000 home. (Picture below) This made us $12,000 in up front profit, will generate $600 a month cash flow and $26,000 on the back end. In order to make the large down payment on this home, our tenant buyer needed to sell their other home first. Guess who bought it? Yes, we bought it at a huge discount and wholesaled it to make a few more thousand. We added an invoice in the form of an addendum to the contract to ensure when they closed on their old home we would definitely get paid. We love your system! Thanks for helping us to get to the next level!

Sincerely,

Lauri & Jeff Giles
Real Estate Resources
Mechanicsville, VA

15

AIM HIGH

All of us have a comfort level in which we live and work. That level is determined by several factors and can be changed with practice and time. We have a choice what we do each day, how we spend our time, and how much money we make. This may come as a surprise to people who are convinced their income is someone else's choice, not theirs. Nothing could be further from the truth. Your income is the result of one thing and one thing only: *what you choose to do with your time.*

"But, Ron, you don't understand. I have a job. I'm not in control of my salary; my boss is. He tells me when to come to work and how much I can make." I guess you're right. You're not in control, and maybe you never will be—at least not without a major attitude change. If you're reading this book, it means you know the opportunities available to you as a real estate entrepreneur. So if you're still employed, you've chosen to be. No one forced you. It's your decision, and therefore you have chosen to exchange dollars for time—a surefire recipe for being broke.

Does this mean I think every one of you should immediately quit your job and start doing real estate? Absolutely not. This business is not for everyone. Being in *any* business for yourself is also not for everyone. Besides, if you can't do this part-time, you won't do it full-time either.

Time is not the controlling factor. Doing the *right* things determines your income, not how many hours you work.

Maybe you aren't employed any longer, and you're feeling pretty smug because you're now on your own flying free. No job! No boss! No traffic jams! No one giving you orders! Well, congratulations! But before you get too full of yourself, maybe we'd better look a little closer. You see, there is a downside. You have no job, which means no paycheck and no boss making decisions for you. You're on your own to decide what you do every day and worse is that there's no one to blame when you screw up.

It's you against the world. You're on fire. You haven't been this excited in a long time. No place to report to in the morning. You can do what you darn well please. You see, my friend, that's what scares me. What will you do with all this newfound freedom? How long will it be before you fill your days with activities that accomplish nothing except filling your days?

If you're not careful, your poor time management habits and low expectations will lead you right back to doing no more than just making a living. You'll replace your old job with a new one and simply change bosses. A new doofus will replace the old one.

Have I hurt your feelings? Tough! Get over it. Remember, I'm on your side. We're in this together, and it's my job to help make you better than all the employed or unemployed drones just drifting out there waiting to die. Just because you no longer have a job doesn't mean you're going to be rich. Rich people don't waste all day thinking like a job slave or don't spend their time killing time. *The rich focus on what produces the most revenue with the least work.*

If it will make you feel any better, I'm no different from you. I wasted a lot of years killing time, and that's why I'm so adamant that *you* don't do the same. So let's talk about getting off to a good start. If you're way past a start, let's discuss amending your ways so you can begin making more money.

Incidentally, making more money has nothing to do with having more time. It involves using the time you have in the best way you can. Whether you work part-time or full-time, you have a choice of the real estate deals you participate in. You can either make a few thousand dollars because you feel comfortable with the easy stuff or you can make a hundred times more using no more money or extra time to do so. Again, you get to choose. No one else.

Let me explain: For years I dealt with low-priced junkers, usually in low-income areas. I'd either wholesale for $2,000 to $6,000 or retail for $15,000 to $20,000. It was all I knew, my comfort zone. The thought of buying anything worth over $60,000 petrified me. I wouldn't even let myself think about it. I was happy making two or three times more than what I used to make from my job, so why bother doing anything better and upset the apple cart?

Besides, I had bought and sold hundreds of houses. I had to be smarter than anyone else I knew. The more money I made, the more I allowed myself to think bigger. Gradually I learned there was more to the business than cheap junkers and small dollars. I began to learn the pretty house business. My threshold kept rising higher and higher as I learned that *it's just as easy to make more as it is to make less.*

Now you may be thinking it was easier to make more because I had more money to work with. That's the same stupid thinking that held me back all those years. As I've said before:

If you can't make money without money, you can't make money with money!

Recently I decided to work some deals with students in all parts of the country. When I see them at events, I suggest they call me to discuss those larger house deals they're presently throwing away because the numbers scare them. I tell them if the deal were doable, I might agree to be their partner.

Consequently, some called me with deals. At this time, I have about 10 or 15 deals in various stages of production, and I'll use a couple of them to prove my point. In many cases, it's not the lack of money holding you back; it's the lack of knowledge about how to structure the deals so you don't need money!

In Atlanta we found a preforeclosure worth $300,000 in a lovely area; the loan was $196,000 and $27,000 in arrears. The second deal was $28,000 and delinquent. The first had filed foreclosure and stopped because the owner told the lenders he had a plan to bring the payment current. During this time, the owner called my student and finally said he'd deed the house to him if he wished. The student let the deal pass because the numbers were scary and the exit strategy wasn't clear.

Then I got involved. We now own the house without a dime out of pocket to the first mortgage, and we haven't made a payment yet. The second owner agreed to discount to $4,000 from $28,000, so the total debt is about $200,000. The house sold for $265,000 and will close in two weeks. We let it go cheap instead of spending $15,000 on repairs. We also feel by the time it closes, the first mortgage will get discounted $25,000 to $50,000.

The net profit will be between $65,000 and $115,000. The total cash outlay was $4,000 because we chose to pay off the second mortgage while they were willing to discount $24,000 before they learned the house was sold. That was a good example of leveraging our brains instead of our wallets. Incidentally, how many houses will you wholesale to make $65,000 to $115,000? We only did one.

It costs nothing to aim high—but wait! That's only one little deal. I personally negotiated another student deal in Orlando. The $910,000 appraisal the seller gave us was one year old. He agreed to sell for what he owed: $513,000. The house is in a gated community on 2.8 acres with a screened-in pool and tennis court. It has 7,500 square feet of beautiful living space and looks even nicer as the seller is leaving behind $25,000 worth of furniture.

We're raising the money to buy from a private lender who learned the business from me several years ago. This same lender is available to anyone in his area. Nothing special happened because I was involved— nothing except the deal is now done instead of lost. We didn't need a dime of our own money or credit to do this deal. It just took guts and a clear vision of the exit strategy. More than anything, it took expanding out of our comfort zone.

What's the next deal? I don't know, but I bet it's better than the last house you flipped. I'm sure it's better than your last year's W-2 showed. But don't worry. I can't expect something like this to come your way, can I? After all, there's too much competition where you live, and it probably won't work there anyway. Surely there aren't any sellers with more expensive houses that would even consider selling for less than retail price.

Yes, I'm being sarcastic. At the same time, I hope I'm making a point you soon won't forget: *Do what everyone else does and you can expect to get what they get. Do what they fear, and they'll wish they had what you've got.*

Don't you think it's time to get your head out of the sand and begin to think much bigger? It's free. Figure out what scares you and fix it. If it's lack of money, it can and will be fixed with more knowledge.

The more you learn, the more you earn.

Here's a brief recap of a few more deals presently in the works with students. A $300,000 house in lovely shape with a $145,000 mortgage that's $17,000 behind. The seller has deeded it to us. We won't put up a dime. You figure the profit. Here's another $300,000 home requiring $10,000 in repairs. We paid $112,000 in cash borrowed from a private lender. A $500,000 house on the ocean; seller agreed to finance for $435,000 at 6 percent with nothing down! We're trying to raise the money for the down payment, chuckle, chuckle! A house worth $180,000 with a balance of $135,000 that's current. Seller is deeding and will wait until we sell it when she'll net $10,000, which was previously agreed on.

A house in Florida worth $1,100,000 that needs about $50,000 in work for which we paid $650,000 and borrowed $725,000 from a private lender. We sold the house for $1,050,000 and netted about $280,000, which I split with my student partner. It was a good day for her and me and the IRS. She had thrown this deal aside with no intention of buying it before she and I discussed it at one of my training events. I told her to go home and get it under contract and we'd work it together. She did, we did, and voilà—$280,000 rose from the ashes like a phoenix.

I think you get the picture. If you don't, make sure you get into my live trainings. These events will open new doors for you. Many past attendees are now millionaires.

Speaking of millionaires, how many deals do you need per year such as I've previously discussed to make a million bucks? Not many. Good news! They're more plentiful and easier to do than junkers. All you need to do is expand your comfort zone just a little and increase your ability to construct and present offers. You can make more or continue to make less. It's your choice.

BEWARE OF DREAM STEALERS

I've known many investors and entrepreneurs. I've seen every possible scenario, from overnight success to plodding, sit-on-your-butt-and-do-nothing failure. I've known people who would get off to a great start and then fade away, and some who would dawdle around and never

He got off to a slow start, but now he's in the race.

Mark Schmale, *Kent, Washington*

Dear Ron,

I've been intending to write you a thank you letter for the last year and a half. It's just not procrastination that's delayed it. Frankly, I made so many mistakes on my first 3 properties, that my profit was too low to feel very proud of. They certainly didn't measure up to most of the deals I've heard or read about from other students. By the way, the mistakes I made were mostly things that you taught not to do, but either ignored or forgot. Dumb!!

Well, with your training and support, and my persistence (Roni kicking me in the behind), houses 4 & 5 have sold in February and March, generating profits of $14,000 and $13,000 respectively. And I've bought houses 6,7, & 8 in the last 2 weeks; which will generate $20,000 each. And I'm still making offers, just like you told me to.

Thank you for the training and support you and your staff have provided. You have opened the doorway to amazing profession and lifestyle. All I had to do was step through it. I know that part of the reason that you teach is the satisfaction you get when you see the results of your work. Well, I want you to know what an impact you've had on my life, and how grateful Roni and I are. Thank you.

I just enrolled in your new Paper Power boot camp, and I can't wait. I'll bring the cigars!

seem to get anywhere. I've known those who made a very successful living and even a few who became *super*wealthy.

Is there a magic formula for success? I wish I could tell you there is. It could have saved me a whole lot of headaches over the years and would have made me an awful lot of money. However, from years of experiencing my own successes and failures, as well as witnessing those of others, I have identified a few mistakes that can short-circuit an entrepreneur's rise to fortune. I've compiled a list of the most common roadblocks you'll face on the road to becoming a successful real estate entrepreneur. You may be one of the fortunate few who never finds yourself faced with any of these roadblocks, but it's more likely you'll recognize parallels in your own situation in my following discussion.

My goal here is to put you in a position where you can identify these pitfalls. Then, when you encounter them (and you *will*), you'll be armed with the ability to direct yourself around them and get back on track . . . *immediately*. You won't have to worry about these things hindering you from achieving your goals. So, let's go down the list of potential roadblocks:

1. Lack of focus. I define focus as concentrating on only the work you must do to succeed in your business, avoiding all distractions and not getting sidetracked by every "great idea" that pops up. It's not easy. The world we live in today is filled with things that beg for our attention. We live in what's being called the "Information Age," and that's great except the bombardment of information makes it hard for most of us to sift through the junk and come up with the good stuff. That's why most of us have a problem staying focused—even when we're trying to concentrate on something we know will make us wealthy. There are a million ways to make a million bucks, and every day a new avenue for riches is presented to us. But I've learned through trial and error (*lots* of error) that the only way to make something work is to filter out everything else and stick with what I know works.

I become frustrated when I see people with tremendous potential for this business get off track with a so-called get-rich-quick scheme (and there are a *lot* of them—just watch a little late-night television). If you dabble in one business, jump to another, and then try something else that's completely different, you're not likely to be successful at any of them. Focus takes work, determination, and discipline. Sometimes it hurts, such as those times when you have to leave your family to make $5,000 or $10,000 for them, when you could be watching *Seinfeld* reruns with them at home. Believe me, when your increased income starts showing up in trips to Disney World, new clothes, cars, and so on, your spouse and kids won't have a problem with your jaunts away from home.

2. Getting into the rental business before your cash flow needs are met.

When I first got started in real estate, I decided to buy all the rental property I could, figuring that, with a lot of tenants in a lot of houses, the cash would just fall into my lap every month.

That was the biggest single mistake I made for a very simple reason—I just wasn't ready. Like me, many beginning real estate investors get into the rental business because they think it's a quick path to wealth. But it's not; it's slow and long term. Soon after I built my "rental empire" in 1982, I discovered that my daily cash flow needs weren't being met. I had a huge amount of capital tied up in equity and a thin stream of income. And I had a family to feed!

Don't get me wrong; I've got nothing against rental property as an investment. I'll probably have them myself until the day I die. However, if you haven't built a cash cushion, you'd better get really good at buying properties dirt cheap. And even when you do, you'll discover a million ways to deplete your cash flow: broken toilets, leaky roofs, peeling paint, ragged carpeting, yada-yada-yada; it all eats big holes in your income stream. Even if you do have enough ready cash to get into the rental game, you have to know what you're doing. For instance, do you know about "professional tenants" who make a living "getting over" on landlords? These creeps know the landlord tenant code and eviction laws inside out, and they can make your life a living hell before you finally get them out of your house. If you want to become a professional landlord, you'd better understand how the game is played and get the education necessary to deal with all of the potential problems.

My advice: Make some fast cash by quick turning a few houses before you get yourself mired down with rentals. Get into some low-risk, high-return deals before you start piling up equity and dealing with tenants. Then, when you do become a superlandlord, your chances of retiring on your rental income will be much better.

Give yourself a year to learn the ropes, a year to find out what to buy and keep, where and how. It takes a little time to get acquainted with real estate, and you won't shorten that time by becoming an instant landlord. What you will do is take a seminar from current landlords who began before you did and are now passing their mistakes down the line to you. One deal done incorrectly could cost you more than the tuition for all the training we have at the Financial Freedom Academy and then some. What's the rush? Relax! Learn the ropes and then build your empire on a solid foundation.

3. Listening to poor advice. You probably already know this is a potential roadblock. As you go through life, there will never be a shortage of people who want to give you advice. Your parents, your spouse, friends, in-laws, kids all have opinions about what you're doing and what they think you *should* be doing. Very often, the value of their advice is worth exactly what you paid for it . . . *nothing!*

I'm not saying these do-gooders aren't honest, intelligent, and well-intentioned. However, you must ask yourself if these folks are *qualified* to give you advice. Have they had any experience in what you're doing? It seems to be human nature for people to offer advice on subjects they know nothing about. What baffles me is how often the recipients of this so-called wisdom will listen to it and even act on it without ever questioning the credentials of those giving it.

Through many painful experiences, I've learned that when you take advice from people who don't know any more about the subject matter than you do, the quality of that advice is, at best, suspect. Plus, very often, listening to unqualified advice can have a negative impact on your focus (see roadblock #1).

So who *should* you be listening to? I believe in taking advice only from people who are: (1) qualified experts in their field and (2) making a whole lot more money than I am. And those people are out there. Don't be afraid to seek help—just be careful where you go to get it even if you have to pay for it. I think you'll find that if you pay for the opinion of a bonafide expert, the advice you receive will be more than worth the price.

4. Listening to negative thinkers and deadheads. Nothing kills the entrepreneurial spirit like negativity. With all of the challenges you face in business, you need to keep a positive, upbeat, enthusiastic attitude about what you're doing. It's the only way you'll be able to perform at your best. Negative thinkers and deadheads only suck the energy out of

This couple got the deed and then discounted the second mortgage to net about $50,000.
George Stevenson and Susan Dietz, *North Carolina*

		Arrears	Monthly Payment	Monthly Rent
ARV	$275,000			$ 2,050
1st mortg	$203,270	$10,867	$ 1,515	$ 1,515
2nd mortg	$ 24,137	$ 1,061	$ 317	$ 0
Potential Equity	$ 47,137	$		
Sales Price	$275,000			
1st mortg payoff	$203,000	**Monthly Cash Flow**	**$ 535**	
Promised to Seller	$ 10,000	Annual Cash Flow	$6,420	
Cash Invested	$ 16,300	**Yield on Invested Cash**	**39.4%**	
Equity when we sell	**$ 45,700**			

Ron,

Here is a deal we found by marketing to pre-foreclosures. The seller called us needing help. This is a combination of "Get the Deed" and buying delinquent paper in the same deal, both are techniques that we learned from you. This is a 2800 sq ft high end "Pretty House".

The house already had (and continues to have) a great tenant renting for $2,050/mth. Apparently the seller chose not to pay the mortgage because he was in foreclosure. He agreed to deed us the house subject to the liens and we gave him a 0 interest 0 payment note for $10,000 (of his equity) that is payable when we sell the house. We bought an assignment of the 2nd mortgage for $5,000 and paid the arrears on the 1st to reinstate the mortgage. The best part is that we now have a $535 monthly cash flow because the 2nd is gone. That's a close to 40% yield on the cash we have in the deal, and doesn't include the $45,000+ expected profit when we sell.

Thanks so much for showing us what the possibilities are in this business. Naturally, as we learned at the recent MIS class in Jax, we will be asking for a big discount on the Note that we gave the seller before we pay him.

We started our training with our first class from you, the one-day Foreclosure class that you held with Jeff Kallar in Atlanta. We've already done more than 5 deals this year, and keep advancing towards our goal of becoming a "transaction engineer".

You truly are a Millionaire Maker. Now we just need to get another 10 like this one, and we can retire.

you and bring you down to their own miserable level. These are usually people who have failed in their own life and find pleasure trying to make failures out of those around them. They'll make you question yourself, doubt what you're doing, and, if you listen to them, eventually give up entirely.

I'm sure when you first told friends and family you were going to be a real estate entrepreneur, you heard: "You really believe that stuff they sell on TV?" or "You can't make money in real estate; the market's too slow." Or maybe "There's not enough appreciation to make a profit, and didn't they change the tax laws or something?" Yes, the "Larry Losers" of this world have all the answers, don't they? Meanwhile, they're working three jobs and won't answer the phone at night for fear it will be a bill collector. I don't think your true friends or your family would intentionally hurt you or bring you down. Usually they think they have your best interests at heart. However, in the process of "trying to make you see all sides" or "just giving you a few facts about the real world," they're pouring buckets of ice water on the fire you need to keep burning in order to keep on succeeding.

It may be nearly impossible to completely cut yourself off from these people. I suggest you simply tell them in firm, no-nonsense terms you appreciate their interest but have no use for their negative, sarcastic, or skeptical comments. Sure, it can be a rough thing to do and some of them may be offended, but if they really care about you, they'll get the message.

One of the best ways to avoid negativity is to seek out positive and supportive people. Find successful people or a group with common interests with whom you can share ideas; it's important to discuss successes and failures with people who are genuinely in tune with what you're doing. Pick out the winners and connect with them. When you become a successful real estate entrepreneur (and you *will*), one of your greatest rewards will be to share your blueprint for success with others. "What goes around comes around." Before you know it, that sharing will attract people to you like a magnet. I can't tell you the many profitable deals that have come my way through people who wanted to hang around me because I was willing to share my knowledge.

5. Lack of action. There's an old saying: "Even a turtle won't get anywhere until he sticks his neck out." Another old saying that I made up is: "You're never going to get rich sitting on your behind and waiting for it to come to you." *You* have to make it happen. *You* have to get things started. *You* have to put the wheels in motion. And if they get stopped, guess who has to get them started again. *You* guessed right.

Movement, action, activity, progress . . . they're essential in any successful business. Without activity on your part, nothing positive will happen for you. It starts with that first call, that first conversation with a seller, even the first visit to a Realtor. But your ship can't come in if it never gets launched.

By action, I don't mean running in place. Sure, you can go to the seminars and listen to the tapes so often that you memorize everything I've ever said. You can acquire all the tools you need to do this business. But then the time comes to fish or cut bait, and you find yourself standing by the creek bank watching the water flow by. My friend, all the education in the world is worthless until you put it into practice.

The best time to start is now. And I mean *right now.* I want you to get up after you've finished reading this book and do something that will get you going on your first deal. Just do it. You'll be surprised how taking a tiny step will propel you forward toward your goals. The more actions you take, the more results you'll get.

6. Wasting time with unmotivated sellers. They may be interesting. They may be wonderful people. They may have heartbreaking stories to tell. But if they're not motivated to sell, they're wasting your precious time and sucking dollars out of your pocket. If you waste enough of your time waltzing around with people who aren't serious about doing business, then you're not going to be *in* business for very long. It's just that simple.

Unmotivated sellers will think up so many reasons "why not" and give you so much baloney that you'll soon become convinced this business doesn't work for you but only for others. I can't stress enough that you must avoid unmotivated sellers like the plague. But to avoid them, you have to learn to recognize them and move on. It shouldn't take you more than five minutes to prequalify a seller.

7. Fear of making an offer. Being afraid or unwilling to contact sellers and to construct offers is probably the most serious problem you can develop. Taken to the extreme, it can stop your career dead in its tracks.

I've identified four basic concerns that prevent most people from making offers:

1. What if I can't, or decide not to, close (there are typically no contingencies in our contracts)?
2. What if I get a counteroffer?
3. What if my offer gets rejected?
4. (My favorite) What if my offer gets accepted?

Let's tackle some of these in no special order. When you think about it, what is the worst thing that can happen to you if you don't close on a transaction? What does the seller do? Comes out and holds your kids ransom until you buy the property? Or sends "Guido the Enforcer" to break your legs? Of course not! The worst that will happen is the seller keeps your earnest money deposit. It's a loss, but my point is this: It ain't life or death. Besides, your deposit should be an amount you're willing to walk away from in the event you could not, or decided not to, close. It shouldn't be an amount of money that would ruin you financially if you lost it. Just keep the amount of earnest money you offer on a property to a minimum. The lower your deposit, the lower your risk.

A surefire remedy for overcoming the fear of having a deal fall through: Make lots of offers. If you're out there making a lot of offers, you'll be less likely to live or die by any one deal.

How do you handle a rejected offer? First of all, you should be prepared for rejection and accept it as just part of the business. A seller may reject an offer for one of a million different reasons. Sometimes you can determine the reason and correct it, but at other times there is simply no explanation. I often wished I could read sellers' minds to figure out why they rejected my offer.

Second, you shouldn't take a rejected offer personally. In most cases, the seller is not rejecting you—only the offer. Remember: some will; some won't; so what; someone's waiting! Learn what you can from a rejected offer and move on.

For those with fragile egos, I'd like to reprogram the way you feel about rejection. Let's assume you made 12 offers, only one was accepted and you retailed that house for a modest $12,000 profit. Do you realize for each offer you made, you earned a whopping $1,000? Yes, in spite of all that rejection, you still made $1,000 on each of your offers. The underlying logic is it took making all those offers to raise the odds of one being accepted. When you look at it from that perspective, the question becomes: How many offers (at $1,000 profit each) do you want to make today?

What if my offer gets accepted? This is my favorite because it seems ironic that someone who wants to be in this business would be nervous about having an offer accepted. Yet I've often had students ask me: "Oh, no, Ron, they've accepted my offer; what the heck do I do now?"

The problem is obvious: Students with this fear haven't completed their homework, don't have the financing end of their business together, or are lacking the proper education altogether. By doing their homework, I mean evaluating the house and working the numbers to determine if it's a good deal and knowing what exit strategies are available. If they're not sure whether it's a good deal or what they're going to do with the house once they've bought it, I can understand why they would be a little edgy when an offer is accepted.

One of the biggest reasons students have a fear of an offer being accepted is this: "Where am I going to get the money when the deal does go through?" These people just don't fully understand how we do things in the quick turn business. If you have this concern, you'll soon learn that money is necessary only if you intend to buy, rehab, and retail the property. And my Wholesale/Retail Cash Flow System reveals the many ways to access other people's money for retailing deals. When you make offers on houses to wholesale, owner finance, lease option, or option, you have no need for substantial cash, including your own.

Let's take a look at wholesaling houses. If you become good at finding deals and tying them up under contract, you'll have no problem wholesaling a house to someone else for quick cash. I have students all over the country picking up from $5,000 up to $20,000 or more by finding the bargains and passing them along to other investors.

Wholesaling houses creates an instant cash profit, and the only cash required is an earnest money deposit. You don't need credit or partners, and it makes no difference where you are in life. All you have to do is go out and find the deals. So when you make an offer, there is absolutely no excuse for you to worry about where the money is going to come from if you know you can always wholesale the house. And when you learn how easy it is to raise the money, you'll be able to convert your ability to find the deals into larger sums of money through retailing houses.

8. Fear of making a mistake. Nobody wants to appear incompetent or foolish, which is why we all fear messing up. But you might as well just learn to live with it, because in spite of all your efforts, it's going to happen. The best of us make errors.

Your objective should be to get as much education and experience as you can. That's the best way to keep mistakes to a minimum. A good education by a qualified instructor in your area of interest will alert you to potential pitfalls. A good teacher has the requisite background and experience and will have made all the common mistakes. He or she will be able to warn you away from the career killers as well as the nuisance errors.

Now that I've convinced you mistakes are coming, don't let them bog you down. When you mess up, roll with it, learn from it, and move on. Don't worry about looking foolish to other people. They haven't seen your bank account.

9. Procrastination. Like a lot of people, I used to be bad about putting things off, but I've found an excellent way to overcome this tendency. That way is to use a daily planner. I'm talking about one of those books where you write down everything you have to accomplish in calendar fashion so that, not only do you remember everything you're supposed to accomplish, but you get a kick to make you do it *today*.

Not only will a planner help cure your procrastination; it will also help organize your life in general. You may have your own system for remembering important things. You may rely on your memory, scraps of paper, strings around your fingers, your spouse, or other crazy reminders of your daily duties. What I'm talking about is not a haphazard, hit-or-miss method but real organization.

A good planner allows you to enter all of your appointments and your to-do lists every day. You can see how your week or month is shaping up and more efficiently schedule appointments that will improve your productivity. You'll also want to use the planner to record events, conversations, meetings, and any new ideas so you don't have to remember all those important details.

How does a planner help you overcome procrastination? Well, every day I write down my to-do list, and when I accomplish each item, I check it off the list. If I fail to get to anything, I make sure to put it on the top of the next day's list. I find myself doing even unpleasant tasks just to get

Donna and Jon McVety, *Fort Myers, Florida*

REALTY SERVICES
Property Management Company

Professional Residential Property Managers Since 1978 • Certified Community Association Managers

Buy & Hold Long Term Wealth Building Strategies

Jon & I met Ron LeGrand at a Financial Freedom Workshop in Tampa. We were impressed with his presentation and knowledge and decided to pursue training with him. My contract with the University of Vermont was ending and I needed to have an alternative to employment. I was 52 and my husband Jon was 56. We had a small property management company in Lee County, Florida and were already buying properties.

Ron taught us a system of accumulating better properties at a faster pace. Since our strategy was buy and hold for long term appreciation and current cash now and since we were experienced and trained property managers and had a rehab team in place, we set the following goals: to acquire 100 properties, become platinum members, buy the house of our dreams, mentor others, stop foreclosure whenever possible for our clients and relieve financial distress, be able to take liberal time off and travel to Egypt and Russia, before we went on Social Security. We achieved all those goals and more. And we had fun doing it.

Jon and I are a team. We work very well together. Ron's training gave us an edge over our competition. We became bolder and took on more complex deals. And of course, we earned bigger profits. In October we bought an elaborate home on an acre worth three quarters of a million dollars.

You never stop learning. We've been working with Ron for 10 years and still enjoy putting together killer deals. We have time for our families, our company, tennis, and volunteer work. We still admire Ron's feisty, determined spirit and his ability to dream.

Donna & Jon McVety
Realty Services
Fort Myers, FL

them off my list. That may sound silly and simple, but it works. Sooner or later, rewriting the same task will get to be a pain in the neck, and you'll find yourself becoming more efficient at getting through your entire list every day.

A planner also helps when you have a big project to work on. If you feel overwhelmed, the chances are good you'll avoid the project and put it off. I suggest you break large projects into smaller, more manageable tasks that can be accomplished on a daily basis. You'll be amazed at how quickly a big job gets whittled away using this method.

Let me warn you that using a planner only works if you use it on a daily basis, and the hardest part is incorporating it into your daily life. However, once you get used to it, you'll wonder how you ever got along without it. My planner sits on my desk when I'm in the office and is the first thing that goes into my briefcase when I leave. I'm sure I refer to it 40 to 50 times a day. You'll find, however, there are times when you can't use your planner—when you're driving, for instance. For these times, I suggest a handheld tape recorder. Some of my best ideas have come to me while driving. All I have to do is switch on the recorder and dictate a message to myself. I've composed long letters and reports this way. Time is money after all, so don't waste valuable productivity just because you're in your car.

10. Incomplete education. A big problem I see often is people attempting to do this business with an incomplete education. And this leads to two related problems: (1) Action without complete knowledge of procedures and strategies will get you in trouble, and (2) an incomplete education will cause you to leave money on the table.

I'm not suggesting that you have to spend several years getting a real estate education before you do deals. A complete mastery of the hundreds of techniques available to buy houses isn't necessary. In a very short time, you can learn a simple real estate technique that allows you to make money. All I'm suggesting is this: Before you use any technique or strategy, make sure you fully understand it, or you may be headed for another "seminar."

Once you become active in this business, you'll run across a lot of different buying situations. For example, some sellers might owe a lot of money, or don't want to hold paper, or want all cash, or have a house in good shape or bad shape. If you know only one technique to put a deal together, you're going to miss some lucrative deals. You won't be able to create a profitable transaction from the situation at hand with the limited real estate knowledge you possess.

"The only thing that can keep you from becoming successful in this business is located right between your ears."

Ron LeGrand

That's why I recommend you never stop learning. Make your real estate training an ongoing process. You should read books, listen to courses, go to seminars, and join real estate clubs to further your education. By the way, not all of your education will be free. A good education isn't cheap; you'll have to spend money on books, tapes, and seminars. You might even come across a deal where you have to give up some of the profits to a partner because he or she has the expertise to put the transaction together and you don't.

I know what you may be thinking: "Yeah, right, you just want to sell me more of your stuff." While I am in the education business, I can almost guarantee you this: If you don't spend the time and money it takes to get educated, you'll go to a "seminar" sooner or later. And the seminar I'm talking about is not a planned one, but a real-life, hurt-like-hell, cost-you-a-lot-of-bucks seminar. Getting your education up front and avoiding real-world seminars is a lot more pleasant and ultimately cheaper. How do you think I know that?

11. Poor communication skills. Some students believe they won't be able to do this business because they have a hard time communicating. Hogwash! You don't even need to speak or write English. As a matter of fact, you can be bedridden and illiterate and still make money in real estate. I know this is a brash statement, but I can say it because I've seen students with communication problems make successful deals. You see, it's not necessary to talk directly with sellers or buyers to make money with my quick turn system. If you have a tough time communicating, for whatever reason, a good Realtor will be your key to success. A Realtor can handle just about all of the paperwork and can communicate information for you during the negotiation process. If you don't have a good command of the English language, seek out a Realtor who is bilingual in your native language and English. Your local board of Realtors can help you find one.

Let me explain my statement about making money even if you're bed-ridden and an explanation of how I currently do transactions. In the seminar business, I find myself on the road all the time. So if I'm in Chicago, there's no way I could be looking for houses to buy in Florida, right? Wrong! My Realtor pulls leads on houses out of the MLS computer system and faxes them to me. I'll pick out the properties that look like good candidates for purchase and send someone out to inspect and take pictures of them. When I return from my trip, I work up my offers and give them to my Realtor to submit to the sellers.

When a seller accepts my offer, the next step is settlement. If I'm going to wholesale the house, I do a simultaneous closing and immediate sale to another investor. Again, the closing agent faxes the settlement paperwork to me for my approval. If I'm going to retail the house, I call my contractor and get a repair bid. When I get an acceptable bid, I have the house repaired, write a couple of checks, and then put the house back on the market to be sold by a Realtor. When I get an offer, it goes through my Realtor to me. After I accept the offer, I again handle the settlement process through the fax machine and wait for my check to arrive by a courier.

So you see, I can easily buy and sell houses without ever meeting the sellers, personally seeing the houses, or even shaking hands with the buyers. All it takes is my phone, a fax machine, a checkbook, and a helper. If you ran your business like this, wouldn't it free up more of your time to do more deals? I suggest you do just that. Put in place the things that allow you to run your business as I just described. Remember, you should be doing only the things that you alone can do—such as making offers. Running around looking at houses, dropping off contracts, and getting repair estimates are things you can train other people to do. You'll free up more time to make more offers, and you'll make more money!

12. Fear of failure. One of the biggest fears I run into is the fear of failure, but you should actually have a greater fear of growing old without pursuing your dreams. The easiest thing to do is nothing, but it is the most costly. It costs you the thrill of the chase. Doing nothing robs you of your self-respect and sense of self-worth. It also deprives you of the feeling of excitement and sheer thrill of achievement. Yes, it even deprives you of the experience of making mistakes. But that experience is the essence of growth. In my opinion, the absolute worst thing you can do is nothing. So get out there and give it a try. Ask yourself what the worst is that can happen to you. You make a few mistakes, you fumble around a little bit, and you learn something in the process. Hey, you might even lose a few bucks. So what! Believe me, it'll be worth your while to make it work. You will look back and say to yourself, "You know, that really wasn't so bad after all."

What worries me is your letting a few roadblocks stop you and turn you into one of those seminar junkies who go to every class but rarely put what they learn into action. It's up to you. You are the person in control of your future and the only thing that can stop you from becoming successful in this business is located right between your ears! So you decide and be sure and let me know if there is anything I can do to help you.

SUCCESS TIPS

- Take care of your cash flow needs first, before you try to build wealth. Keep working until your real estate cash flow is equal to or exceeds your income from a job. Then you don't have to worry about making a living. You can start making money.

- Stay focused! Stay on track! Stick to your game plan! If it works, don't even think of anything else; just keep doing it. Don't stray and, above all, keep heading for your goal.

- Take advice only from someone who is making more money than you. Learn from people who are doing. Don't be afraid to ask for help. All the experts use expert advice—it saves money.

- Make your profit going in. Profit is not borrowed money. Borrowed money has to be paid back. Negotiate good deals and don't depend on appreciation.

- Movement is the key. You have to get out and do things. You'll make mistakes, but don't let them stop you. You have to keep moving. Start somewhere. You may not get rich quick, but if you don't start, you'll never get rich.

- Avoid listening to negative thinkers and deadheads. They are everywhere. The people who are closest to you are usually the most negative. Many people will never understand what you're doing if you're doing it right. Leave them in your dust; don't let them bury you in their dirt.

- Deal only with motivated sellers. I have probably said this a dozen times in this book. But if you ever catch yourself wasting time with a seller and feeling generally discouraged in looking for deals, the root of the problem is almost always a lack of seller motivation. You don't want to chase dead-end leads. So screen sellers well over the phone before you drive anywhere.

- Make a lot of offers. Don't get bogged down in doing the wrong things. Concentrate on activities that produce the most income. Nothing produces more than making offers. If you don't make offers, you won't make deals.

- Make a reservation to attend the very next live training you can at our Financial Freedom Academy. This valuable hands-on training cannot be found anywhere else. It will save you thousands of dollars in mistakes and give you a focused, easy-to-follow plan to generate cash. You simply cannot afford the mistakes that come with trial and error when such an inexpensive quick-start opportunity is available. Take action now. You'll be glad you did.

- Call or write my office for more information on our full line of training material and events.

"Man's mind, once stretched by a new idea,
never regains its original dimensions."

Oliver Wendell Holmes

40 deals in their first year.
Rick and Peggy Catlin, *Grand Junction, Colorado*

Dear Ron,

My husband and I started studying your courses. In February 2002 my husband stopped working as a mechanic and started buying and selling property full time. Within our first year we had contracts on 40 properties. We have been giving properties with quit claim deeds, worked deals on three properties that were in foreclosure, two the week they were scheduled for auction. Found our dream home and moved in. We would have never been able to afford this home without the knowledge we gained with your courses. Here is a picture of our home.

Thank you,

Rick L. Catlin
Peggy J. Catlin
Grand Junction, CO

P.S. This is just one of the checks we received in the last 6 months.

STEWART TITLE OF GRAND JUNCTION	FIRST NATIONAL BANK OF THE ROCKIES GRAND JUNCTION, CO 81508 82-154/1021	0123
ESCROW ACCOUNT (970) 243-3070 521 ROOD AVENUE GRAND JUNCTION, CO 81501-0178	GF NO. 03006694	CHECK DATE 01-000012 09/26/2003

NINE THOUSAND THREE HUNDRED SIX And 93/100 DOLLARS

CHECK AMOUNT

$9,306.93

PAY TO THE ORDER OF   RICK L. CATLIN

VOID IF NOT USED WITHIN 90 DAYS

ASSIGNMENT OF CONTRACT FOR PURCHASE AND SALE

In reference to the contract for puchase and sale dated _____

between _____ or Assigns, Buyer, and

_____ Seller, concerning property described as:

_____

_____

_____

Buyer hereby assigns all rights to said contract for sale and purchase to

_____ Assignee in exchange for compensation

in the amount of $_____.

Buyer/Assignor	Date	Assignee	Date

Buyer/Assignor	Date	Assignee	Date

PRIVATE LENDER SCRIPT

Do you have an IRA or any other investment capital that's not getting you _____% return safely?

No—Move On

Yes—I buy and sell single-family houses here in _____ and I sometimes borrow short-term funds from individuals such as yourself to purchase and rehab these houses.

Your money is secured by a first mortgage (trust deed) and I pay _____% interest. It's closed by professionals with title insurance, fire insurance, appraisal, and other proper documentation and I never borrow more that 65% of the value of the house.

Does this sound interesting to you?

BIRD DOG

Make $2,000 a Month

NO CREDIT—NO MONEY—VERY LITTLE KNOWLEDGE

- Write down the phone numbers on all For Sale by Owner (FSBO) signs, then call those numbers and get information sheets completed.

- Fill out information sheets on any and all houses for sale by private owners. Do this for FSBOs and any other houses you can find.

- Submit those sheets to my office.

YOU GET $250 IF WE BUY

- Make up an information sheet on all vacant houses not listed with REALTORS®, especially if the houses are run down.

- Try to locate owner's name, address, and phone number.

- Submit sheets to my office.

For Bird Doggers!

YOU GET $250 if we buy and you furnished owner's information.

YOU GET $100 if we buy and you did not furnish owner's information.

PROPERTY INFORMATION SHEET

Submitted by: _____

Date: _____ Phone: _____

Address: _____

Area: _____

This is an FSBO: _____ Listed: _____

Other: _____

Owner's name: _____ Owner's Phone: _____

Owner's address: _____

_____

Asking price: $_____

Terms: _____

Existing mortgages:

1st

$_____ Lender _____ Rate _____ Pmt _____ FHA/VA/Conv _____

2nd

$_____ Lender _____ Rate _____ Pmt _____ FHA/VA/Conv _____

Does house need repairs? _____ General description of repairs: _____

_____

_____

Bedrooms _____ Baths _____ Construction _____

Central Heat _____ Central Air _____

Garage _____ Range _____ Refr _____

Is the house: Vacant _____ Occupied _____

EXTRAS: _____

Comments:

_____

_____

LETTER TO
AN OUT-OF-STATE OWNER

Your Name
Address
City, State, ZIP

Dear Homeowner:

We are a group of investors who buy and sell houses in the Jacksonville area. Through public records, we are aware of the property you own here in Jacksonville. If you are interested in selling and need FAST CASH, please call Bob at (   )   -   or, if you prefer, you can fill out the bottom portion of this letter and mail it to us at the address above. We guarantee you an offer, and we will be in contact with you as soon as we receive the information listed at the bottom.

We are looking forward to doing business with you, and have a **GREAT NEW YEAR!**

Sincerely,

Your Name

- -

__ YES, I am interested in selling my property located at _____

I am asking $_____ for the property. It is (   ) Occupied (   ) Vacant.

NAME: _____

ADDRESS: _____

CITY: _____ STATE: _____ ZIP: _____

PHONE #: _____

NOTES: _____

_____

_____

We will inspect the property from the exterior and call you shortly with an offer.

LETTER TO REALTORS

[Print on Professional Letterhead]

Dear Realtor,

You've got a reputation of being one of the most successful and aggressive real estate agents in town. That's why I'm writing to you today.

Remember when you first started in the business? All the old pros told you "it's a numbers game." Just keep filling up the pipeline—your listing book, and a certain number of them will sell.

Or put another way, <u>you've got to kiss a lot of frogs before you find a prince.</u>

You know what I mean by "frogs," don't you? All those listings you know will never sell. Maybe it's a real ugly house? Maybe it needs a lot of repairs? Maybe it's in a war zone rather than a good neighborhood? Or any of the other countless maybes.

But for whatever reason, lots of houses don't sell. And a lot more simply aren't worth too much of your time and effort.

<u>Why not let me be your garbage disposal?</u>

I want to buy all those "unsellable" houses.

My name is XXXXX. I'm a real estate investor, not a Realtor, who specializes in buying and selling "haunted houses." Not just the kind with spirits (although I'm not afraid of ghosts), but the ones that seem haunted <u>because they just won't sell.</u>

Look. You're a professional. You can generally find a buyer for most people who want to sell their home. But when you find those houses that just won't move—for whatever reason—you no longer have to chalk it up to another kissed frog and write off your investment with time and effort.

I've got a better solution . . . a solution that can put cash in your pocket. <u>And all you have to do is make a simple phone call.</u>

You see, I specialize in solving those seemingly unsolvable problems that keep houses from selling. And I don't care what neighborhood the house is in or how many repairs it needs. In fact, sometimes "the uglier, the better."

But here's the best part . . . I'm associated with a group of private investors. We use private funds to buy our houses so you don't have to worry about long, drawn-out loan approvals. In fact, when we buy houses, it's frequently for all cash and we normally close within 48 to 72 hours. And of course you get full commission.

Like you, I'm a professional, so you don't have to deal with all the hand-holding and mollycoddling necessary with typical buyers. And I can work with you just about any way you want.

But I'm involved in more successful real estate closings than your typical agent. And that involvement is usually as the buyer.

We generally buy between five and ten houses a month, so you know I'm not just fooling around. It's how I make a living.

Look. I want to buy more houses and you want to sell more houses. It's a match made in heaven.

I want to become a major source of income for you, and I've identified several ways to do this . . .

When you find a situation where the owner doesn't have enough equity in the house to pay you commission (and they're not willing to "go out of pocket"), give me a call. You've got nothing to lose.

Often I can negotiate a purchase with people like this. If that's the case, <u>I'll pay you a referral fee.</u>

When you find a house that's run down, or in a bad neighborhood, or won't sell for a high enough price to make it worth your time . . . give me a call.

I'll buy it and pay you a referral fee, plus your full commission.

And I'm not just talking about the frogs covered with warts either. I'll buy just about anything, including "cream puffs." When you have a situation where someone needs to sell a house fast—like yesterday—call me. I can do a deal like greased lightning. Please don't be under the impression I have to steal these houses to be interested. Sometimes I pay retail price for the pretty ones. If you'll send me the frogs, I'll tell you right over the phone if I'm interested or not.

What about houses that have serious damage such as from a fire or flood? Call me. Or those cases where people are behind in their payments, have liens on the property, or are even in foreclosure? Call me. I can usually do the deal.

We can usually close in a few days, and the best part is you don't have to do any work. When you refer me to a house and I buy it, you'll get free money.

You don't have to do anything but make one simple phone call. It's a way for you to get paid for the effort you've already invested—effort that, before I came along, would have simply gone down the drain. Wouldn't you rather run it through a "garbage disposal" that spits out cold, hard cash to you? And that's only the beginning . . .

We still have to sell all these houses. I'll be honest with you; sometimes the profit in our houses is so slim we can't afford to use a real estate agent. But many times we get a house cheap enough that we can use an agent; and if we develop a working relationship, you'll be that agent.

I'll give you a call in a few days to discuss in more detail how I can help you make more money. Or if you have some of those "stinky deals" right now, give me a call at 555-5555.

Sincerely,

Your Name

P.S. Please don't try to prejudge what I would be interested in. I'm not a normal seminar graduate, wanna-be real estate investor. I buy all kinds of houses in all areas and conditions. I have multiple purchase plans available and an unlimited supply of capital. I'm deadly serious about what I do. It's my business, not a game. You've never met a more qualified prospect to buy a house. Don't wait until one of your associates tells you how easily they collected a commission you could have had.

P.S. Isn't it time you started getting paid for all those deals you worked on but didn't sell? Call me today.

SAMPLE FLYER

I Buy Houses
(904)555-9240
www.yourwebsitehere.com

Any Area—Any Condition—Any Size

- Been Transferred
- Need to Move
- Behind on Payments
- In Foreclosure
- Need to Sell
- Moving Out of State
- Need Extra Money Now

If You Need to Sell Fast
Call Me <u>Now</u>!

<u>Private Investor</u>
I am not a real estate agent and I am not
associated with any real estate firm.

<u>P.S.</u>
Please keep this flyer with your important papers and if the
need arises, I'll be glad to help you in the future.

SAMPLE BUSINESS CARD

"I'll Buy or Lease Your House"
(See reverse side for exciting news . . .)

Your
Photo
Here

Your Name
Your Company
Address
City, State Zip

Phone: (555)555-5555
Fax: (555)555-5555

Do you want to sell your house quickly and still get a fair price?

Is your house vacant or in need of repairs? Are you in foreclosure or behind on payments? Are you facing a divorce, bad tenants, or liens?

They're common problems. Here's a perfect solution . . .

I buy houses in any condition, price range, or area from people in situations just like yours.

I can pay cash and close in as little as 3 days with no real estate commission fees.

<u>I'm not a Realtor</u>. I'm associated with a group of investors that buys several houses a year and wants to buy more. You'll get a **quick sale at a fair price with no hassles.** Call now.

TELEPHONE QUESTIONNAIRE FOR POTENTIAL BUYERS

Date: _____ Source of call: _____

Name: _____

Address: _____

City: _____ State: _____ ZIP: _____

Phone: W _____ H _____

What is the maximum down payment available? _____

What price range? _____

Maximum payment affordable? _____

What areas are acceptable? _____

How many bedrooms and bathrooms required? _____

Construction preferred? ___ Frame ___ Brick ___ Concrete block

Is a garage mandatory? _____

How is credit? ____ Good ____ Fair ____ Poor

When are you ready to buy? _____

What is the problem (if there is one)? _____

_____

How many square feet are needed? _____

Other requirements: _____

_____

_____

_____

_____

Comments: _____

_____

_____

LETTER TO ATTRACT BUYERS

Special financing programs including owner financing. Quick closing!

"Do Not Sign Another Rent Check
Until You Consider
This Letter and My Promise:
I Can Help YOU
Buy and Own Your Own Home, Right Now,
Regardless of Your Financial Circumstances."

Dear Renter,

My name is (your name), and I have a very exciting promise for you. You can stop flushing away your rent money every month, stop making your landlord rich, and buy a home of your very own right now, and I can help you every step of the way. In fact, I do most of the work for you.

Imagine: A home of your own! A fenced yard for the kids. A garage for your car. Enough room for your stuff. All on a quiet street. Privacy, comfort.

Why Now?

I have lots of lenders sitting on too much money—imagine that!—and they are eager to make more home loans right now. Interest rates are low. The time couldn't be better to get financing for your new home, and if the lenders won't do it, I'll probably finance you myself.

What about Credit Problems?

Even if you do <u>not</u> have perfect credit or are self-employed, there are loans available for you. Whatever your current situation, there's a home loan just right for you—and I'll find it for you.

Won't I Need a Big Down Payment?

You do <u>not</u> need a large chunk of money for a down payment. If you've been held back by the idea that you have to save up $10,000, $20,000, or more to put down to buy a good home, I'll show you how to avoid that altogether. You'll need a little money but you'll be surprised how little.

In fact, I have several houses right now where you can do some repairs yourself and build sweat equity if that appeals to you.

I own these houses so I can build a plan to suit your needs. All you need to do is find a house you like, tell me what you have to work with, and let me work my magic.

**Every Month You Wait,
You're Flushing Your Hard-Earned Money
Right Down the Toilet**

Renting is <u>wasting</u> money. You make your landlord rich, but you do nothing for yourself. By putting those exact same dollars into a "house payment" instead of "rent," you create "equity" . . . Value that you own, that later can send your kids to college, finance the start-up of your own business, or pay for your retirement. Be your own landlord and build up a future of financial security. I'll even show you easy strategies to speed up the payoff of your home without making extra payments. And as a homeowner, you get tax breaks that renters never get.

You can use home ownership as the "foundation" of a complete change in your finances.

Being a Homeowner Makes You Feel Good!

In addition to the smart financial reasons for buying your own home instead of renting, you will feel better about yourself, your spouse, and your family. You can decorate your home just as you please. You'll enjoy inviting people over to your home.

<u>**There's no reason to wait. I can help you buy one of our homes RIGHT NOW!**</u>

For many people—maybe even you—the government will even step in to help with the down payment, with low-interest financing, and in other ways. Very few people know that the government is eager to help them buy their first home. I can help you get every benefit available for first-time homebuyers.

**Why Not Explore This Idea?
What Do You Have to Lose?**

Once you call me, we can have a brief discussion, at which time I'll collect the information I need from you to create a Profile—then I will talk about what I have available and what's coming up soon. We'll do all this over the phone with absolutely no obligation.

You can call my office at any time at (555)555-5555; if we're not in, leave a message and we'll get right back to you.

Sincerely,

Joe Homebuyer

P.S. I know that the natural tendency is to set my letter aside to think it over—but then it may get lost, you may forget about it. So please, call right away. I'll make you this promise. If you're serious about buying a home and have income to pay for it, there's no one in Jacksonville better qualified to help fulfill your dreams of home ownership. You'll see why when we talk.

AUTHORIZATION TO RELEASE INFORMATION

(Use for credit check or acquiring information concerning a loan.)

I/We hereby authorize you to release to _____ any and all information that they may require for the purpose of a credit transaction. You may reproduce this document to acquire reference from more than one source.
Thank you.

Signature	Soc. Sec. #	Date

Signature	Soc. Sec. #	Date

affidavit A written statement or declaration sworn to or affirmed before an authorized person.

agreement of sale A written agreement in which the purchaser agrees to buy and the seller agrees to sell. Terms and conditions are included in the agreement.

alienation clause Also known as a due-on-sale clause. This is a provision that allows a lender to demand payment of the balance of a loan in full if the collateral is sold.

amortization mortgage A debt for which the periodic repayments are used to reduce the principal outstanding as well as to pay off the current interest charges.

apportionment The adjustment of the income, expenses, or carrying charges of real estate that is usually computed to the date of closing of title so that the seller pays all expenses to that date. The buyer assumes all expenses from the date on which the deed is conveyed to the buyer.

appraisal An estimate of a property's value made by an appraiser who is usually presumed to be an expert in this work.

appraisal by comparison An estimate of value made by comparing the sale prices of other similar properties.

assignment The method or manner by which a right or contract is transferred from one person (the assignor) to another (the assignee).

assumption of mortgage This occurs when a person takes title to property and assumes the payment of an existing note or deed of trust.

balloon payment A final installment payment that pays off a debt.

beneficiary The person who receives or is to receive the benefits of a certain act.

bird dog/bird dogger A person who looks for houses that potentially fit the guidelines of the properties you prefer to purchase. Bird doggers will bring the information you require and you will reimburse them for their efforts on whatever basis you have agreed on.

bona fide In good faith; without fraud.

capital gain or loss The difference between the basis price (cost plus purchase expenses) of a capital asset and its sales price.

caveat emptor Let the buyer beware. The buyer must examine the goods or property and buy at his or her own risk.

chain of title A history of the conveyances and encumbrances affecting a land title from the time it was granted or as far back as records are available.

client The principal, the one who employs and compensates a broker.

closing date The date on which the buyer takes over a property.

cloud on the title An outstanding claim or encumbrance that, if valid, would affect or impair the owner's title.

codicil An addition to, or amendment of, a will.

collateral Additional security pledged for the payment of a debt.

commission A fee charged for brokerage services.

commitment A pledge; a promise; an affirmation agreement.

complaint 1. In civil law, the initial statement of the facts on which a complaint is based. 2. In criminal law, the preliminary charge made against the accused.

comps See *appraisal by comparison.*

condemnation The acquisition of private property for public use with fair compensation to the owner. See also *eminent domain.*

conditional sales contract A contract for the sale of property stating that although delivery is to be made to the buyer, the title is to remain vested in the seller until the conditions of the contract have been fulfilled.

consideration Anything given as an inducement to enter into a contract, such as money or personal services. Any contract, lease, obligation, or mortgage may subsequently be modified without consideration provided that the change is made in writing and signed.

contract A legally enforceable agreement.

covenants Agreements written into deeds and other instruments promising performance or nonperformance of certain acts or stipulating certain uses or restrictions on a property.

debt service Annual amount to be paid by a debtor for money borrowed.

deed An instrument in writing, duly executed and delivered, that conveys title to real property.

deed restriction A restriction imposed in a deed to limit the use of the land. A deed might include clauses preventing the sale of liquor or defining the size, type, value, or placement of improvements.

default Failure to fulfill a duty or promise or to discharge an obligation; omission or failure to perform an act. In property foreclosure, usually the failure to pay loan installment repayments when they become due.

defeasance clause The clause in a mortgage that permits the mortgagor to redeem his or her property on payment of the obligations to the mortgagee.

defendant The party sued or called to answer in any lawsuit, civil or criminal.

deficiency judgment When the security for a loan is sold for less than the amount of the loan, the unpaid amount (the deficiency) is held by law (the judgment) to be the liability of the borrower unless the new owner has assumed the debt.

due-on-sale See *alienation clause.*

earnest money Down payment made by a purchaser of real estate as evidence of good faith.

easement A right that may be exercised by the public or individuals on, over, or through the property of others.

eminent domain A right of the government to acquire property for public use. The owner must be fairly compensated.

encroachment A building, part of a building, or obstruction that intrudes on the property of another.

encumbrance Any right to or interest in property interfering with its use or transfer or subjecting it to an obligation. In connection with foreclosure property, the most likely encumbrances are mortgages and claims for unpaid taxes.

equity In real estate, the difference between the value of a property and the amount owed on it. Also called the owner's interest.

equity loan Junior (subordinate) loan based on a percentage of the equity.

escrow A written agreement between two or more parties providing that certain instruments or property be entrusted to a third party to be delivered to a designated person upon the fulfillment or performance of some act or condition.

estate The degree, quantity, nature, and extent of interest (ownership) that a person has in real property.

estoppel certificate An instrument executed by the mortgagor setting forth the status of, and the balance due on, the mortgage as of the date of the execution of the certificate.

eviction A legal proceeding by a landlord to recover possession of real property.

exclusive agency An agreement to employ one broker only. If the sale is made by any other broker, both are entitled to commissions.

exclusive right to sell An agreement to give a broker the exclusive right to sell for a specified period. If a sale during the term of the agreement is made by the owner or by any other broker, the broker holding the exclusive right is, nevertheless, entitled to compensation.

executor A person or a corporate entity or any other type of organization named in a will to carry out its provisions.

fee (fee simple, fee absolute) The absolute ownership of real property. This type of estate gives the owner and his or her heirs unconditional power of disposition.

FHA Federal Housing Administration. See *FHA mortgage loan.*

FHA mortgage loan Mortgage loan insured by the Federal Housing Administration.

fiduciary A person who transacts business or handles money or property on behalf of another. The relationship implies great confidence and trust.

first mortgage Mortgage that has priority as a lien over all other mortgages. In cases of foreclosure, the first mortgage will be satisfied before other mortgages are paid off.

foreclosure A procedure whereby property pledged as security for a debt is sold to pay the debt in the event of default in payments or terms.

grace period Additional time allowed to perform an act or make a payment before a default occurs.

grantee The party to whom the title to real property is conveyed; the buyer.

grantor The person who conveys real estate by deed; the seller.

habendum clause The "to have and to hold" clause that defines or limits the quantity of the estate granted in the deed.

HUD Department of Housing and Urban Development. This agency has a broad mission in the entire housing industry. The specific area of interest to you, as an investor, is its involvement in subsidizing rents for low-income housing and the marketing of repossessed houses. Many of HUD repossessions provide excellent investment opportunities.

hypothecate To use something as security without giving up possession of it.

installments Parts of the same debt, payable at successive periods as agreed; payments made to reduce a mortgage.

intestate A person who dies before making a will or whose will is defective in form.

irrevocable Incapable of being recalled or revoked; unchangeable; unalterable.

joint tenancy Ownership of property by two or more persons, each of whom has an undivided interest with or without the right of survivorship.

judgment Decree of a court declaring that one individual is indebted to another and fixing the amount of such indebtedness.

junior mortgage A mortgage second in lien (subordinate) to a previous mortgage.

land contract In reality, a land contract is a promise to pay. In other words, if you buy a house under a land contract, you promise to pay an agreed-on amount on or before a specific date. Once the terms have been fulfilled, the seller will then deed the property to you.

landlord One who rents property to another.

land trust A means of taking control of a property anonymously. The only name that will appear on public records is the name of the trust and, usually, the name of the trustee. A land trust provides some asset protection in that it requires a good deal of digging via legal channels to discover if a person is the beneficiary of a trust.

lease A contract whereby for a consideration, usually termed *rent,* one who is entitled to the possession of real property transfers such rights to another for life, for a term of years, or at will.

leasehold The interest given to a lessee of real estate by a lease.

lessee A person to whom property is rented under a lease.

lessor One who rents property to another under a lease.

lien A legal right or claim on a specific property that attaches to the property until a debt is satisfied.

life estate The conveyance of title to property for the duration of the life of the grantee.

lis pendens A legal document filed in the office of the county clerk giving notice that an action or proceeding affecting the title to a property is pending in the courts.

LTV (loan-to-value ratio) Refers to the amount of money loaned on a property relative to its actual value. For example, a loan of $20,000 on a $40,000 house would have a 50 percent LTV.

marketable title A title that a court considers so free from defect that the court will enforce its acceptance by a purchaser.

mechanic's lien A claim made to secure the price of labor done on, and materials furnished for, uncompensated property improvement.

moratorium An emergency act by a legislative body to suspend the legal enforcement of contractual obligations.

mortgage An instrument in writing, duly executed and delivered, that creates a lien on real estate as security for the payment of a specified debt, which is usually in the form of a bond.

mortgage broker One who is paid to match borrowers with lenders.

mortgagee The party who lends money and takes a mortgage to secure payment.

mortgagor A person who borrows money and gives a mortgage on his or her property as security for the payment of the debt.

multiple listing An arrangement among members of a board of REAL-TORS® whereby brokers bring their listings to the attention of the other members. If a sale results, the commission is divided between the broker providing the listing and the broker making the sale.

nonqualifying assumption A mortgage or deed of trust that does not contain a due-on-sale clause, thereby allowing transfer of title freely without permission from the lender.

obsolescence Loss in value as a result of reduced desirability and usefulness of a structure because its design and construction have become obsolete.

open listing A listing given to any number of brokers with commissions payable only to the broker who secures the sale.

open mortgage A mortgage that has matured or is overdue and is therefore "open" to foreclosure at any time.

option A right given for a consideration to purchase or lease a property on specific terms within a specified time. If the right is not exercised, the option holder is not subject to liability for damages. If exercised, the grantor of the option must perform.

payoff letter A letter from a lender stating the current balance due on an account; also referred to as an estoppel letter or certificate.

performance bond A bond used to guarantee the specific completion of an endeavor in accordance with a contract.

personal property Any property that is not real property.

plat book A public record containing maps of land showing the division into streets, blocks, and lots and indicating the measurements of the individual parcels.

points Discount charges imposed by lenders to raise the yields on their loans. One (1) point equals one percent (1%) of the loan amount.

prepayment clause A clause in a mortgage that gives a mortgagor the privilege of paying the mortgage indebtedness before it becomes due, either with or without a prepayment penalty.

proration Allocation of closing costs and credits to buyers and sellers.

purchase money mortgage A mortgage given by a grantee or any other lender in partial payment of the purchase price of real estate.

quiet title suit A suit in court to ascertain the legal rights of an owner to a certain parcel of real property.

quitclaim deed A deed that simply conveys the grantor's rights or interest, if any, in real estate; generally considered inadequate except when interests are being passed from one spouse to the other.

real estate board An organization whose members consist primarily of real estate brokers and salespersons.

REO (real estate owned) Property acquired by a lender through foreclosure and held in inventory.

real estate syndicate A partnership formed for a real estate venture. Partners may be limited or unlimited in their liability.

real property Land and generally whatever is erected on or affixed thereto.

REALTOR® A term used to identify active members of the National Association of REALTORS®(NAR), This term is commonly used to refer to anyone licensed to sell real estate. However, the term *REALTOR®* applies only to dues-paying members of NAR.

recording The act of writing or entering, in a book of public record, instruments affecting the title to real property.

recourse The right to claim against an owner of a property or note.

red lining The refusal to lend money within a specific area for various reasons. This practice is illegal because it discriminates against credit-worthy people who happen to live there.

release clause A clause found in a blanket mortgage that gives the owner of the property the privilege to pay off part of the debt and thus free part of the property from the mortgage.

repo A shortened or slang version of repossession, which occurs when a lender takes possession of the collateral that was security for a loan.

right of redemption Right to recover property transferred by a mortgage or other lien by paying off the debt either before or after foreclosure; also called equity of redemption.

right of survivorship Right of the surviving joint owner to succeed to the interests of the deceased joint owner. This right is a distinguishing feature of a joint tenancy or tenancy by the entirety.

RTC (Resolution Trust Corporation) An organization set up by the federal government to market houses from the inventory of federally insured, defunct banks and other lending institutions.

sales contract A contract by which a buyer and seller agree to the terms of sale.

second mortgage A mortgage made by a homebuyer in addition to an existing first mortgage. The order of recording determines the seniority of the lien.

seller financing Refers to the owner of a property who agrees to carry a mortgage on the property that he or she is selling so that the buyer doesn't have to obtain any or all of the financing from another source or lending institution.

specific performance A remedy in a court of equity compelling a defendant to carry out the terms of an agreement or contract.

split funding A technique whereby an investor offers a small amount of cash to close a deal with the balance due at a later date in a form other than extended monthly payments.

statute of frauds Law requiring certain contracts to be made in writing or partially complied with in order to be legally enforceable.

subdivision A tract of land divided into lots or plots.

subordination See *subordination clause.*

subordination clause A clause in a mortgage that gives priority to a mortgage taken out at a later date. The seller agrees to go into a second, third, or fourth position allowing the buyer to obtain new financing senior to the seller's lien without paying off the lien from the proceeds.

substitution of collateral Taking an existing mortgage on one property and transferring it to another.

survey The process by which a parcel of land is measured and its area ascertained; also the blueprint showing the measurements, boundaries, and area.

tax sale Sale of real property after a period of nonpayment of real estate taxes.

tenancy at will A license to use or occupy lands and tenements (permanent and fixed property) at the will of the owner.

tenancy by the entirety An estate that exists only between husband and wife with equal right of possession and enjoyment during their joint lives and with the right of survivorship.

tenancy in common An ownership of realty by two or more persons, each of whom has an undivided interest without the right of survivorship.

testate Condition when a person dies leaving a valid will.

title company A firm that examines title to real estate and/or issues title insurance.

TPA (third-party administrator) One who is approved to administer funds from a retirement program. You must use a TPA to access money from your retirement accounts for self-directed activities.

without recourse Words used in endorsing a note or bill to denote that the future holder is not to look to the endorser in case of nonpayment.

wrap (wraparound loan) A new loan encompassing any existing loans.

IMPORTANT INFORMATION

Ron LeGrand, Global Publishing Inc., and the Financial Freedom Academy offer a full range of training on every aspect of real estate investing, business management, asset protection, tax reduction, entity structuring, estate planning, business, and personal growth.

You may order a free Financial Freedom Academy Curriculum Guide by calling **800-567-6128.**

In addition, you may subscribe to our interactive Coaching/Mentoring program for eight weeks to accelerate your learning curve with a one-on-one coach, weekly lesson plans, and accountability controls to work with you on operating your business and actually buying properties.

An ongoing support system called Financial Freedom Network (FFN) is available with a long list of benefits including free Web sites, annual retreats, teleconference calls, support meetings, and numerous other benefits. All the details for FFN can be found at **http://www.goffn.com.**

Partnerships are available to all students with a minimum of training where Ron and his staff joint venture with students anywhere in North America on real estate deals on a 50/50 split.

Mortgage loans to buy and rehab junkers as well as luxury homes are available to students from our equity loan company. These loans are based on collateral, not credit, and make it easy to pay cash for any wholesale deal you find.

Numerous one-day workshops and two-hour presentations are available. Ron himself does the presenting at some, and his hand-picked professors speak at others. Some are open to the public and others are sponsored by associations and companies for their own members.

Each year Global Publishing Inc. hosts an annual Customer Appreciation Celebration for its customers and clients held in a location such as Orlando or Las Vegas.

You may also subscribe to a free electronic newsletter by going to **http://www.globalpublishinginc.com** and logging on. It's loaded with valuable tips, techniques, and resources at no cost to you.

For more information on any items above or current news, please contact:

Global Publishing Inc.
9799 Old St. Augustine Road
Jacksonville, FL 32257

Phone: 888-840-8389   9 AM-5 PM EST
Fax: 888-840-8385   24 Hours
Sales: 800-567-6128   9 AM-9 PM EST

Web sites:
http://www.ronlegrand.com (general information)
http://www.globalpublishinginc.com (general information)
http://www.goffn.com (Financial Freedom Network)
http://www.freewealthtraining.com (free workshops)

Free CD Order Form
of Ron LeGrand Interviews

As my way of saying thanks for buying this book, I'd be pleased to send you any or all of the CDs below, each worth $19.95, at no charge to you except for $11.95 S&H total. But there's a catch. Not a big catch, just a small favor. All I ask is you tell your friends about my book and maybe give them a polite nudge to get them to buy. My wife and kids would appreciate it.

Check the CDs you'd like:

❑ **How You Can Be a Quick Turn Real Estate Millionaire Without Previous Experience**
This frank discussion with *Mentor Magazine* explores the lucrative world of quick turn real estate and where the really big money is made, including behind-the-scenes secrets rarely disclosed elsewhere.

❑ **Everything You Ever Wanted to Know About Land Trusts**
This interview answers every question ever asked about how, why, and when to use land trusts to buy real estate and discusses the risks you take if you don't.

❑ **How to Sell Houses on Auto Pilot**
You'll see how an amazing ex-UPS employee buys and sells 5 to 10 houses each month and never talks to a buyer or shows a house.

❑ **How to Bomb Proof Your Assets**
This interview with a national attorney who specializes in asset protection, estate planning, tax reduction, and entity structuring could save you a fortune and be the difference between keeping or losing a lifetime of wealth.

❑ **Where to Get the Money**
This interview explains where you can get all the money you'll need to buy and rehab properties, regardless of your credit or financial condition. It contains the secrets banks don't want you to know, and Ron explains how he got started with no money or credit and overcame bankruptcy to buy over 40 houses his first year.

Please Print Clearly

Name: _____ Spouse: _____

Address: _____

City: _____ State: _____ Zip: _____

Phone: (_____) _____ Fax: (_____) _____

E-mail: _____

Please charge credit card _____, exp. date _____ $11.95 for S&H.

Authorized Signature _____

(Must have the information above. No PO Boxes please. S&H covers one or all CDs.)

No phone orders will be accepted.

Order online at **http://www.ronlegrand.com/freeinfo.htm**
Fax this completed order form to: **888-840-8385** or **904-262-1464** (24 hours/7 days a week).
Mail this completed order form with check to:
Global Publishing, Inc., 9799 St. Augustine Road, Jacksonville, FL 32257

Would you like to be a ❑ **Full Time or** ❑ **Part Time investor?**

What would you expect to make your first year? _____

What would stop you? _____

When would you like to start? _____

Share the message!

Bulk discounts
Discounts start at only 10 copies. Save up to 55% off retail price.

Custom publishing
Private label a cover with your organization's name and logo.
Or, tailor information to your needs with a custom pamphlet
that highlights specific chapters.

Ancillaries
Workshop outlines, videos, and other products are available on
select titles.

Dynamic speakers
Engaging authors are available to share their expertise and insight
at your event.

**Call Dearborn Trade Special Sales at
1-800-245-BOOK (2665)
or e-mail trade@dearborn.com**